RELIGIOUS APPROACHES TO HUMAN RIGHTS

RELIGIOUS APPROACHES

to

HUMAN RIGHTS

Martin Davie

Exploring Religion & Society

Oxford Centre for Religion and Public Life Publications

OXFORD

First published in Great Britain in 2016 by
Oxford Centre for Religion and Public Life Publications, an imprint of
Select Academic Publishing Oxford Ltd
Registered Office (not for trade): 5, South Parade, Oxford, OX2 7JL

**For further information contact:
The Oxford Centre for Religion and Public Life,
21 High Street, Eynsham, Oxfordshire OX29 4HE
or through the website:**

www.ocrpl.org

The Oxford Centre for Religion and Public Life warmly acknowledges
inspiration from and partnership with Grassroots conservatives
www.grassrootsconservatives.org
in developing this research project and with them express our grateful
thanks to the Cross Trust for its financial support for the research and
the Tufton Trust for its financial support for the publication.

ISBN 978-0-9935529-0-8

Contents

FOREWORD

Human rights occupy a central place in contemporary international politics and social discourse. They are the basis for much judicial activity to bring about social change, some of which particularly impinges on freedom of religious belief and practice and national self-determination.

The Universal Declaration of Human Rights was developed to override claims of national sovereignty in the Nuremberg trials after the Second World War. It insists on a moral standard from which nations and their agents cannot and should not claim immunity on the grounds of obeying a nation's law and carrying out its policies.

But now human rights activism has achieved such hegemony in contemporary political discourse that it challenges all policy and law-making, even if resulting from the democratic political process, and conflicts with and overrides other valid moral claims. Judgments are handed down from human rights courts to override national sovereignty and moral awareness in many areas of legitimate national determination. It is this that has prompted calls for a Bill of British Rights.

Many countries violate the human rights treaties they ratify. Governments are rightly held to account for implementing the rights they solemnly agreed to uphold. Foreign governments and international bodies are lobbied to intervene and enforce compliance even to the extent of replacing governments. Several governments use vague definitions of rights and human well-being to stress that a local view should trump any international understanding. This makes human rights all but unenforceable in such contexts. The very weak enforcement of human rights is increasingly an international scandal.

Samuel Moyn, in his brilliant work, *The Last Utopia: Human Rights in History* (Harvard University Press, 2010), identifies utopian origins to the contemporary expressions and excesses of the human rights movement. He argues that it was only when utopian ideologies like socialism and anti-colonialism failed in the 1970s that human rights activism gained its pre-eminent position in political discourse, creating an unchallengeable moral horizon which became the key moral guide to political behaviour.

A distinction must be recognised between the rights of citizens as members of a nation state that derive from their own legislature, and the universal rights of humans that are given to every human person regardless of their nation's laws. This distinction, and the failure to recognise it, is often the basis of conflicts around human rights. For example, the right to religious freedom is often in conflict with various expressions of current human rights equality legislation in the United Kingdom. This is because the right to religious freedom is held to be a right of human beings and not solely granted by a state's laws. Thus it is held to be superior to those rights granted to a citizen by their state. Similarly an international environmental convention can also produce a set of rights and put pressure on nations to adopt and implement them. Not all rights are legislated by the state.

Such a conflict, and others, require a thorough examination of the grounding and authority of human rights.

A natural rights theory derived from secularism and Western liberalism has provided the basis of much contemporary interpretation of human rights. However, secular utopias no longer provide a compelling basis or narrative. Natural rights, understood for example as 'self-evident' in the United States and France, were undermined by secularism and Western liberalism since they were related to no transcendent reality, and therefore became a matter of power struggles between interest groups with no means of arbitration between them.

Furthermore, the humanitarian assumptions of secularism and Western liberal society were themselves undermined as society de-linked itself from its Christian religious roots. Thus, any transcendent validation of human identity has been eroded. How and why are human rights superior to the rights of future generations, animal rights and the 'rights' of the environment? A human life is no longer sacred but may be sacrificed to other pressing or more powerfully exercised rights. Egregious violations of human rights, extending even to genocide, perpetrated by both state and non-state actors, have increased dramatically.

Does the notion of human rights have a future, given the challenges it faces? We need to turn again to examine religions as a possible source to recover, ground and shape human rights and moderate between conflicting claims for a post-secular age.

This study, commissioned by the Oxford Centre for Religion and Public Policy and Grassroots conservatives, and carried out by Martin Davie with input from others, suggests that if the idea of human rights is to survive in the 21st century it must take the contribution of religions seriously. Ways are offered here in which that can be done.

Vinay Samuel and Chris Sugden
Oxford Centre for Religion and Public Life

Executive Summary

PURPOSE

To help secure a strong foundation for, and wide acceptance of, the concept of human rights necessary for the development of a British Bill of Rights.

SYNOPSIS

The concept of human rights was developed as a powerful tool to promote human flourishing. Religion has recently come to be perceived as a barrier to human rights and been subject to sustained attack. However religion is needed to provide a robust philosophical foundation for human rights, and is a vital component of the human flourishing that human rights aim to achieve.

Religions vary in the basis on which they give support to human rights. Yet, all religions have come to support in principle the concept of basic human rights, and any Bill of Rights must be drafted in religiously intelligible terms. Christianity has been the main driver for the development of human rights and is the prime guarantor of freedom of religion for all. So we need to celebrate this nation's Christian heritage as we work together with people of all faiths and none to draft a British Bill of Rights able to promote human flourishing.

FORMAT OF REPORT

Outlines the relationship between religion and human rights in the contemporary world, focussing on the six major world religions: Christianity, Judaism, Islam, Hinduism, Buddhism and Sikhism. Leaders from all six religions have been consulted in preparing this report.

- Chapter 1: What is meant by the term 'human rights'. Development from the Universal Declaration of Human Rights in 1948 to the present day.
- Chapters 2-7: How each religion has responded to the development of human rights since 1948; how they understand human rights in the light of their worldview; the diversity of approaches within each religion, and areas of tension over human rights.
- Chapter 8: Why religion and human rights should not be seen in opposition to each other. The vital contribution of religion to human flourishing which is the aim of human rights.
- Appendices: Full texts of statements about/declarations of human rights from each tradition. The 1998 'Universal Declaration of Rights' produced jointly across religious traditions.

THE PLACE OF RELIGION

Religion has increasingly come under attack in contemporary Europe, including the UK. This assault on the free exercise of religious conviction is in large part driven by a human rights agenda which sees religion and human rights as intrinsically antithetical. The growing threat of terrorist activity rooted in an Islamist ideology has led many governments to conclude that religion can be dangerous and that the best way to counteract this danger is by suppressing the dissemination of 'extremist' religious ideas. This combination of a secular rights ideology and fear of Islamic terrorism risks undermining the very rights that activists and Western governments seek to promote.

The originators of the modern concept of human rights were seeking to promote human flourishing in the face of political tyranny. Rights language was a tool to bring this about. The decision as to what makes for human flourishing, and hence what 'rights' people should have, must be decided by each individual or group on the basis of their religious or philosophical convictions. In this debate, a secular approach has no greater *a priori* claim to validity than a religious approach. Secularism can itself be described as a 'religious' approach in that it is a pattern of practice rooted in a commitment to a particular view of the world and the place of human beings in it.

DIFFERENCES BETWEEN THE RELIGIONS

The question of why a human being has value underpins any concept of human rights. Each religion gives a different answer:

- **Christianity**: Human beings are created in God's image. As one created in God's image, value is not dependent on performance; each human being is of infinite value, *per se*. God values them enough to become incarnate in Jesus Christ in order to die to redeem them.
- **Judaism**: Human beings are created in God's image. As a son of God, value is not dependent on performance; each human being is of infinite value, *per se*.
- **Islam**: Human beings are created by God with the ability to obtain knowledge, engage in conceptual thinking and decide whether they will believe in God and submit to him. As a subject of God, the value of each human being is conditional upon submission to God.
- **Hinduism**: God is present in all human beings, all of whom work to maintain the cosmos. Of all creatures, humans are best poised to achieve escape from the birth/death/reincarnation cycle.
- **Buddhism**: Human beings are the 'precious birth' because of all forms of re-incarnation they are the best poised to achieve enlightenment/ Buddhahood.
- **Sikhism**: All human beings are created by the one God.

These cannot be reduced to a single 'religious account' of human value, nor can their differing understandings of the nature of human existence and relationship to God all be true. Yet, each provides a basis for giving value to human beings in a way that a secular materialist viewpoint which sees human beings as the accidental product of an unthinking and uncaring universe does not. The most robust basis for human rights comes from the Judaeo-Christian understanding which ascribes infinite and unconditional worth to human beings.

RELIGION AND STATE

Four basic models:

1. **Only one religion permitted.** Provides a strong, coherent and universally accepted moral framework which can help to promote human flourishing. But no place for freedom of religion and belief, a vital component of human flourishing.

2. **Secular state.** Claims to be neutral, but is a version of model 1, promoting the secular worldview/religion. Its denial of God and/or an objective transcendent moral law means that it fails to provide a strong and coherent basis for identifying what is good for human beings and hence what is needed for human flourishing.

3. **General encouragement to religion, without endorsing one in particular.** Can enable human flourishing, allowing freedom of speech, religion and belief. However, lack of a coherent understanding of human flourishing threatens community cohesion.

4. **One religion is established, with freedom for the exercise of all religions and none.** This can provide the state with a clear and coherent account of human flourishing while allowing space for dissent and the free exercise of religion and belief.

The UK follows model 4 with the establishment of the Church of England, which serves as the guarantor of freedom of religion for all, and is seen by other religions as a bulwark against the totalitarian tendencies of a secular state.

PUBLIC POLICY IMPLICATIONS

We need to end the attack on religion, and instead publicly celebrate this nation's Christian heritage which provides a coherent and inspiring vision of human flourishing. We need to work together with churches and those of all faiths and none to strengthen a common commitment to duties and responsibilities based on the consensus about human rights developed since 1948.

Chapter One

WHAT IS MEANT BY HUMAN RIGHTS?

1.1   THE DEFINITION OF A HUMAN RIGHT

When thinking about the concept of human rights it is important to understand that the term 'human rights' has come to be used in a very specific sense.

Someone who is a member of the National Trust has the right to visit properties owned by the Trust without having to pay an entry fee; someone who has a valid United Kingdom driving licence has the right to drive a car in the United Kingdom; someone who has been ordained as a priest in the Church of England has the right to preside at Church of England services of Holy Communion. All of these are rights but they are not 'human rights'.

This is because they do not have the combination of three factors that mark something out as a human right. Unlike the limited rights given in the three examples in the previous paragraph, a human right is a right that applies to all human beings everywhere, that is recognised by international and national conventions and treaties and that is legally enforceable under international and national law.

Thus, Article 5 of the Universal Declaration of Human Rights adopted by the United Nations in 1948 declares that 'No one shall be subjected to torture or to cruel, inhuman or degrading treatment or punishment.'[1] Under this Article there is an absolute right not to be tortured that is applicable to all human beings regardless of sex, nationality, ethnicity or any other qualification.

This right has subsequently been enshrined in a number of international

13

conventions. Thus, Article 3 of the European Convention on Human Rights of 1950 and Article 7 of the International Covenant on Civil and Political Rights of 1966 repeat the prohibition on torture contained in the Universal Declaration of Human Rights. This prohibition was further reinforced by the United Nations Declaration on the Protection of All Persons from Being Subjected to Torture and Other Cruel, Inhuman or Degrading Treatment or Punishment of 1975 and the 1984 Convention against Torture and Other Cruel, Inhuman or Degrading Treatment. These later statements define torture as:

> ... any act by which severe pain or suffering, whether physical or mental, is intentionally inflicted by or at the instigation of a public official on a person for such purposes as obtaining from him or a third person information or confession, punishing him for an act he has committed or is suspected of having committed, or intimidating him or other persons.[2]

They also make the infliction of torture a criminal offence under international law and under the national law of the nations that have signed the 1984 convention.

All this means that the right not to be tortured is a human right. It applies to all human beings, it is recognised by international conventions and it is legally enforceable. As noted above, all other human rights, such as the right to life, the right to respect for private and family life and the right to freedom of expression have similar characteristics.

1.2 THE HISTORY OF HUMAN RIGHTS

1.2.1 The Universal Declaration of Human Rights

Although the contemporary concept of human rights has a long pre-history,[3] human rights in the modern sense came into existence with the adoption by the United Nations of the Universal Declaration of Human Rights in 1948. This declaration, which was a response to the totalitarianism of the 1930s and 40s was the first time that an international body had set out the fundamental rights and freedoms shared by all human beings.

The Charter of the United Nations, agreed in 1945, declared that one of the purposes of the United Nations was 'promoting and encouraging respect for human rights and for fundamental freedoms for all without distinction as to race, sex, language, or religion.'[4] The United Nations Commission on Human Rights then established a committee, chaired by Mrs Franklin Roosevelt, the widow of American President Franklin D. Roosevelt, to draw up a draft declaration of human rights which would set out the rights and freedoms referred to in the Charter. The draft declaration produced by the commission was sent to the member states of the United Nations for comment and the final text was agreed at a meeting of the United Nations held in Paris in December 1948 with eight of the fifty member states abstaining but none voting against.[5]

The Declaration consists of a preamble and thirty articles. The preamble explains the purpose of the Declaration. It states that 'recognition of the inherent dignity and of the equal and inalienable rights of all members of the human family is the foundation of freedom, justice and peace in the world' that 'disregard and contempt for human rights have resulted in barbarous acts which have outraged the conscience of mankind' and that 'it is essential, if man is not to be compelled to have recourse, as a last resort, to rebellion against tyranny and oppression, that human rights should be protected by the rule of law.' Consequently, it says, the General Assembly of the United Nations proclaims the Declaration:

… as a common standard of achievement for all peoples and all nations, to the end that every individual and every organ of society, keeping this Declaration constantly in mind, shall strive by teaching and education to promote respect for these rights and freedoms and by progressive measures, national and international, to secure their universal and effective recognition and observance, both among the peoples of Member States themselves and among the peoples of territories under their jurisdiction.[6]

The thirty articles that follow set out a range of universal rights and freedoms. These articles can be usefully divided into five sections.

Articles 1 and 2 set out the foundation for everything that follows by declaring that 'All human beings are born free and equal in dignity and rights' and that everyone is entitled to all the rights and freedoms set forth in this Declaration, regardless of who they are or which country they belong to. In other words there are some rights to which all human beings are entitled and which are in that sense universal.

Articles 3-11 cover the right to life, to freedom from slavery and to proper treatment under the law. Article 3 says that everyone has the right to 'life, liberty and security of person.' Article 4 states that no one should be enslaved; Article 5 prohibits torture and 'cruel, inhuman or degrading treatment or punishment.' Articles 7-11 declare that everyone has the right to equal treatment and protection by the law, that they have the right to legal remedy for the infringement of their rights, that they should not be subject to 'arbitrary arrest, detention or exile,' and that they have the right to a fair and public trial and should be presumed innocent until proved guilty.

Articles 12-17 cover the rights of the individual in civil and political society. They guarantee the rights to privacy, freedom of movement, asylum, nationality, marriage and family life and ownership of property.

Articles 18-21 cover the right to freedom of 'thought, conscience and religion,' freedom of expression, freedom of 'peaceful assembly and association' and the right to take part in the government of one's country either directly or by freely choosing representatives.

Articles 22-27 cover social, economic and cultural rights. These rights are the right to social security, to work, to a fair wage and to union membership, to 'rest and leisure', to 'a standard of living adequate for the health and well-being of himself and his family', to education, to participating in cultural life and scientific advancement and to the protection of copyright.

Finally, articles 28-30 set out the necessary framework for the exercise of these rights and freedoms. Article 28 states that everyone 'is entitled to a social and international order in which the rights and freedoms set forth in this Declaration can be fully realized.' Article 29 says that everyone has responsibility to the community, that their freedom should only be limited 'for the purpose of securing due recognition and respect for the rights and freedoms of others and of meeting the just requirements of morality, public order and the general welfare in a democratic society' and that the rights and freedoms in the Declaration may not be exercised 'contrary to the purposes and principles of the United Nations'. Article 30 adds that nothing in the Declaration allows any 'State, group or person' to act in a way that is intended to destroy any of the rights and freedoms which the Declaration contains.[7]

1.2.2 The International Bill of Rights

The Universal Declaration of Human Rights was a statement of principles. In order to put these principles into practice it was decided after the Declaration had been adopted to produce a legally binding multilateral treaty on human rights to complement it. The United Nations' Commission on Human Rights was given the task of producing this treaty, but eventually political disagreement about including all kinds of rights in one treaty led the General Assembly of the United Nations to draft two separate covenants which were finally produced in 1966.

The first of these was the International Covenant on Economic, Social and Cultural Rights. As Andrew Chapman explains, this Covenant of thirty-one articles 'covers human rights in areas including education, food, housing and health care, as well as the right to work and to just and favourable conditions of work. A state that becomes a party to the Covenant agrees to takes steps for the progressive realization of these rights to the full extent of that state's available resources.'[8]

An optional protocol to this Covenant enables the United Nations' Committee on Economic, Social and Cultural Rights set up under that Covenant to receive and consider communications from citizens of states that have signed the protocol who believe that their rights under the Covenant have been violated and who have not been able to find any domestic remedy.

The second was the International Covenant on Civil and Political Rights. As Chapman further explains, this Covenant of fifty-three articles 'safeguards rights such as rights to life, liberty, fair trial, freedom of movement, thought conscience, peaceful assembly, family and privacy. It also prohibits slavery, torture, cruel, inhuman and degrading treatment and punishment, discrimination, arbitrary arrest and imprisonment for debt.'[9]

There are two optional protocols to this Covenant. The first enables the United Nations' Human Rights Committee, to receive and consider communications under the same terms as the protocol to the first Covenant mentioned above. The second, which was added in 1989, aims at the abolition of the death penalty and states that no one within the jurisdiction of a nation that has signed the protocol may be executed.

The two covenants finally came into force in 1976 and together with the original Universal Declaration of Human Rights they form what is known as the International Bill of Human Rights which is the basic foundation for human rights around the world today.

1.2.3 Other United Nations Conventions on Human Rights

As well as the two covenants already mentioned, there are also a number of United Nations conventions which are legally binding on those states that sign up to them and which cover a variety of human rights issues. The 1984 Convention against Torture and Other Cruel, Inhuman or Degrading Treatment or Punishment has already been mentioned, but in addition there are the 1966 International Convention on the Elimination of All Forms of Racial Discrimination, the 1979 Convention on the Elimination of All Forms of Discrimination against Women, the 1989 Convention on the Rights of the Child, the 1990 International Convention on the Protection of the Rights of All Migrant Workers and Members of Their Families, the 2006 International Convention for the Protection of All Persons from Enforced Disappearance, and the 2006 Convention on the Rights of Persons with Disabilities.

As an example of the contents of these conventions, the Convention on the Rights of Persons with Disabilities is intended to 'promote, protect and ensure the full and equal enjoyment of all human rights and fundamental freedoms by all persons with disabilities, and to promote respect for their inherent dignity.'[10] In order to achieve this goal the states that sign the convention 'undertake to ensure and promote the full realization of all human rights and fundamental freedoms for all persons with disabilities without discrimination of any kind on the basis of disability.'[11]

In specific terms this means that they undertake:

a. To adopt all appropriate legislative, administrative and other measures for the implementation of the rights recognized in the present Convention;
b. To take all appropriate measures, including legislation, to modify or abolish existing laws, regulations, customs and practices that constitute discrimination against persons with disabilities;
c. To take into account the protection and promotion of the human rights of persons with disabilities in all policies and programmes;
d. To refrain from engaging in any act or practice that is inconsistent with the present Convention and to ensure that public authorities and

institutions act in conformity with the present Convention;

e. To take all appropriate measures to eliminate discrimination on the basis of disability by any person, organization or private enterprise;

f. To undertake or promote research and development of universally designed goods, services, equipment and facilities, as defined in Article 2 of the present Convention, which should require the minimum possible adaptation and the least cost to meet the specific needs of a person with disabilities, to promote their availability and use, and to promote universal design in the development of standards and guidelines;

g. To undertake or promote research and development of, and to promote the availability and use of, new technologies, including information and communications technologies, mobility aids, devices and assistive technologies, suitable for persons with disabilities, giving priority to technologies at an affordable cost;

h. To provide accessible information to persons with disabilities about mobility aids, devices and assistive technologies, including new technologies, as well as other forms of assistance, support services and facilities;

i. To promote the training of professionals and staff working with persons with disabilities in the rights recognized in this Convention so as to better provide the assistance and services guaranteed by those rights.[12]

Like the two previous covenants these conventions have optional protocols which give the citizens of those states who have signed the protocol the right to communicate with the United Nations Committee monitoring the convention if they feel their rights under the convention have been violated and have not been able to achieve a domestic remedy.

1.2.4   Regional Human Rights Instruments

In addition to the global human rights instruments established under the United Nations system a number of regional human rights instruments have also developed in Africa, in North and South America and in Europe. In all three cases there is a charter or convention based on the Universal Declaration of Human Rights setting out an overall framework of human rights and additional charters and conventions dealing with specific issues.

In the case of Europe the fundamental instrument is the Convention for the Protection of Human Rights and Fundamental Freedoms, more generally known as the European Convention on Human Rights.

This convention was drawn up by the Council of Europe after the Second World War and came into force in 1953. It consists of fifty-nine articles which are grouped into an introductory article and three subsequent sections.

The introductory article, Article 1, lays down the obligations of signatory states to 'secure to everyone within their jurisdiction the rights and freedoms defined in Section I of this Convention'.[13] Section I, Articles 2-18, then set out what these rights and freedoms are. They are:

• The right to life (Article 2)
• The prohibition of torture or inhuman or degrading treatment or punishment (Article 3)
• The prohibition of slavery and forced labour (Article 4)
• The right to liberty and security of person (Article 5)
• The right to a fair trial (Article 6)
• No punishment except where a law has been broken (Article 7)
• The right to respect for private and family life (Article 8)
• Freedom of thought, conscience and religion (Article 9)
• Freedom of expression (Article 10)
• Freedom of assembly and association (Article 11)
• The right to marry (Article 12)
• The right to an effective remedy when rights and freedoms have been violated (Article 13)
• The prohibition of discrimination (Article 14). This prohibits people from being deprived of the rights and freedoms contained in the convention on the basis of grounds such as 'sex, race, colour, language, religion, political or other opinion, national or social origin, association with a national minority, property, birth or other status.'[14]

Some of these rights and freedoms (such as the right not to be tortured) are absolute. Others are qualified. Thus Article 11 allows restrictions to be placed on the freedom of assembly and association 'such as are prescribed by law and are necessary in a democratic society in the interests of national security or public safety, for the prevention of disorder or crime, for the protection of health or morals or for the protection of the rights and freedoms of others.'[15]

The absoluteness of the rights and freedoms set out in the Convention is further qualified by Articles 15 and 16 of Section I. Article 15 allows states to derogate from the provisions of the Convention in times of 'war or other public emergency.' However no derogation is allowed in the case of Article 2 'except in respect of deaths resulting from lawful acts of war, or from Articles 3, 4 (i) ('No one shall be held in slavery or servitude') and 7. Article 16 allows states to place restrictions on the political activities of non-citizens (Articles 10, 11 and 14 notwithstanding). Articles 17 and 18 then go on to say, however, that nothing in the Convention should be interpreted as allowing a 'state, group or person' to seek to destroy the rights and freedoms set out in the Convention or to limit them further than the convention allows.

Section 2, Articles 19-51, sets up the European Court of Human Rights to protect the rights and freedoms contained in the Convention.

Section 3, Articles 52-59, contains a series of miscellaneous provisions relating to the Convention, including how it will come into force and how a state will be able to 'denounce' (i.e. exit from) the Convention.

Since it was originally written fifteen protocols have been added to the Convention. These can be divided into two groups. First there are those protocols that amend the framework for the operation of the Convention. Thus, Protocol 11 gives the European Court of Human Rights jurisdiction over all states that have ratified the Convention and also introduces a provision allowing individuals to bring cases directly to the Court. Secondly, there are protocols that have expanded the rights covered by the Convention. Thus, Protocol 1 adds the right to peaceful enjoyment of one's possessions, to education and to regular, free and fair elections.

In addition to the European Convention on Human Rights and its protocols there are also a number of other European charters and covenants concerning human rights that most, but not all, European states have signed. These are:

• The Charter of Fundamental Rights of the European Union (2009)
• The Convention on Action against Trafficking in Human Beings (2008)
• The European Charter for Regional or Minority Languages (1992)
• The European Convention for the Prevention of Torture and Inhuman or Degrading Treatment or Punishment (1987)
• The European Social Charter (1961), and Revised Social Charter (1996)
• The Framework Convention for the Protection of National Minorities (2009)

The European Social Charter covers the sort of social rights that are in the Universal Declaration of Human Rights but were not included in the European Convention on Human Rights. The basic rights contained in the Charter are housing, health, education, full employment, reduction of working hours, equal pay for equal work, parental leave, social security, social and legal protection from poverty and social exclusion, the free movement of persons, the rights of migrant workers and the rights of people with disabilities.

1.2.5 Britain and Human Rights

The United Kingdom was one of the leading supporters of the development of human rights after World War II and to date it has signed most, but not all, of the human rights instruments listed above. It has signed:

- The Convention on the Elimination of All Forms of Racial Discrimination
- The International Covenant on Civil and Political Rights
- The International Covenant on Economic, Social and Cultural Rights
- The Convention on the Elimination of All Forms of Discrimination against Women
- The United Nations Convention against Torture
- The Convention on the Rights of the Child
- The Convention on the Rights of Persons with Disabilities
- The European Convention on Human Rights
- The European Social Chapter (and its revised form)
- The European Convention for the Prevention of Torture
- The European Charter for Regional or Minority Languages
- The Framework Convention for the Protection of National Minorities
- The Convention on Action against Trafficking in Human Beings.

It has also signed some, but not all, of the protocols attached to these instruments and has incorporated some, but not all, of these protocols into British law.[16]

1.2.6 The Human Rights Act of 1998 and the Equality Act of 2010

Countries such as the United States, South Africa and Germany that have written constitutions have rights written into these constitutions. Thus Chapter 1 of the German Constitution begins with an article on human dignity that declares that the German people 'acknowledge inviolable and inalienable human rights as the basis of every human community, of peace, and of justice in the world.'[17] Subsequent articles in the chapter set out these rights in more detail. Article 3, for example, is on 'Equality' and it states:

1. All humans are equal before the law.
2. Men and women are equal. The state supports the effective realization of equality of women and men and works towards abolishing present disadvantages.
3. No one may be disadvantaged or favoured because of his sex, parentage, race, language, homeland and origin, his faith, or his religious or political opinions. No one may be disadvantaged because of his handicap.[18]

Because the United Kingdom does not have a written constitution it has no equivalent constitutional statement about human rights. Its legal support for human rights instead takes the form of specific pieces of parliamentary legislation.

The two most important of these are the Human Rights Acts of 1998 and the Equalities Act of 2010.

The Human Rights Act incorporates into British Law the rights set out in the European Convention on Human Rights in Articles 2-14, in the three Articles of the first protocol and in protocol 13 (the abolition of the death penalty).

Under the Act these rights form part of United Kingdom law in three ways:

1. All United Kingdom law must be interpreted, so far as possible, in a way that is compatible with these rights.

2. If an Act of Parliament breaches these rights, the courts can declare the legislation to be incompatible with human rights. This does not however invalidate the law. It is up to Parliament to decide whether to amend the law in the light of the court's declaration, but Section 10 of the Act contains provision for 'remedial action' to be taken to amend legislation in order to make it compatible with human rights.
3. It is unlawful for any public authority to act incompatibly with these rights (unless it has a statutory duty to act in that way), and anyone who believes their rights have been violated can bring court proceedings

against the authority in question.

The Act defines a 'public authority' as '(a) a court or tribunal, and (b) any person certain of whose functions are functions of a public nature.'[19] Examples of such authorities include police officers, prison staff, local authorities, government departments, statutory bodies such as the Office of the Information Commissioner, and providers of nursing and personal care.

If the courts find that a public authority has acted unlawfully they can declare this to be the case and either cancel the decision or prevent the public authority from acting in a particular way. They can also award compensation.

In making decisions about human rights the courts must 'take into account' any decisions made by the European Court of Human Rights, but only to the extent that the Court considers them to be relevant.[20] This does not mean that decisions of the European Court bind British courts. It merely requires the courts to take into account relevant legal judgments in the way that courts normally do when interpreting legislation.

Under section 19 of the Act any Minister who is bringing a Bill before Parliament must make a written statement before the Second Reading of the Bill that states either 'that in his view the provisions of the Bill are compatible with the Convention rights' or 'that although he is unable to make a statement of compatibility the government nevertheless wishes the House to proceed with the Bill.'[21]

This part of the Act is intended to encourage Ministers and the Civil Service to consider the human rights implications of proposed legislation before it is introduced and to encourage informed parliamentary debate about the human rights implications of a proposed piece of legislation.

In addition to the Human Rights Act, human rights in the United Kingdom are also protected by the Equality Act of 2010. In line with the prohibition of discrimination in Article 7 of the Universal Declaration of Human Rights, Article 26 of the International Covenant on Civil and Political Rights and Article 14 of the European Convention on Human Rights, and building on previous British anti-discrimination legislation, this act makes it illegal to discriminate against people on the basis of their age, disability, gender re-assignment, marriage or Civil Partnership, race, religion or belief, sex or sexual orientation.[22]

It also places an obligation on 'public authorities' to 'have due regard to the desirability of exercising them [rights] in a way that is designed to reduce the inequalities of outcome which result from socio-economic disadvantage' when they are 'making decisions of a strategic nature' about the exercise of their functions.[23] Furthermore, because the United Kingdom has signed the European Convention on Human Rights, people in this country have the right of appeal to the European Court of Human Rights if they believe that their human rights have been violated. However, they must have previously exhausted all possible remedies in the British courts.

1.3.   THE PROPOSAL FOR A BRITISH BILL OF RIGHTS

Since 2007 there has been a debate about whether the Human Rights Act should be replaced by a British Bill of Rights and Responsibilities and, if so, what this would mean in terms of the United Kingdom's membership of the European Convention on Human Rights and Britain's relationship to the European Court of Human Rights.

The Conservative Party's Election Manifesto for the 2015 General Election declared:

> The next Conservative Government will scrap the Human Rights Act, and introduce a British Bill of Rights. This will break the formal link between British courts and the European Court of Human Rights, and make our own Supreme Court the ultimate arbiter of human rights matters in the UK.[24]

After the Conservative Party won the election the Minister for Justice, Michael Gove was given the task of putting this pledge into effect.

At the time of writing it is not yet clear what the specific proposals for the replacement of the Human Rights Act will involve, but what is clear is that they will not involve the abolition of human rights. What they will do is propose changes in the framework within which human rights are decided and protected. It is also worth remembering that even if the Human Rights Act is abolished Britain will still remain a party to the European Convention on Human Rights, the United Nations International Bill of Human Rights and to other human rights instruments, and that the Equality Act of 2010 will remain in force unless repealed or amended.

1.4.   RELIGION AND HUMAN RIGHTS

In his famous book *After Virtue* Alisdair MacIntyre decried the idea that there are human rights. 'Rights which are alleged to belong to human beings as such and which are cited as a reason for holding that people ought not to be interfered with in their pursuit of life, liberty and happiness' are in his view a fiction. As he sees it, 'there are no such rights, and belief in them is one with belief in witches and unicorns.'[25]

What we have seen in this chapter makes it clear that McIntyre is wrong. Human rights are not just a fiction. Unlike unicorns, they are a reality. That is to say, there are a number of rights, theoretically shared by all human beings, which are set out in, and guaranteed by, a number of instruments of international and national law.

Furthermore, because these rights are part of international and national law they are in theory, and increasingly in practice, legally enforceable. People who believe that their human rights have been violated can and do seek and receive redress through national and international courts and those who have violated human rights have been punished for doing so. Human rights violations continue to be widespread (for example, it is estimated that some eighty-one governments around the world continue to practise torture), but they are increasingly being challenged.

The fact that human rights have developed in this way also reflects another reality, which is a growing, although not yet universal, consensus that human rights should exist and should be protected. The reason that governments have been willing to develop the human rights instruments outlined in this chapter and to give human rights legal protection is because of an increasing international movement in favour of human rights. This movement, consisting of concerned individuals and campaigning organisations such as Amnesty International, Human Rights Watch, and the International Service for Human Rights, has supported the development of human rights and has sought to ensure that these rights are enforced in practice. This growing popular support for human rights is sometimes referred to as the development of a 'human rights culture'.

Human rights and the growth of support for human rights are thus important realities in the world today.

Another important reality is the existence of religion. Most people in the world today are religious. This is shown, for instance, by the comprehensive demographic survey produced by the Pew Research Center's Forum on Religion and Public Life in 2012 which suggested that in 2010 there were 5.8 billion religiously affiliated adults and children around the world, making up 84% of the global population of 6.9 billion people.[26]

The study suggested that there were 2.2 billion Christians (32% of the world's population), 1.6 billion Muslims (23%), 1 billion Hindus (15%), nearly 500 million Buddhists (7%) and 14 million Jews (0.2%). In addition, it said, more than 400 million people (6%) practise various folk or traditional religions, including African traditional religions, Chinese folk religions, Native American religions and Australian aboriginal religions. An estimated 58 million people – slightly less than 1% of the global population – belong to other religions, including the Baha'i faith, Jainism, Sikhism, Shintoism, Taoism, and Zoroastrianism, to mention just a few.

It is true that the same survey showed that approximately one-in-six people around the globe (1.1 billion, or 16%) have no religious affiliation. This makes them the third-largest group worldwide, behind Christians and Muslims, and about equal in size to the world's Roman Catholic population. However, not all the unaffiliated are non-religious. Many of those who describe themselves as unaffiliated hold some form of spiritual or religious belief even if they do not identify with a particular religious tradition.

Furthermore, additional work by the Pew Research Center has suggested that the number of people who are religiously unaffiliated is likely to fall rather than rise over the next few decades. It suggests that it will fall from 16.4% to 13.2% of the world's population by 2050.[27]

Although Britain is one of the world's less religious societies, even in this country a majority of the population describe themselves as religious. Thus, in the 2011 census 59.3% of the population of England and Wales described themselves as Christian, 4.8% described themselves as Muslim, 1.5 % described themselves as Hindu and 2.1 % described themselves as belonging to some other religion. This means that 67.7% of the population described themselves as religious as opposed to the 25.1% that said they had no religion.[28]

Although the degree of religious commitment by people who describe themselves as religious varies, there can be no doubt that what these figures point to is the fact that a majority of the world's population is religious and this means that the way they understand the world and act in it will be shaped to a greater or lesser extent by their religious belief.

The realities just highlighted, the fact that since World War II there has been a growth in human rights and in a human rights culture and the fact that the majority of the world's population have a religious affiliation, raise questions both for those who are supportive of human rights and for those who are religious (groups which can obviously often overlap).

For those who are supportive of human rights the question that needs to be addressed is how human rights, which can often be couched in language that is legal and secular, can be expressed in terms that make sense to those who have religious belief. Recent events in the Middle East have shown once again how important this is. If a religious group such as the so-called Islamic State comes to view human rights as something that is alien to their religion this can lead to very serious human rights violations. This is an extreme example, but it underlines the more general point that the continuing development and maintenance of a human rights culture will depend to a large extent on convincing people of religious faith that human rights matter in terms of their particular religious tradition.

For those who are religious the question that needs to be addressed is how they can make sense of the reality of the existence of human rights in terms of their religious tradition. As we have said, human rights are something that actually exist and religious people have to think how they understand them in terms of their religion just as they have to think how they understand other aspects of the world in the light of what they believe.

The remainder of this report will provide the basic groundwork to enable people to start to answer these questions by looking at how human rights have come to be understood in the six major religious traditions in this country – Christianity, Judaism, Islam, Hinduism, Buddhism and Sikhism. Each of these religions will be considered in a separate chapter and there will then be a concluding chapter that summarises what has been learnt and looks at the implications of this for the development of human rights in this country.

Notes

[1] Universal Declaration of Human Rights, Article 5 at http://www.ohchr.org/EN/UDHR/Pages/Language.aspx?LangID=eng

[2] Declaration on the Protection of all Persons from Being Subjected to Torture and other Cruel, Inhuman or Degrading Testament or Punishment, Article 1 at http://www.ohchr.org/EN/ProfessionalInterest/Pages/DeclarationTorture.aspx

[3] See the discussion in Micheline Ishay, *The History of Human Rights: From Ancient Times to the Globalization Era*, Berkeley: University of California Press, 2004.

[4] The Charter of the United Nations, Article 1:3 at http://www.un.org/en/sections/un-charter/chapter-i/index.html

[5] For the history of the drafting of the Universal Declaration of Human Rights see John Humphrey, *Human Rights and the United Nations: A Great Adventure*, Dobbs Ferry: Transnational, 1984 and Johannes Morsink, *The Universal Declaration of Human Rights: Origins, Drafting and Intent*, Philadelphia: University of Pennsylvania Press, 2000.

[6] Universal Declaration of Human Rights, Preamble at https://www.un.org/en/documents/udhr/

[7] The full text of these articles can be found at https://www.un.org/en/documents/udhr/

[8] Andrew Clapham, *Human Rights, A Very Short Introduction*, OUP: 2007, e-edition, ch.2.

[9] Ibid., Ch. 2.

[10] Convention on the Rights of Persons with Disabilities, Article 1 at http://www.un.org/disabilities/convention/conventionfull.shtml

[11] Ibid., Article 4.

[12] Ibid., Article 4.

[13] European Convention on Human Rights, Article 1 at http://conventions.coe.int/treaty/en/Treaties/Html/005.htm

[14] Ibid., Article 14.

[15] Ibid., Article 15.

[16] A useful table of the Human Rights instruments signed by the United Kingdom can be found at https://en.wikipedia.org/wiki/Human_rights_in_the_United_Kingdom

[17] The German Constitution, Article 1 at http://www.servat.unibe.ch/icl/gm00000_.html

[18] Ibid., Article 3.

[19] The Human Rights Act, 6 (3) at http://www.legislation.gov.uk/ukpga/1998/42/contents

[20] Ibid., 2 (1) a.

[21] Ibid., 19 (1).

[22] The Equality Act 2010, Part 2 at http://www.legislation.gov.uk/ukpga/1998/42/contents

[23] Ibid., Part 1(1)

[24] *The Conservative Party Manifesto 2015*, p.60.

[25] Alisdair MacIntyre, *After Virtue: A Study in Moral Theory*, 3ed, Notre Dame, Indiana: University of Notre Dame Press, 2007, pp.66-67.

[26] Pew Research Center, *The Global Religious Landscape: A Report on the Size and Distribution of the World's Major Religious Groups as of 2010*, Washington DC: Pew Research Center, 2012.

[27] Pew Research Center, 'The Future of World Religions: Population Growth Projections, 2010-2050', April 2015 at http://www.pewforum.org/2015/04/02/religious-projections-2010-2050/

[28] The Office for National Statistics, 'Religion in England and Wales 2011', http://www.ons.gov.uk/ons/rel/census/2011-census/key-statistics-for-local-authorities-in-england-and-wales/rpt-religion.html

Chapter Two

CHRISTIANITY AND HUMAN RIGHTS

2.1   CHRISTIAN INFLUENCE ON THE DEVELOPMENT OF HUMAN RIGHTS

There can be no doubt that there was a major Christian influence on the development of human rights in the period during and after World War II.

As scholars such as Mary Anne Glendon,[1] Samuel Moyn[2] and John Nurser[3] have shown, the development of the Universal Declaration of Human Rights in 1948 and the European Convention of Human Rights of 1953 built upon the work of Christian activists such as the Roman Catholic Jacques Maritain and the Lutheran Frederick Nolde and the support of the Roman Catholic Church and the fledgling World Council of Churches.[4] They saw the development of human rights as a way of preserving Christian values and as a giving space for the proclamation and practice of the Christian faith in a world in which the old idea of Christendom was no longer viable and in which there was a continuing threat to the Church and to Christian values from Communist totalitarianism. Furthermore, one of the key figures who shaped and promoted the 1948 Declaration was the Lebanese Christian philosopher and diplomat Charles Malik.

There have been Christian thinkers who have had strong reservations about the concept of human rights on the grounds that (a) the assertion of rights undercuts the sheer unmerited benevolence of Christian love and (b) that it encourages antagonistic individualism.[5]

However, Christian majority nations around the globe have generally been supportive of the development of human rights with Christian majority nations in Europe and North America pioneering the development of such rights.[6] In addition the major Christian churches have been unsurprisingly enthusiastic about human rights. Three examples will serve to illustrate this.

2.2.1   The Lambeth Conference 1948

The first example is the three resolutions on human rights passed by the Lambeth Conference of the bishops of the Anglican Communion in 1948 in support of what was then the proposed Universal Declaration on Human Rights. These resolutions are as follows:

Resolution 6
The Conference declares that all men, irrespective of race or colour, are equally the objects of God's love and are called to love and serve him. All men are made in his image; for all Christ died; and to all there is made the offer of eternal life. Every individual is therefore bound by duties towards God and towards other men, and has certain rights without the enjoyment of which he cannot freely perform those duties. These rights should be declared by the Church, recognized by the state, and safeguarded by international law.

Resolution 7
The Conference declares that among such rights are security of life and person; the right to work, to bring up a family, and to possess personal property; the right to freedom of speech, of discussion and association, and to accurate information; and to full freedom of religious life and practice; and that these rights belong to all men irrespective of race or colour.

Resolution 8
The Conference endorses the proposed Covenant on Human Rights, now before the United Nations, and declares it necessary for full religious freedom that:

a) every person shall have the right to freedom of religion, conscience, and belief, including the right, either alone or in community with other persons of like mind, to hold and manifest any religious or other belief, to change his belief and to practise any form of religious worship and observance, and he shall not be required to do any act that is contrary to such worship and observance; and that

b) every person of full age and sound mind shall be free, either alone or in community with other persons of like mind, to give and receive any form of religious teaching, and in the case of a minor the parent or guardian shall be free to determine what religious teaching he shall receive.

The Conference believes that the above rights should be subject only to such limitations as are internationally recognised as necessary to protect public order, morals, and the rights and freedoms of others. Any such limitations should be clearly defined by law, and there should be appeal concerning them before impartial courts of justice.[7]

2.2.2 *Pacem in Terris*

The second example is the Encyclical *Pacem in Terris* promulgated by Pope John XXIII in 1963. Building on the natural law tradition of the Roman Catholic Church, this encyclical declares that the created nature of human beings, and the dignity bestowed on them as a result of their being the objects of the saving work of Jesus Christ, require support for the sorts of rights and freedoms set out in the Universal Declaration of Human Rights and European Convention on Human Rights.

The encyclical states that:

Any human society, if it is to be well-ordered and productive, must lay down as a foundation this principle, namely, that every human being is a person, that is, his nature is endowed with intelligence and free will. Indeed, precisely because he is a person he has rights and obligations flowing directly and simultaneously from his very nature. And as these rights and obligations are universal and inviolable so they cannot in any way be surrendered.

If we look upon the dignity of the human person in the light of divinely revealed truth, we cannot help but esteem it far more highly; for men are redeemed by the blood of Jesus Christ, they are by grace the children and friends of God and heirs of eternal glory.[8]

It then goes on to argue that these foundations lead to a range of personal, social, economic and religious rights:

... we see that every man has the right to life, to bodily integrity, and to the means which are suitable for the proper development of life; these are primarily food, clothing, shelter, rest, medical care, and finally the necessary social services. Therefore a human being also has the right to security in cases of sickness, inability to work, widowhood, old age, unemployment, or in any other case in which he is deprived of the means of subsistence through no fault of his own.

By the natural law every human being has the right to respect for his person, to his good reputation; the right to freedom in searching for truth and in expressing and communicating his opinions, and in pursuit of art, within the limits laid down by the moral order and the common good; and he has the right to be informed truthfully about public events.

The natural law also gives man the right to share in the benefits of culture, and therefore the right to a basic education and to technical and professional training in keeping with the stage of educational development in the country to which he belongs. Every effort should be made to ensure that persons be enabled, on the basis of merit, to go on to higher studies, so that, as far as possible, they may occupy posts and take on responsibilities in human society in accordance with their natural gifts and the skills they have acquired.

This too must be listed among the rights of a human being, to honor God according to the sincere dictates of his own conscience, and therefore the right to practice his religion privately and publicly. For as Lactantius so clearly taught: 'We were created for the purpose of showing to the God Who bore us the submission we owe Him, of recognizing Him alone, and of serving Him. We are obliged and bound by this duty to God; from this religion itself receives its name.' And on this point Our Predecessor of immortal memory, Leo XIII, declared: 'This genuine, this honorable freedom of the sons of God, which most nobly protects the dignity of the human person, is greater than any violence or injustice; it has always been sought by the Church, and always most dear to Her. This was the freedom which the Apostles claimed with intrepid constancy, which the Apologists defended with their writings, and which the Martyrs in such numbers consecrated with their blood.'

Human beings have the right to choose freely the state of life which they prefer, and therefore the right to set up a family, with equal rights and duties for man and woman, and also the right to follow a vocation to the priesthood or the religious life.

The family, grounded on marriage freely contracted, monogamous and indissoluble, is and must be considered the first and essential cell of human society. From this it follows that most careful provision must be made for the family both in economic and social matters as well as in those which are of a cultural and moral nature, all of which look to the strengthening of the family and helping it carry out its function.

Parents, however, have a prior right in the support and education of their children.

If we turn our attention to the economic sphere it is clear that man has a right by the natural law not only to an opportunity to work, but also to go about his work without coercion.

To these rights is certainly joined the right to demand working conditions in which physical health is not endangered, morals are safeguarded, and young people's normal development is not impaired. Women have the right to working conditions in accordance with their requirements and their duties as wives and mothers.

From the dignity of the human person, there also arises the right to carry on economic activities according to the degree of responsibility of which one is capable. Furthermore -- and this must be specially emphasized -- the worker has a right to a wage determined according to criterions of justice, and sufficient, therefore, in proportion to the available resources, to give the worker and his family a standard of living in keeping with the dignity of the human person. In this regard, Our Predecessor Pius XII said: 'To the personal duty to work imposed by nature, there corresponds and follows the natural right of each individual to make of his work the means to provide for his own life and the lives of his children; so fundamental is the law of nature which commands man to preserve his life.'

The right to private property, even of productive goods, also derives from the nature of man. This right, as we have elsewhere declared, 'is an effective means for safeguarding the dignity of the human person and for the exercise of responsibility in all fields; it strengthens and gives serenity to family life, thereby increasing the peace and prosperity of the State.'

However, it is opportune to point out that there is a social duty essentially inherent in the right of private property.

From the fact that human beings are by nature social, there arises the right of assembly and association. They have also the right to give the societies of which they are members the form they consider most suitable for the aim they have in view, and to act within such societies on their own initiative and on their own responsibility in order to achieve their desired objectives.

And, as we Ourselves in the encyclical *Mater et Magistra* have strongly urged, it is by all means necessary that a great variety of organizations and intermediate groups be established which are capable of achieving a goal which an individual cannot effectively attain by himself. These societies and organizations must be considered the indispensable means to safeguard the dignity of the human person and freedom while leaving intact a sense of responsibility.

Every human being has the right to freedom of movement and of residence within the confines of his own country; and, when there are just reasons for it, the right to emigrate to other countries and take up residence there. The fact that one is a citizen of a particular State does not detract in any way from his membership in the human family as a whole, nor from his citizenship in the world community.

The dignity of the human person involves the right to take an active part in public affairs and to contribute one's part to the common good of the citizens. For, as Our Predecessor of happy memory, Pius XII, pointed out: 'The human individual, far from being an object and, as it were, a merely passive element in the social order, is in fact, must be and must continue to be, its subject, its foundation and its end.'

The human person is also entitled to a juridical protection of his rights, a protection that should be efficacious, impartial and inspired by the true norms of justice. As Our Predecessor Pius XII teaches: 'That perpetual privilege proper to man, by which every individual has a claim to the protection of his rights, and by which there is assigned to each a definite and particular sphere of rights, immune from all arbitrary attacks, is the logical consequence of the order of justice willed by God.'[9]

2.2.3 World Council of Churches statement on the 60th anniversary of the Universal Declaration of Human Rights

The third example is the statement issued by the Executive Committee of the World Council of Churches in September 2008 to mark the 60th anniversary of the Universal Declaration of Human Rights.

This statement notes the statement about the theological basis of human rights made by the Assembly of the World Council of Churches held in Nairobi in 1975:

Our concern for human rights is based on our conviction that God wills a society in which all can exercise full human rights. All human beings are created in the image of God, equal and infinitely precious in God's sight and ours. Jesus Christ has bound us to one another by his life, death and resurrection, so that what concerns one concerns us all.[10]

It then goes on to say:

Fully aware of the interconnection and interdependence of human rights and human dignity, the executive committee of the World Council of Churches, meeting in Lübeck, Germany, 23-26 September 2008:

A. *reaffirms* its commitment to the Universal Declaration of Human Rights and to the principles enshrined within it;

B. *regrets* the huge gap which continues to exist between declarations on human rights and implementation, and the tragic human suffering this represents as a result of extensive violation of human rights;

C. *requests* governments to adopt, ratify and respect international and regional instruments for the promotion and protection of human rights, to monitor compliance with them in their own countries and around the world, and to underwrite that commitment with human and financial resources;

D. *urges* governments to take all necessary measures in order to guarantee the effective protection and promotion of the right to freedom of religion or belief and to challenge intolerance or discrimination based on religion or belief in society;

E. *calls* on churches, through education and action, to work to promote human dignity by improving public understanding of human rights violations and of the human rights protection mechanisms and urges member churches and their governments to cooperate with the UN and other governments and non-governmental bodies in this regard;

F. *commends* the ongoing work of the churches and ecumenical organizations for the promotion and protection of human rights and urges them to continue to stress the linkages between universally accepted standards of human rights and the Christian commitment to human dignity;

G. *acknowledges* human rights advocacy work to be an essential and integral component of the worldwide struggle and yearning for peace with justice and an important part of the ministry of the church.[11]

In addition to this formal support for human rights by the churches, churches and individual Christians have been and are involved in the work of Christian human rights organizations such as Christian Solidarity Worldwide,[12] Action by Christians Against Torture,[13] and Release International,[14] as well as secular human rights organizations such as Amnesty International and Human Rights Watch and have been heavily involved in campaigns such as the Campaign for Civil Rights in the United States, the campaign against Apartheid in South Africa, the campaigns against human rights abuses in Central and Southern America and most recently the campaign for the rights of migrants and asylum seekers.

2.3 THE CHRISTIAN THEOLOGICAL FRAMEWORK FOR HUMAN RIGHTS

These examples show the way in which Christian majority nations, Christian churches and Christian groups and individuals have been generally supportive of the development of human rights. They also highlight the fact that Christian support for human rights is rooted in what Christians believe about the nature and consequent dignity of human beings.

This theological foundation for human rights is helpfully expounded in more detail by the Evangelical Anglican theologian John Stott in a book on Christian ethics *Issues Facing Christians Today*.

In this book he writes that from a Christian perspective the dignity of human beings consists of three relationships which are set out in the biblical account of creation in Genesis 1 and 2:

The first is *our relationship to God*. Human beings are God-like beings, created by his will in his image. The divine image includes those rational, moral and spiritual qualities which separate us from the animals and relate us to God. In consequence we can learn about him from evangelists and teachers (it is a basic human right to hear the gospel); come to know, love and serve him; live in conscious, humble dependence upon him; understand his will and obey his commands. So then, all those human rights we call the freedom to profess, practise and propagate religion, the freedom of worship, of conscience, of thought and of speech, come under the first rubric, of our relationship to God. It is striking that even the deistic leaders of the American and French Revolutions knew this instinctively and referred to the 'Supreme Being' from whom human rights are ultimately derived.

The second unique capacity of human beings concerns *our relationship to one another*. The God who made humankind is himself a social being, one God comprising three eternally distinct modes of personhood. He said: 'Let us make man in our image' and 'It is not good for the man to be alone.' So God made man male and female, and told them to procreate. Sexuality is his creation, marriage is his institution, and human companionship his purpose. So then, all those human freedoms which we call the sanctity of sex, marriage and family, the right of peaceful assembly, and the right to receive respect, whatever our age, sex, race, or rank, come under this second rubric of our relationship to each other.

Our third distinctive quality as human beings is *our relationship to the earth and its creatures*. God has given us dominion, with instructions to subdue and cultivate the fruitful earth, and rule its creatures. So then, all those human rights we call the right to work and the right to rest, the right to share in the earth's resources, the right to food, clothing and shelter, the right to life and health and to their preservation, together with freedom from poverty, hunger and disease, come under this third rubric of our relationship to the earth.[15]

He goes on to say that:

In spite of the risk of over-simplification, we may sum up what is meant by human dignity in these three ways: our relationship to God (or the right and responsibility of worship), our relationship to each other (the right and responsibility of fellowship), and our relationship to the earth (or the right and responsibility of stewardship) – together of course with the opportunity which education, income and health provide to *develop* this unique human potential.

Thus all human rights are at base the right to be human, and to enjoy the dignity of having been created in God's image and possessing in consequence unique relationships to God himself, to our fellow human beings and to the material world. Christians have something important to add to this, namely that our Creator has also redeemed us, at a great personal cost, through the incarnation and atonement of his Son. And the costliness of God's redeeming work reinforces the sense of human worth which his creation has already given us. William Temple expresses this truth with his customary clarity:

There can be no Rights of Man except on the basis of faith in God. But if God is real, and all men are his sons, that is the true worth of every one of them. My worth is what I am worth to God; and that is a marvellous great deal, for Christ died for me. Thus, incidentally, what gives to each of us his highest worth gives the same worth to everyone;

in all that matters most we are all equal.[16]

The right to receive respect to which Stott refers under the heading of 'our relationship to one another' also explains rights to which he does not directly refer, namely the right not to be unjustly accused or imprisoned and the right not to be subject to torture or cruel, inhuman or degrading treatment. Both of these show a lack of respect to the God-given dignity of another human being. Thus the *Catechism of the Catholic Church* declares that 'Torture which uses physical or moral violence to extract confessions, punish the guilty, frighten opponents, or satisfy hatred is contrary to respect for the person and for human dignity.'[17]

2.4   RIGHTS AND AUTONOMY

From a Christian perspective, the fact that human rights have their foundation in the God-given dignity of every human being in the way described by Stott means that human rights are not simply an artificial legal construct. It is true that the form in which human rights have been articulated since 1948 is a human legal construct, but this legal construct has given expression to fundamental truths about what it means to be human and how human beings should behave.

This means, for example, that to deprive someone of food and shelter is wrong not just because human rights law says it is wrong, but because it is intrinsically wrong on the basis of the worth that human beings have before God and the way that he has created them. As bodily creatures human beings require food and shelter in order to survive and it shows a lack of respect to them, and therefore to the God who created and redeemed them, to prevent someone from having them.

The fact that human rights are rooted in the way that God has made human beings also means from a Christian perspective that human rights cannot be seen in terms of each individual human being exercising their own personal autonomy as he or she sees fit. To quote Stott again:

Our value depends then on God's view of us and relationship to us. As a result of this, human rights are not unlimited rights, as if we were free to be and do absolutely anything we like. They are limited to what is compatible with being the human person God made us and meant us to be. True freedom is found in being our true selves as authentic human beings, not in contradicting ourselves.[18]

The fact that human rights are ultimately the right to be the person God made us and meant us to be has three implications from a Christian viewpoint.

First, because human beings have been created to know, love and serve God it follows that human beings can only fulfil the end for which they were made if this is what they do. As a result, even if human beings are materially prosperous and are free from every kind of material oppression they have failed to achieve the proper fulfilment of their humanity if they lack a right relationship with God.

Furthermore, Christian theology has traditionally held on the basis of the teaching of the New Testament that this kind of relationship is only achievable through Jesus Christ. Only through the victory over sin achieved by Jesus' death and resurrection and through the power of the Holy Spirit given by Jesus to those who believe in him are human beings able to know, love and serve God as they were created to do.

For this reason the freedom of religion that is guaranteed in the International Bill of Rights and in the European Convention on Human Rights is for Christians something that is fundamental to the rights of human beings. There have been long periods in Christian history in which Christians have held that it is right to impose observance of the Christian religion by law. However, by the time that the Universal Declaration of Human Rights came to be written there had been a re-discovery of the theological truth insisted on by many of the Church Fathers of the early centuries of the Christian era that a relationship with God is something that by its very nature requires free consent and that therefore religious compulsion is wrong in principle, and also an acceptance that the best guarantee of freedom to practise the Christian religion was by guaranteeing religious freedom for all.

Because seeking to spread the Christian faith to all people everywhere in accordance with Jesus' Great Commission recorded in Matthew 28:18-20 is a fundamental part of the Christian religion and because Christian discipleship is something that cannot be confined to participation in church services, but has to be lived out in every aspect of life it is also the case that from a Christian viewpoint freedom of religion has to involve more than simply freedom to worship. It has to involve the freedom to propagate the Christian faith, including to those who belong to other religions, and the freedom to live out the faith in everyday life. This is why recent cases in Britain in which Christians have been prohibited from wearing a cross at work or from sharing their faith with others in the course of their work has been seen by many Christians as a violation of freedom of religion.[19]

Secondly, because human beings have been created by God to live in relationship with others it is impossible from a Christian viewpoint to consider the rights of individuals without also considering what is good for other people and for humanity as a whole.

A Christian approach to rights would say that it is not acceptable to make the good of the individual subservient to the good of a nation, a state or a political party. The growth of Christian support for human rights in the 1940s was in large part a protest against the way in which Fascist and Communist forms of totalitarianism were seen to have done this. Each individual has his or her own dignity bestowed on them by God and this dignity cannot be infringed to serve the greater good of some wider body of people. That is why, for example it would not be right to torture or unjustly imprison someone for the sake of seeking to keep a country safe from the threat of terrorism.

On the other hand, it is equally true that from a Christian perspective the rights of individuals need to be exercised in ways that will enable every other individual to flourish as well. There can be no place for a selfish autonomy that pursues a purely individual fulfilment.

Roman Catholic social teaching has helpfully described this right balance between the good of the individual and the good of the community as a whole in terms of the need to seek the 'common good'. The *Catechism of the Catholic Church* explains the concept of the common good in the following terms:

> In keeping with the social nature of man, the good of each individual is necessarily related to the common good, which in turn can be defined only in reference to the human person:
>
> Do not live entirely isolated, having retreated into yourselves, as if you were already justified, but gather instead to seek the common good together.

By common good is to be understood 'the sum total of social conditions which allow people, either as groups or as individuals, to reach their fulfillment more fully and more easily.' The common good concerns the life of all. It calls for prudence from each, and even more from those who exercise the office of authority.[20]

The Catechism goes on to say that the common good involves three essential elements:

First, the common good presupposes *respect for the person* as such. In the name of the common good, public authorities are bound to respect the fundamental and inalienable rights of the human person. Society should permit each of its members to fulfill his vocation. In particular, the common good resides in the conditions for the exercise of the natural freedoms indispensable for the development of the human vocation, such as 'the right to act according to a sound norm of conscience and to safeguard ... privacy, and rightful freedom also in matters of religion.'

Second, the common good requires the *social well-being* and *development* of the group itself. Development is the epitome of all social duties. Certainly, it is the proper function of authority to arbitrate, in the name of the common good, between various particular interests; but it should make accessible to each what is needed to lead a truly human life: food, clothing, health, work, education and culture, suitable information, the right to establish a family, and so on.

Finally, the common good requires *peace,* that is, the stability and security of a just order. It presupposes that authority should ensure by morally acceptable means the *security* of society and its members. It is the basis of the right to legitimate personal and collective defence.[21]

The *Catechism* also argues that the common good has to be seen in universal terms, embracing not only what is good for each individual nation, but what is good for all people everywhere:

Human interdependence is increasing and gradually spreading throughout the world. The unity of the human family, embracing people who enjoy equal natural dignity, implies a *universal common good*. This good calls for an organization of the community of nations

CHRISTIANITY AND HUMAN RIGHTS

able to 'provide for the different needs of men; this will involve the sphere of social life to which belong questions of food, hygiene, education ... and certain situations arising here and there, as for example ... alleviating the miseries of refugees dispersed throughout the world, and assisting migrants and their families.'[22]

Thirdly, from a Christian perspective rights that are granted by law, but which are not compatible with the way that God has created human beings to be, lack moral validity. There are two particular areas in which this is an issue for many Christians at the moment.

2.5   AREAS OF TENSION OVER HUMAN RIGHTS

The first area is the area of what is known as 'reproductive rights'. These are defined by the World Health Organisation as:

...the basic right of all couples and individuals to decide freely and responsibly the number, spacing and timing of their children and to have the information and means to do so, and the right to attain the highest standard of sexual and reproductive health. They also include the right of all to make decisions concerning reproduction free of *discrimination, coercion* and *violence.*

Reproductive rights are not mentioned in the Universal Declaration of Human Rights or the European Convention on Human Rights, but they have come to be widely recognised as rights since 1968 when the Proclamation of Tehran issued after the United Nations' International Conference on Human Rights declared, 'Parents have a basic human right to determine *freely* and *responsibly* the number and the spacing of their children.'[23]

There are two issues in relation to the idea of reproductive rights where many Christians have moral problems.

The first issue is the use of artificial contraception to limit the number of children or to prevent childbirth entirely. Many Christians hold that the decision about whether or not to use artificial contraception is something that should be left to couples to decide.

Thus, Resolution 115 of the Lambeth Conference of Anglican Bishops of 1958 declares:

> The Conference believes that the responsibility for deciding upon the number and frequency of children has been laid by God upon the consciences of parents everywhere; that this planning, in such ways as are mutually acceptable to husband and wife in Christian conscience, is a right and important factor in Christian family life and should be the result of positive choice before God. Such responsible parenthood, built on obedience to all the duties of marriage, requires a wise stewardship of the resources and abilities of the family as well as a thoughtful consideration of the varying population needs and problems of society and the claims of future generations.[24]

On the other hand, many other Christians, particularly, but by no means exclusively, in the Roman Catholic tradition, would hold that while it is morally acceptable to regulate childbirth by means of 'periodic continence' based on 'self-observation and the use of infertile periods',[25] it is morally wrong to use artificial forms of contraception. In the words of the *Catechism of the Catholic Church*:

> ... every action which, whether in anticipation of the conjugal act, or in its accomplishment, or in the development of its natural consequences, proposes, whether as an end or as a means, to render procreation impossible' is intrinsically evil.[26]

The reason it is seen as morally wrong is because an openness to the creation of a new life is seen as an integral part of the total self-giving that sexual activity is meant to involve and the use of artificial contraception goes against this. In the words of Pope John Paul II:

> ... the innate language that expresses the total reciprocal self-giving of husband and wife is overlaid, through contraception, by an objectively contradictory language, namely, that of not giving oneself totally to the other. This leads not only to a positive refusal to be open to life but also to a falsification of the inner truth of conjugal love, which is called upon to give itself in personal totality.... the difference, both anthropological and moral, between contraception and recourse to the

rhythm of the cycle . . . involves in the final analysis two irreconcilable concepts of the human person and of human sexuality.[27]

The second issue is that of abortion. Many Christians would see abortion, though always regrettable, as something that should be left to the decision of the woman concerned and would argue that it can be justified as a least-worst option in circumstances where the physical or mental well-being of the woman is at risk or it is known that the pregnancy would result in a baby who is severely handicapped.

On the other hand, many other Christians, again particularly but not exclusively Roman Catholics, would argue that a child is a person from the moment of conception and that abortion involves depriving that person of the right to life. Abortion can never therefore be morally justified.

There is also a more general concern among many Christians that an emphasis on reproductive rights has led to a culture in which sexual activity is separated from the intention to found a family and that this separation has had damaging social consequences. By encouraging men in particular to have sex without any intention or expectation of marriage or parental responsibility it has led to an increasing number of children living in poverty in homes headed by single mothers.

The second area in which many Christians judge that there is a tension between human rights and what is morally and theologically justifiable is the area of equality. As in the case of reproductive rights there are two specific issues involved. The first is the issue of equality between the sexes.

There is universal agreement amongst Christians that as people created in God's image and as the objects of the saving work of Jesus Christ women have equal human dignity to men. Where there is disagreement is over the question of whether the equal human dignity that men and women possess means that the roles which they exercise should be identical.

Many Christians would argue that this is the case. They would say that there should be equality between men and women in all areas of life including the ministry of the Church with no fixed distinction of role between women and men. Christians who take this view feel comfortable with the way that such a view of sexual equality has become an integral part of much contemporary thinking about human rights.

On the other hand, many other Christians would say that the equal human dignity possessed by men and women does not preclude a God-given distinction between the roles that men and women should exercise, particularly in family life and the ministry of the Church. They would say that men should exercise a leadership role both in the family (as 'head' of the household) and in the Church and that it is contrary to Scripture and Christian tradition for women to be ordained as ministers, priests or bishops. Those who take this view are concerned that the current emphasis on sexual equality does not recognise the idea of differentiation of roles between men and women and will lead to increasing social pressure on Christians to change their traditional teaching and practice in this regard. They would point, for example, to the political pressure placed on the Church of England to bring in women bishops after the General Synod voted against legislation to allow this in November 2011.

The second is the issue of equality for gay and lesbian people. As before, there would be universal agreement amongst Christians that those who identify themselves as gay or lesbian have equal dignity to any other human being. Therefore the general rights that apply to all human beings apply to them as well. Where there is disagreement is over what this should mean in practice.

An increasing number of Christians, particularly but not exclusively in the Western world, would argue that the equal human dignity of gay and lesbian people has to be reflected in equality of treatment in both society and in the Church. Thus they would say that gay and lesbian relationships should be accorded parity of esteem with heterosexual relationships through, for instance, the recognition of such relationships as a form of marriage and that being in a sexually active gay or lesbian relationship should not be a bar to ordination.

On the other hand, a majority of Christians worldwide would argue that gay and lesbian relationships are wrong in principle because sexual activity should be confined to marriage and God has established marriage as a relationship between a man and a woman (see Genesis 1:26-28 and 2:18-25). They would therefore argue that such relationships should not be given parity of esteem either by the state or by the Church and would therefore oppose both same-sex 'marriage' and the ordination of those who are in sexually active same-sex relationships.

Those who take this second view are increasingly concerned that the growing emphasis in Western society on the right to equality for gay and lesbian people will result in an erosion of religious freedom in that those Christians who are conscientiously opposed to gay and lesbian sexual activity and to same-sex 'marriage' will not be permitted to articulate their views freely in the public square or to give expression to their opposition in the way they behave. For example, it is argued, Christians in the teaching profession and national and local government are increasingly fearful of facing disciplinary action if they express disapproval of same-sex relationships and there is now a series of well-documented cases in which those running guest houses have had cases brought against them for not allowing same-sex couple to share a double room, and florists, bakers and photographers have had cases brought against them for refusing to supply goods and services for same-sex weddings.

Christians who are concerned about this issue would argue that there needs to be proper balance of rights so that the right of gay and lesbian people to conduct their private lives as they see fit is balanced by the right of Christian and other religious people to freely express their moral opposition to same-sex relationships and to act in a way that avoids giving tacit support to such relationships. They would also argue that it would be wrong for the state to seek to encourage or coerce churches or other religious bodies into accepting such relationships.

A third and final area in which there can be seen to be tension between the way in which human rights have developed and the conviction of some Christians is over the issue of capital punishment. As noted in the first chapter, protocols to the International Covenant on Civil and Political Rights and to the European Convention on Human Rights commit States to the abolition of the death penalty. An increasing number of Christians have come to support this position. For example, in March 1990 the World Council of Churches adopted a declaration unconditionally opposing the death penalty.

This declaration states, 'Recognizing that all human beings are created, in taking away a human life, the state usurps the will of God.' It goes on to say that the WCC 'declares its unconditional opposition to capital punishment, and calls upon all States to abolish it and to sign and promptly ratify the International Covenant on Civil and Political Rights concerning the abolition of the death penalty' and

...calls on member churches, in cooperation with other faiths and non-governmental organizations:

- to advocate the abolition of the death penalty in States where it remains legal;

- to oppose efforts to restore the death penalty in States where it is now abolished;

- to support international efforts towards the universal abolition of the death penalty;

- develop theological and biblical arguments to help their members, and others, in their efforts to abolish the death penalty and to refute the theological and biblical arguments advanced by supporters of the death penalty;

- to encourage and support each other in these efforts by sharing ideas, resources and solidarity.'[28]

However some Christian churches continue to argue that imposition of the death penalty is legitimate. Thus the Southern Baptist Convention (the world's largest Baptist church and the largest Protestant denomination in the United States) passed a resolution in 2000 that stated its continuing support for the death penalty.

This resolution stated that 'God forbids personal revenge (Romans 12:19) and has established capital punishment as a just and appropriate means by which the civil magistrate may punish those guilty of capital crimes (Romans 13:4)' and that the Convention therefore supported a 'fair and equitable use of capital punishment by civil magistrates as a legitimate form of punishment for those guilty of murder or treasonous acts that result in death.'[29] Other conservative Protestant churches would take a similar position.

Those who take this view obviously oppose the idea that respect for human rights necessitates the abolition of the death penalty. As they see it the death penalty serves justice and the common good.

Notes

[1] Mary Anne Glendon, *A World Made New: Eleanor Roosevelt and the Universal Declaration of Human Rights*, New York: Random House, 2001.

[2] Samuel Moyn, *Christian Human Rights*, Philadelphia: University of Pennsylvania Press, 2015.

[3] John Nurser, *For All Peoples and Nations – Christian Churches and Human Rights*, Washington DC: Georgetown University Press, 2005.

[4] The text of Article 18 of the Universal Declaration of Human Rights on freedom of thought conscience and religion was contributed by the WCC's Commission of the Churches on International Affairs.

[5] For these points see Nicholas P. Wolterstorff, 'Christianity and Human Rights', in John Witte Jr and Christian Green (eds), *Religion and Human Rights*, Oxford: OUP, 2012, Ch.2.

[6] There is undoubtedly an issue about the extent to which such nations have lived up to their formal support for human rights in practice, but the official support of nations such as, for example, the United States, Great Britain and Germany for human rights is clear.

[7] Text in Roger Coleman (ed) *Resolutions of the Twelve Lambeth Conferences 1867-1988*, Toronto: Anglican Book Centre, 1992, pp. 92-93.

[8] Pope John XXIII, *Pacem in Terris*, 1963, paragraphs 9-10. Text at http://papalencyclicals.net/John23/j23pacem.htm

[9] Ibid., paragraphs 11-25.

[10] World Council of Churches, Statement on Universal Declaration of Human Rights, 2008. Text at http://www.oikoumene.org/en/resources/documents/executive-committee/2008-09/statement-on-universal-declaration-of-human-rights. The full text of this statement is at Appendix 1 of this report.

[11] Ibid.

[12] Christian Solidarity Worldwide, http://www.csw.org.uk/home.htm

[13] Action by Christians Against Torture, http://acatuk.org.uk/

[14] Release International, http://www.releaseinternational.org

[15] John Stott, *Issues Facing Christians Today*, Basingstoke: Marshalls, 1984, pp.144-145.

[16] Ibid., quoting Archbishop William Temple, *Citizen and Churchman*, London: Eyre and Spottiswoode, 1941, pp. 74-75. For a more detailed statement of the argument put forward by Stott see Roger Ruston, *Human Rights and the Image of God*, London: SCM, 2004.

[17] *Catechism of the Catholic Church*, paragraph 2297, London: Geoffrey Chapman, 1994, p. 494.

[18] Stott, op.cit. p.145.

[19] See, for example, the cases listed in the 'employment' section of the Christian Concern website at http://www.christianconcern.com/our-concerns/employment?page=2

[20] *Catechism of the Catholic Church*, paragraphs 1905-1906, p.418.

[21] Ibid., paragraphs 1907-1909, pp. 418-419. Italics in the original.

[22] Ibid., paragraph 1911, p.419. Italics in the original.

[23] Proclamation of Tehran, 16 at http://web.archive.org/web/20071017025912/http://www.unhchr.ch/html/menu3/b/b_tehern.htm

[24] Text in Coleman (ed), op.cit. p.147.

[25] *Catechism of the Catholic Church*, paragraph 2370, p.508.

[26] Ibid., paragraph 2370, p.508.

[27] John Paul II, Familiaris Consortio, 1981, paragraph 32 text at http://w2.vatican.va/ content/john-paul-ii/en/apost_exhortations/documents/hf_jpii_exh_19811122_familiaris-consortio.html. This exhortation does not carry the same theological authority as the Catechism, but it does explain the thinking behind it.

[28] See The Evolution Of The Christian Position On The Death Penalty, at http://www.fiacat.org/the-evolution-of-the-christian-position-on-the-deathpenalty

[29] http://www.sbc.net/resolutions/299

Chapter Three

Judaism and Human Rights

3.1 JEWISH SUPPORT FOR HUMAN RIGHTS

Just as there can be no doubt that there was a strong Christian influence on the development of the concept of human rights, so also there can be no doubt that there was a strong Jewish influence as well.

As Lord Sacks has argued, the emergence of the tradition of thinking about human rights in the 17th and 18th centuries in the writings of men such as Thomas Hobbes, John Locke and Thomas Jefferson that would eventually lead to the development of human rights legislation in the 20th century was due to the influence of the Hebrew Bible:

> The concept of rights entered the West in the 17th and 18th centuries. When Hobbes and Locke were writing their treatises, the book they had in front of them was the Hebrew Bible. When Thomas Jefferson sat down to write the immortal words of the American Declaration of Independence – "We hold these truths to be self-evident, that all men are created equal and are endowed by their Creator with certain unalienable rights" – he was not drawing on the philosophy of ancient Greece. Neither Plato nor Aristotle would have understood them, convinced as they were that some people were born slaves.
>
> Those truths were self-evident to only a mind steeped in the book of Genesis, with its revolutionary statement that all human beings are made in the image of God; in the Book of Exodus with its assertion that the true God is one who liberates slaves; and in the prophets of

ancient Israel whose message of human dignity, justice, and peace still resonates today.

The language of human rights is universal, but it speaks with a Jewish accent.[1]

The waves of persecution that Jewish people suffered in the 19th and 20th centuries, culminating in the Holocaust, led to a strong Jewish concern about the need to establish safeguards for human rights in order to prevent such persecution continuing to happen either to Jews or to others. In line with this concern, the American Jewish Committee was one of the leading bodies arguing in the 1940s that the United Nations should produce a statement of universal human rights, and the French Jewish jurist Renee Cassin was one of the key drafters of the Universal Declaration of Human Rights. He was awarded the Nobel Peace Prize in 1968 for his work on the Declaration.[2]

Jewish support for human rights has subsequently been shown by the official endorsement of human rights by the State of Israel, a state which seeks to give expression in its national life to the beliefs and values of the Jewish people.

The Declaration of Independence of the State of Israel in May 1948 put human rights at the heart of what it said about the nature of the new state. It declared that:

> The State of Israel will be open to the immigration of Jews from all countries of their dispersion; will promote the development of the country for the benefit of all its inhabitants; will be based on the precepts of liberty, justice and peace taught by the Hebrew Prophets; will uphold the full social and political equality of all its citizens, without distinction of race, creed or sex; will guarantee full freedom of conscience, worship, education and culture; will safeguard the sanctity and inviolability of the shrines and Holy Places of all religions; and will dedicate itself to the principles of the Charter of the United Nations.[3]

The State of Israel subsequently became a signatory to the Universal Declaration of Human Rights and the International Bill of Rights and importance of human rights is also emphasised in the 1992 Basic Law of the State of Israel which is concerned with 'Human Dignity and Liberty'. Article 1 of this Basic Law states that the purpose of the law 'is to protect human dignity and liberty, in order to establish in a Basic Law the values of the State of Israel as a Jewish and democratic state.'

Articles 2-7 then go on to state:

2. There shall be no violation of the life, body or dignity of any person as such.

3. There shall be no violation of the property of a person.

4. All persons are entitled to protection of their life, body and dignity.

5. There shall be no deprivation or restriction of the liberty of a person by imprisonment, arrest, extradition or otherwise.

6.   (a) All persons are free to leave Israel.

       (b) Every Israel national has the right of entry into Israel from abroad.

7.   (a) All persons have the right to privacy and to intimacy.

       (b) There shall be no entry into the private premises of a person who has not consented thereto.

       (c) No search shall be conducted on the private premises of a person, nor on the body or personal effects.

       (d) There shall be no violation of the confidentiality of conversation, or of the writings or records of a person.[4]

A number of key rights, such as the right to equality, to freedom of speech and to freedom of religion, are not listed in the Basic Law. However, these rights are given to the residents of Israel by general principles of Israeli law which existed before this Basic Law and which go back to the Declaration of Independence. It has also been argued that these rights are implicitly included under the 'right to dignity' in clauses 2 and 5.

As well as this official emphasis on human rights at the heart of the law of the State of Israel, the presence of a vigorous Jewish human rights culture is also shown by the existence of a range of Jewish human rights organisations in Israel and elsewhere that campaign for human rights both in Israel and the Occupied Territories and in the world as a whole. Four examples will illustrate the nature and activity of these organisations.

Rabbis for Human Rights is an Israeli human rights organisation. As its name suggests, it is an organisation of Israeli rabbis who represent a variety of different traditions within Judaism but who are united in a common commitment to human rights. Its website declares:

> ... we derive our authority from our Jewish tradition and the Universal Declaration of Human Rights. Our mission is to inform the Israeli public about human rights violations, and to pressure the State institutions to redress these injustices. In a time in which a nationalist and isolationist understanding of Jewish tradition is heard frequently and loudly, Rabbis for Human Rights give expression to the traditional Jewish responsibility for the safety and welfare of the stranger, the different and the weak, the convert, the widow and the orphan.[5]

B'Tselem – the Israeli Information Centre for Human Rights in the Occupied Territories – is an Israeli human rights group which seeks to 'document and educate the Israeli public and policymakers about human rights abuses in the Occupied Territories, combat the phenomenon of denial prevalent among the Israeli public, and help create a human rights culture in Israel.' Its aim is 'to change Israeli policy in the Occupied Territories and ensure that its government, which rules the Occupied Territories, protects the human rights of residents there and complies with its organisations under international law.'[6]

The Jacob Blaustein Institute for the Advancement of Human Rights is an American institute organised under the aegis of the American Jewish Committee which works 'to strengthen human rights through the United Nations and other intergovernmental bodies.' It centres its work on the following areas:

1. Clarifying basic human rights concepts, principles, and issues;
2. Building national and international procedures and institutions to assess compliance with international human rights standards;
3. Defending human rights defenders and advancing the techniques they bring to their work;
4. Networking, constituency building, and capacity development;
5. Advocacy and educational training;
6. Participating in the work of international human rights bodies.[7]

In 1974 the Institute, together with the Canadian Jewish Congress and the Consultative Council of Jewish Organisations issued a Declaration on Judaism and Human Rights.

Section I of this Declaration sets out a basic Jewish commitment to human rights. This states:

> In the light of the contributions Judaism and the Jewish experience have made to human rights, we affirm:
>
> Human rights are an integral part of the faith and tradition of Judaism. The beliefs that man was created in the divine image, that the human family is one, and that every person is obliged to deal justly with every other person are basic sources of the Jewish commitment to human rights.
>
> The struggles of Jews for freedom from oppression and discrimination in the modern era have helped advance the cause of human rights for all.
>
> Jews and Jewish organizations have significantly aided efforts to secure national and international protection of human rights and freedoms.
>
> We accordingly reaffirm our long-standing dedication to the advancement and protection of fundamental rights and freedoms for all persons.[8]

Subsequent sections of the Declaration go on to affirm Jewish support for the Universal Declaration of Human Rights, for the interdependence of civil, political, economic and cultural rights, for the war against poverty, for progress in human rights law and for the elimination of racial, ethnic and religious discrimination.

Reflecting specific Jewish human rights concerns, the Declaration also highlights the importance of the struggle against anti-Semitism and the importance of the preservation of cultures.

On the former, reflecting the situation which existed in 1974, it declares:

> The current manifestation of anti-Semitism in various parts of the world, whether open or under one or another guise, are to be condemned and combated, in keeping with the International Conventions on the Elimination of Racial Discrimination. Vicious libels about Jews and Judaism are being disseminated in some countries, including certain Arab states and the Soviet Union. It is incumbent on all governments,

citizen groups and private persons to desist from any anti-Semitic activity and to do all they can to curb it.[9]

On the latter it states that:

Many agreements between two or more nations, including the International Covenant on Civil and Political Rights, confirm the right of each of the world's religious, ethnic and linguistic groups to preserve its unique cultural heritage; but this right is often denied in practice. Jewish minorities in particular have suffered grievously from such denials in some countries. All states should undertake or intensify action to safeguard the rights of all groups to their cultures, according to the existing commitments.[10]

Rene Cassin is a UK charity founded in the memory of Rene Cassin that seeks to 'promote and protect universal human rights, drawing on Jewish experience and values' through 'a combination of advocacy, policy analysis, public campaigning and education and building the capacity of activists and lawyers to promote and protect human rights.'[11] Its vision is for 'a world where everyone fully enjoys all their human rights as enshrined in the Universal Declaration of Human Rights and members of the Jewish community are actively engaged in promoting and protecting these rights.'[12]

Among its current campaigns are campaigns on the issues of the detention of asylum seekers, equal rights for Gypsies, Roma and Travellers, genocide, slavery and trafficking.

3.2   THE JEWISH THEOLOGICAL FRAMEWORK FOR THINKING ABOUT HUMAN RIGHTS

The basis for Jewish thinking about human rights is the Hebrew Bible and the tradition of Jewish reflection on its teaching contained in the *Mishnah*, the *Talmud* and subsequent Jewish writings. The Jewish tradition of thought contained in these sources provides three fundamental foundations for human rights.

3.2.1   God the Creator

The first foundation for Jewish human rights thinking is the conviction found throughout the Hebrew Bible from Genesis 1 onwards, that there is one creator God who is the sovereign ruler over the world that he has made.

As Elliot Dorff notes in his essay 'A Jewish perspective on human rights', this basic conviction 'that God both created the world and owns it' means that:

> The whole drama of life, from the viewpoint of Judaism, is not played out on the stage of individuals with inherent inalienable rights; it is rather played out on the stage of both positive and negative duties to God. So, for example, the right to life is not phrased as such in the Torah; rather as God told Noah in the early chapters of Genesis, God forbids both suicide and murder and will punish those who engage in either: 'For your own life blood I will require a reckoning for ... human life, of every man for that of his fellow man! Whoever sheds the blood of man, by man shall his blood be shed; for in his image did God make man.' (Gen 9:5-6)[13]

For Judaism, therefore, thinking about rights means primarily not thinking about the rights I have, what is owed to me, but about the duties I have to others arising from my paramount obligation to live in obedience to God.

To quote Dorff again, 'the mapping of duties onto rights is not completely congruent.' This is because we may have duties to others based on our obligation to God that go beyond legal rights:

> I may have duties to God vis-à-vis you even though you do not have a legal right to expect something of me. So, as Jewish commentators note, Leviticus 19 specifies a number of duties to other people with mention of 'I am the Lord' following the duty, thus indicating that we have these duties because God commands them even though they cannot be enforced by human courts. Such duties include our obligations to leave crops for the poor and to refrain from cursing the deaf, putting a stumbling block before the blind, or spreading gossip about someone else. Moreover, even if there were a complete one-to-one mapping of duties onto rights, my frame of mind is completely different if I begin

by assuming that I have duties towards others rather than rights I can demand from others; in the former, Jewish mode, I owe the world, while in the latter, American mode, the world owes me.[14]

3.2.2 The creation of human beings in God's likeness

The name of the Israeli human rights group B'Tselem means 'In the image' and this reflects the fact that the second foundation for Jewish thinking about human rights is the conviction expressed in Genesis 9:6 and also Genesis 1:26-27 and 5:1-2 that God created all human beings in his image and likeness. Jewish thought sees the belief that human beings are created in God's image as having two ramifications. Firstly, as we have already seen, it means it is wrong to murder another human being and, secondly, it means that every individual human being has immense value.

The Jewish Rabbis reflected on the fact that according to the Book of Genesis humanity was created in God's image in the person of one human being, Adam, and they came to see this fact as emphasising both the seriousness of murder, since killing one person meant also killing their potential descendants and thus 'an entire world', and the unique value of each human being, since each person individually is made in God's image.

Both these points are made in a famous passage from the *Mishnah* in which witnesses in a case involving the death penalty are warned of the seriousness of what they are doing:

> Know, moreover, that capital cases are not like non-capital cases: in non-capital cases a man may pay money and so make atonement, but in capital cases the witness is answerable for the blood of him [that is wrongfully condemned] and the blood of his descendants [that should have been born to him] to the end of the world.
>
> For so have we found it with Cain that murdered his brother, for it says, 'The bloods of your brother cry out' (Gen. 4:10). It doesn't say, 'The blood of your brother', but rather 'The bloods of your brother' —meaning his blood and the blood of his descendants....
>
> Therefore but a single person was created in the world, to teach that if any man has caused a single life to perish from Israel, he is deemed by Scripture as if he had caused a whole world to perish; and anyone

who saves a single soul from Israel, he is deemed by Scripture as if he had saved a whole world.

Again [but a single person was created] for the sake of peace among humankind, that one should not say to another, 'My father was greater than your father.'

Again, [but a single person was created] against the heretics so they should not say, 'There are many ruling powers in heaven.'

Again [but a single person was created] to proclaim the greatness of the Holy Blessed One; for humans stamp many coins with one seal and they are all like one another; but the King of kings, the Holy Blessed One, has stamped every human with the seal of the first man, yet not one of them are like another. Therefore everyone must say, 'For my sake was the world created.'[15]

As Dorff writes, the Rabbis, following on from the teaching of the *Torah*, the first five books of the Hebrew Bible, saw the belief that all human beings are created in God's image as not just an abstract truth about human nature, but the basis for instruction about how we should treat other people:

Specifically, the Rabbis maintain that because human beings are created in God's image, we affront God when we insult another person. Conversely, 'one who welcomes his friend is as if he welcomes the face of the Divine Presence (jEvruv 5:1). Moreover, when we see someone with a disability, we are to utter this blessing: 'Praised are you, Lord our God…who makes different creatures,' or 'who created us different.' Precisely when we might recoil from a deformed or incapacitated person, or thank God for not making us like that, the tradition instead bids us to embrace the divine image in such people – indeed, to bless God for creating some of us so. Those who suffer from a disability have a right to be angry with God and even to argue with God, as Jews have done from the time that Abraham questioned God's justice in his plans for Sodom and Gomorrah, but the rest of us must look beyond the disability and see the person for the image of God embedded in him or her. Finally, the Rabbis' assertion of human worth is graphically illustrated in their ruling that no one person can be sacrificed to save even an entire city unless that person is named by the enemy or guilty of a capital crime:

Caravans of men are walking down a road, and they are accosted by non-Jews who say to them: 'Give us one from among you that we may kill him otherwise we shall kill you all.' Though all may be killed, they may not hand over a single soul of Israel. However, if the demand is for a single individual like Sheva, son of Bikhri [who according to the biblical story in II Samuel 20 was also subject to the death penalty], they should surrender him rather than be killed. (jTer. 7:20, Genesis Rabbah 94:9).

Thus the doctrine that each person is created in the divine image, with its corollaries that each person is unique and that each person can say 'For me the world was created,' constitute firm foundations for claims of human rights.[16]

3.2.3   The Covenant between God and Israel

The third foundation for Jewish human rights thinking is the conviction that God has made a covenant with the Jewish people on Mount Sinai following their deliverance from oppression in Egypt and that this covenant involves a range of God-given duties to others. To quote Dorff again:

Our duties to one another are rooted not only in God's creation of us in the divine image and as unique individuals, but also in God's covenant with us. God made a covenant with the Jewish people at Mount Sinai consisting of 613 commandments, and many of the Torah's laws guaranteeing specific human rights are included in that list and their expansion at the hands of the Rabbis. We are to cherish human rights, then, as part of our duties to God under our covenant with him and as a way to worship him.[17]

As Edward Kessler has argued, if we look at the commands given to Israel as God's covenant people we find that they have both negative and positive implications:

Negatively, they mean it is wrong to harm a fellow human being deliberately, in any way at all, as expressed by Psalm 34, 'keep your tongue from evil and lips from speaking deceit; depart from evil.' Positively, they require the performance of deeds of loving kindness which, in Jewish tradition, is understood as *gemilut chasadim* (literally, 'the bestowal of loving kindness'). Thus, the quotation from Psalm 34 finishes with, 'and do good.' This was specified in practical terms by Maimonides who wrote that 'it is a positive commandment to visit the sick, to accompany the dead, to dower the bride, to escort one's guest, to attend to all the needs of burial…. These acts are what is meant by *gemilut chasadim* … and they are included in the principle of 'You shall love your neighbour as yourself.' In another rabbinic interpretation from one of the earliest individual statements in the Talmud, *gemilut chasadim* is described as one of the three pillars of Judaism upon which the continued existence of the world depends.[18]

These commands also, he says, enjoin us to:

…show special responsibility towards the weakest members of society: the orphaned, the widowed, the old, the handicapped and the poor. All of these groups are frequently singled out with particular reference to protection. For example, there are detailed instructions concerning the poor tithe as well as a law requiring the farmers to leave corners of the field unharvested so that the poor may help themselves. Micah summarised humanity's responsibility succinctly, 'to do justice, and to love kindness and to walk humbly.' In our times, we should ensure that no-one is left without sustenance, help or opportunity by having laws to provide for health and education, support for the elderly, sick and disabled. Judaism affirms such actions.

We are also reminded that those people who receive our support are our equals. For instance, it is a striking feature of the 15th chapter of Deuteronomy, which deals with the relief of poverty, that whenever it refers to the poor person in need of charity it describes him as *achicha*, your brother, as if to warn the giver against looking upon the recipient as other than equal. Equal mutual respect is something which Judaism demands emphatically because all human beings bear the 'divine seal.' The ideal society, according to Judaism, is a society of freedom and justice; a family of families whose members respect each other as brothers and sisters.[19]

The point that is being made here is not that the commandments given to Israel contain a set of human rights, but that these commandments set out a set of obligations not to harm others, to treat others with loving kindness and to care for those in need, that also find expression in contemporary statements about human rights.

A similar appeal to the obligations contained in God's covenant with Israel is also made, for instance, by Rabbis for Human Rights in the section of their website on 'Judaism and Human Rights'. This states:

> The essence of the Torah, as summarized by Hillel's statement: "What is hateful to you, do not do to your fellow" (Shabbat 31a), reflects the experience and ethical consciousness of the Jewish people. The Torah states explicitly: "Do not wrong a stranger who resides with you in your land. The stranger who resides with you shall be to you as one of your citizens: you shall love the stranger as yourself, for you were strangers in the land of Egypt" (Leviticus 19:33-34). Our historical experience of exile and redemption, as well as our ethical consciousness, must sensitize us to the suffering of others and compel us to defend the rights of all who dwell among us....
>
> Exemplary behavior of Israel is a sanctification of God's name ("Kiddush HaShem"); shameful conduct is a defamation of God's name ("Chilul HaShem"), a term specifically used to condemn the act of robbing a non-Jew (Tosefta B.K. 10). God's name is sanctified through the respect we show for human worth and the dignity of creation.

We are admonished to be holy by leading a moral life in relationship to all:

> "You shall be holy, for I the Lord your God am holy...You shall not pick your vineyard bare, or gather the fallen fruit of your vineyard; you shall leave them for the poor and for the stranger... You shall not steal. You shall not deal deceitfully and falsely with one another... You shall not defraud your fellow. You shall not commit robbery. The wages of your laborer should not remain with you until morning... You shall not take vengeance or bear a grudge against your people. Love your neighbor as yourself, I am God" (Lev. 19:2, 10,11,13,18).[20]

As in Kessler's essay, what we have here is a reminder of the obligations placed upon the Jewish people because of their covenant with God and the argument that these obligations involve respecting the human rights of all with whom we live both negatively, by not doing harm to others, and positively, by showing respect for human worth and caring for those in need.

What we have seen so far is a general argument for a congruence between the obligations of the covenant and human rights. However, Jewish scholars have also argued for detailed congruence between the two.

For example, a former justice of the Israeli Supreme Court, Haim Cohn, has written a book entitled *Human Rights in Jewish Law*[21] which sets out in detail how he thinks that Jewish Law, that is to say the covenant law given to God by Israel as interpreted by the Jewish Rabbinical tradition, provides for a variety of human rights.

This book is in three parts. The first part, 'Rights of Life, Liberty and the Pursuit of Happiness', covers the rights to life, liberty, security of person, privacy, reputation, freedom of movement and residence, marriage and family life, property, work, leisure, freedom of thought, speech, conscience and information, and to education and participation in culture. The second part, 'Rights of Equality', discusses how Jewish law opposes discrimination on account of race, religion, national origin, sex and social and economic status, whilst also providing for special rights and duties to be observed by and between those who are Jewish. The third section, 'Rights of Justice', looks at the insistence of the Jewish tradition on equality before the law, judicial standards, and procedural and legislative safeguards and its prohibition of torture and cruel punishments.

A potential problem with appealing to Jewish law arising from the covenant as the basis for human rights is that the covenant was given by God specifically to Israel. How, then, are the obligations contained in the covenant relevant to those who do not belong to the Jewish people?

Dorff outlines three ways in which the Jewish tradition has addressed this issue.

First, by seeing the Jewish covenant as a model for all nations:

...the Jewish covenant was to be a model for all other nations, as God makes clear in the first mention of it to Abraham: 'Abraham is to become a great and populous nation and all the nations of the earth are to bless themselves by him. For I have singled him out, that he may instruct his children and his posterity to keep the way of the Lord by doing what is right and good' (Ge. 18:18-19). Similarly, Isaiah later was to depict Israel as a 'light unto the nations' (Isa. 49:6). Thus the Jewish covenant was to serve as a model of how all peoples, Jews certainly included, were to treat each other.[22]

Secondly, by developing the idea of a universal covenant between God and all human beings as children of Noah:

...the Rabbis maintained that God made another covenant with all children of Noah, consisting of six prohibitions and one positive command – to wit, the interdiction of murder, incest/adultery, idolatry, tearing limb from a living animal, blasphemy and theft, and the positive command to establish a system of justice. Thus Jews have never been missionary, for according to Jewish theology non-Jews do all that God expects of them by abiding by the Noahide covenant. This non-missionary stance, rooted in the doctrine of the Noahide covenant, is an important foundation for respecting the convictions and rights of others.[23]

Thirdly, by seeing Jewish people as having a responsibility for treating non-Jews, in some respects at least, as if they were Jewish:

....while Jews could only reasonably be expected to fulfill all the 613 commandments toward those fellow Jews who took upon themselves a reciprocal burden, Jewish law specifies that Jews were to bear some of the responsibilities of the Jewish covenant, beyond those of the Noahide covenant, towards non-Jews. Thus according to talmudic law, Jews were to visit the sick among non-Jews, take care of their poor, and to see to their burial if nobody else was available. This was for the 'sake of peace' and also, one would presume, as part of the modelling that Jews were to do.[24]

In his essay 'A Jewish Theory of Human Rights', David Novak illustrates this idea of the application of Torah to non-Jews with reference to the command 'You shall love your neighbour as yourself' (Leviticus 19:18).

He notes that the 'normative Jewish tradition' has seen this command as both part of the reciprocal duty that Jews owe to each other as members of God's covenant people and also as a command that potentially applies to anybody regardless of whether they are a Jew:

> ...it clearly emphasizes that neighbor-love is a Torah right. It is something uniquely commanded to Jews and, therefore, something one Jew can claim from another. Nevertheless, it also teaches that any non-Jew – who could be any human being – could exercise that Torah right when that person is living within enough proximity to Jews to be able to be the object of the Jew's duty to provide neighbor-love to whomever they encounter. In other words, *anybody* could benefit from the beneficence Jews are commanded to provide to *everybody* living in their midst, however temporarily or accidentally. As such, any non-Jew fortunate enough to be so located could enjoy being the object of a Torah duty that can be seen (at least de facto) as his or her exercise of a natural, *universal* right having a particular subject but a universal object. And that is why in rabbinic thought, any non-Jew who publicly accepts what is considered to be basic moral law (called a 'resident sojourner' or *ger toshav* in Hebrew) can be made into enough of a citizen of Jewish polity to be able to enjoy the same civil rights and be obligated by the same duties as a full-fledged Jewish citizen of that polity.[25]

What all this shows us is that the Jewish tradition has taken seriously the particularity of God's covenant with Israel whilst also allowing for the idea that there are God-given rights and duties that are (potentially at least) universal in their scope and can therefore form the basis for the idea of universal human rights.

3.3 AREAS OF TENSION IN RELATION TO JEWISH BELIEF AND PRACTICE AND HUMAN RIGHTS.

Although there is thus Jewish support for human rights and a theoretical basis for the idea of universal human rights in Jewish theology, there are also a number of areas where there is tension in relation to Jewish belief and practice and human rights.

3.3.1 Jewish ritual practice and human rights

There are two areas of Jewish ritual practice where there has been tension. The first is the area of Jewish ritual slaughter of animals and birds – what is known as *shechita*. Under this practice, which is required in order that meat should be kosher and therefore able to be eaten by observant Jews, the trachea, oesophagus, carotid arteries, jugular veins and vagus nerve need to be severed by a swift cut involving a special knife called a *hallaf*.

Because the animal or bird concerned may not be stunned before slaughter the practice of *shechita* is regarded as unacceptably cruel by animal welfare organisations such as People for the Ethical Treatment of Animals Compassion in World Farming and the UK's Farm Animal Welfare Council. In 2014 the Danish government banned the practice of slaughter without prior stunning.

The Jewish response has been to deny that the practice is cruel, because of the swiftness with which they say death ensues, and that any ban on the practice contravenes the right to freedom of religious practice guaranteed under the International Bill of Rights and European Convention on Human Rights. This a particularly sensitive issue for Jewish people because a ban on Jewish ritual slaughter was one of the first anti-Jewish measures introduced by the Nazis in Germany in the 1930s and they fear that the controversy about this issue is part of a re-birth of anti-Semitism.

The second area is the circumcision of Jewish male babies as laid down in Genesis 17:9-14. This is criticised by its opponents as being contrary to the rights of children because it is an assault on their bodily integrity and is potentially detrimental to their health. The Jewish response has been to say that there is no evidence that circumcision raises health issues when carried out in a responsible manner and that what is really underlying such opposition is anti-Semitism and unwillingness to allow freedom of religious practice.

3.3.2 Equality

There are two areas relating to equality where there has been tension. The first is the area of equality between men and women. It is a given within all branches of Judaism that there is a fundamental equality as human beings between men and women because both women and men are created in the image of God. Where there is tension it is over the traditional Jewish distinction between the proper roles of men and women. As Clive Lawton explains, within the Orthodox Jewish community,

> ...women and men have traditionally had clearly defined and separate roles. Women are given total superiority in the home which is the focal point of the development of Jewish life – where children are taught and the table prepared for Shabbat and other festive occasions. Men are given total supremacy in the public aspects of legally bound and ritual practice, in the synagogues and courts.[26]

For those within this tradition this distinction of role does not detract from the essential equality of men and women. For many people outside the Jewish community, however, and for many people belonging to the Liberal and Reform wings of Judaism who have moved away from this distinction of roles to the extent of allowing, for example, women rabbis, there does seem a tension between traditional Jewish practice and the idea of gender-blind equality found in much human rights thinking.

The second is the area of equality for gay and lesbian people. Many in the Reformed and Liberal wings of Judaism are committed to full acceptance of gay and lesbian relationships and of same-sex marriage as an integral part of a commitment to equality. Thus, for example, the 'marriage' section of the Liberal Judaism website declares 'Liberal Rabbis and Liberal Judaism communities delight in celebrating the love of two persons, regardless of gender.'[27]

On the other hand, many in the Orthodox Jewish community hold that while gay and lesbian people have equal dignity as those made in the image of God this does not mean that there should be an acceptance of same-sex sexual relationships or of same-sex marriage. This is because they adhere to the traditional Jewish view that male homosexual relationships (and by extension lesbian relationships as well) are forbidden by Leviticus 18:22 and 20:13 and that Genesis 1 and 2 show that God created marriage to be between a man and a woman. Like their conservative Christian counterparts, Orthodox Jews would be concerned to ensure that a proper balance is struck between the rights of gay and lesbian people and their right to teach and practise their religious convictions in this area. For example, they would want Jewish schools to be able to continue to teach a traditional Jewish approach to marriage and family life.

3.4   ISRAEL

The final and most contentious area of tension is over the existence and practices of the State of Israel.

For many opponents of the State of Israel the very existence of Israel as a specifically Jewish state in fulfilment of the Zionist aspiration for a Jewish homeland is in tension with human rights. This is because, as they see it, the very idea of a Jewish state is racist and inherently discriminatory against non-Jews. On November 10 1975 this point of view found expression in the passing by the General Assembly of the United Nations of Resolution 3379 which '*Determines* that Zionism is a form of racism and racial discrimination.' This resolution was subsequently revoked by General Assembly Resolution 48/46 on 16 December 1991, but the equation of Zionism with racism is one that still has wide currency, particularly amongst supporters of the Palestinian cause.

The Jewish response to this equation is to say that the existence of Israel as a Jewish state is no more inherently racist than the existence of any other nation state. In the words of Chaim Herzog, the Israel Ambassador to the United Nations, addressing the General Assembly in response to Resolution 3379:

The re-establishment of Jewish independence in Israel, after centuries of struggle to overcome foreign conquest and exile, is a vindication of the fundamental concepts of the equality of nations and of self-determination. To question the Jewish people's right to national existence and freedom is not only to deny to the Jewish people the right accorded to every other people on this globe, but it is also to deny the central precepts of the United Nations.[28]

Supporters of Israel would also point out that Israel is not a racist state because non-Jews are entitled to be its citizens and enjoy exactly the same rights as Jewish citizens.

Alongside the legitimacy of the existence of Israel, the issue that is also repeatedly raised is the issue of the actions of the Israeli government and its security forces in relation to the Palestinian people. It is argued by the Palestinians and their supporters, and by Jewish human rights groups such as B'Tselem and Rabbis for Human Rights, that the Government and the security forces have violated the rights of the Palestinians, as laid down in international and Israeli law, through their occupation of Palestinian land and through the way they have reacted to attacks on Israel.

The response from the Government of Israel and its supporters is to say that the issue of the occupation of Palestinian land cannot be separated from the disputed issue of the status of the West Bank, which in turn is something that cannot be settled without a solution to the issue of the continuing threat to the existence of the State of Israel and therefore to the right of the Jewish people to live in peace in their own homeland. They would also argue that the degree of force used by the Israeli armed forces is proportionate to the need to defend the right to life of the citizens of Israel, both Jew and Arab alike.

What we see in this dispute is both a dispute about matters of fact (how have the Israeli government and security forces actually behaved?) and a dispute about how you balance competing sets of rights (how do you balance the rights of the Israelis to peace and security with the right of Palestinians to secure occupation of their own land and to national self-determination?). Most fundamentally, however, it is a question of how Israel can maintain its ideals as set out in its Declaration of Independence in 1948. How can it be a Jewish state that lives at peace with its neighbours and upholds the rights of all its inhabitants regardless of race or religion?[29]

Notes

[1] Jonathan Sacks, 'Human Rights and Wrongs', *Jerusalem Post*, 24 August 2001, at http://www.rabbisacks.org/human-rights-and-wrongs-published-in-the-jerusalem-post/

[2] For the life and work of Renee Cassin see Jay Winter and Antoine Prost, *Renee Cassin and Human Rights*, Cambridge: CUP, 2013.

[3] Declaration of Israel's Independence 1948, at http://stateofisrael.com/declaration/

[4] Basic Law 1992, 'Human Dignity and Liberty', at http://www.knesset.gov.il/laws/special/eng/basic3_eng.htm

[5] Rabbis for Human Rights, 'About Rabbis for Human Rights', at http://rhr.org.il/eng/about/

[6] B'Tselem, 'About B'Tselem', at http://www.btselem.org/about_btselemthe

[7] The Jacob Blaustein Institute, 'About Jacob Blaustein Institute for Human Rights', at http://www.jbi-humanrights.org/jacob-blaustein-institute/jbi-programs.html

[8] Declaration on Judaism and Human Rights, 1974, Section I, at http://hrusa.org/advocacy/community-faith/judaism1.shtm. The full text of the Declaration is in Appendix II of this report.

[9] Ibid., Section II.

[10] Ibid., Section II.

[11] Rene Cassin, 'Who we are', at http://www.renecassin.org/

[12] Rene Cassin, 'Our vision and Mission', at http://www.renecassin.org/

[13] Elliot Dorff, 'A Jewish Perspective on Human Rights' in Joseph Runzo, Nancy M Martin and Arvind Sharma (eds), *Human Rights and Responsibilities in the World Religions*, Oxford: One World, 2003, p. 210.

[14] Ibid., pp. 214-215.

[15] Sanhedrin Chapter 4, Mishnah 5, at mishnahyomit.org/sanhedrin/Sanhedrin 4-5.doc

[16] Dorff, op.cit. p. 213.

[17] Ibid., pp.213-214.

[18] Edward Kessler, unpublished paper on 'A Jewish perspective on the United Nations Universal Declaration of Human Rights'.

[19] Ibid.

[20] Rabbis for Human Rights

[21] Haim Cohn, *Human Rights in Jewish Law*, New York: Ktav, 1984.

[22] Dorff, op.cit. 214.

[23] Ibid., p.214. For a detailed discussion of the idea of the Noahide Covenant see David Novak, *The Image of the Non-Jew in Judaism*, New York and Toronto: Edwin Mellen, 1983.

[24] Ibid., p.214.

[25] David Novak, 'A Jewish Theory of Human Rights', in Witte and Green (eds), op. cit. p.36.

[26] Clive Lawton, 'Judaism', in Peggy Morgan and Clive A Lawton (eds), *Ethical Issues in Six Religious Traditions*, Edinburgh: Edinburgh University Press, 2007, p.198.

[27] http://www.liberaljudaism.org/life-cycle/marriage-civil-partnership.html

[28] Text at http://www.jewishvirtuallibrary.org/jsource/UN/herzogsp.html

[29] For a discussion of the issues involved here see Alexander Yacobson and Amnon Rubenstein, *Israel and the Family of Nations – The Jewish Nation State and Human Rights*, London: Routledge, 2010.

Chapter Four

ISLAM AND HUMAN RIGHTS

4.1 ADDRESSING THE ELEPHANT IN THE ROOM

For many people at the moment the elephant in the room when it comes to the discussion of religion and human rights is the relationship between Islam and human rights. They would see the track record of contemporary Islam as providing clear evidence that religion can be inimical to the humane treatment of human beings that respect for human rights requires.

This problem with the way that Islam is all too often perceived today is noted by the Muslim writer Khaled Abou El Fadl in his 2003 essay 'The Human Rights Commitment in Modern Islam'. He writes:

In recent times, and well before the tragedy of 9/11, Muslim societies have been plagued by many events that have struck the world as offensive and even shocking. Morally offensive events, such as the Satanic Verses and the death sentence against Salman Rushdie; the stoning and imprisonment of rape victims in Pakistan and Nigeria; the public flogging, stoning, and decapitation of criminal offenders in Sudan, Iran and Saudi Arabia; the degradation of women by the Taliban; the destruction of the Buddha statues in Afghanistan; the sexual violation of domestic workers in Saudi Arabia; the excommunication of writers in Egypt; the killing of civilians in suicide attacks; the shooting in 1987 of over four hundred pilgrims in Mecca by Saudi police; the taking of hostages in Iran and Lebanon; the burning to death in 2002 of at least fourteen schoolgirls in Mecca because they were not allowed to escape their burning school while not properly veiled; and the demeaning treatment that women receive in Saudi Arabia, including the ban against women driving cars, as well as many other events, seem to constitute a long Muslim saga of ugliness in the modern world.

For many non-Muslims around the world, Islam has become the symbol for a draconian tradition that exhibits little compassion or mercy toward human beings. When one interacts with people from different parts of the world, one consistently finds that the image of Islam is not that of a humanistic or humane religion. This has reached the extent that, from Europe and the United States to Japan, China, and Russia, one finds that Islamic culture has become associated with harshness and cruelty in the popular cultural imagination of non-Muslims.[1]

Since El Fadl wrote his essay the emergence of hard-line Islamic groups such as Al Shabaab, Boko Haram and particularly Islamic State has added to the problem to which he refers by causing Islam to be associated in the popular imagination of large parts of the non-Muslim world with terrorism, kidnapping and the public beheading of captives – actions which are the antithesis to concern for human rights.

This popular view of Islam as a religion of 'harshness and cruelty' that stands in opposition to human rights obscures the fact that there is a strong tradition within Islam that insists that the humane treatment of others is a religious imperative and that has sought to engage positively from an Islamic perspective with the concept of universal human rights that has emerged since the Second World War.

4.2 THE COMPLEXITY WITHIN ISLAM

In trying to understand Islamic attitudes to human rights it is important to bear in mind Ann Mayer's warning about the complexity of Muslim views on this subject:

Muslim views on the relationship of Islam and human rights are so complex that it is extremely difficult to make valid generalizations about this subject. Shaken by a sudden and as yet incomplete modernization process, the Islamic tradition is in a state of ferment. Exposure to diverse intellectual currents, including liberalism and Marxism, has given rise to different interpretations of Islamic scripture and a range of opinions on any human rights issue.[2]

The complexity of Muslim attitudes to human rights referred to by Mayer includes a variety of different understandings of how Islamic law, Sharia, applies to the issue of human rights. It is often suggested in Western non-Muslim discussion of Islam in human rights that there is a single Islamic law code that is uniformly incompatible with Western conceptions of human rights. In fact, as the Muslim scholar Bassam Tibi explains, this suggestion fails to do justice to a much more diverse reality. There is, he says,

> …no single body of law that constitutes Islamic *shari'a*. Rather, *shari'a* refers to various interpretations of Islamic scripture. That is why *shari'a* can be used to serve modern as well as traditional ends, or to justify the actions of oppressive regimes as well as those of the opposition. There is simply no common understanding of Islamic *shari'a*, particularly with respect to human rights.[3]

In this chapter we shall explore how the complexity to which Mayer and Tibi refer is reflected in the way in which Muslim majority nations have responded to the development of human rights law, in the emergence of different Islamic human rights bodies, in different theological approaches to the relationship between Islamic belief and human rights, and in the points of tension between Islamic thought and practice and liberal views of what constitutes human rights.

4.3   MUSLIM MAJORITY NATIONS AND HUMAN RIGHTS TREATIES

When the General Assembly of the United Nations voted on the Universal Declaration of Human Rights on 10 December 1948, seven countries with Muslim majority populations, Afghanistan, Egypt, Iran, Iraq, Pakistan, Syria and Turkey were among the forty-eight countries that voted in favour. Saudi Arabia, however, was one of the eight countries that abstained, arguing that the Declaration violated Islamic law and failed to take into consideration the cultural and religious context of non-Western countries.

In particular, it argued that Article 16 of the Declaration on equal marriage rights and the clause in Article 18 which stated that everyone has 'freedom to change his religion or belief' were incompatible with Sharia law.

Since 1948 countries with Muslim majorities have become signatories to the various human rights treaties that have been produced by the United Nations.

Afghanistan, for instance, is a signatory to the International Bill of Rights, and the conventions on the Prevention of Discrimination on the Basis of Race, Religion or Belief, and Protection of Minorities, the Elimination of All Forms of Discrimination against Women, Slavery, Torture and other Cruel, Inhuman or Degrading Treatment or Punishment, the Rights of the Child, the Status of Refugees and War Crimes and Genocide.

Egypt is a signatory to the International Bill of Rights and the African Charter on Human and Peoples' Rights and to the conventions on Prevention of Discrimination on the Basis of Race, Religion or Belief, and Protection of Minorities, the Elimination of All Forms of Discrimination against Women, Slavery, Torture and other Cruel, Inhuman or Degrading Treatment or Punishment, Rights of the Child, Freedom of Association, Employment and Forced labour, the Elimination of Discrimination in Education, the Status of Refugees, the Status of Stateless Persons and Genocide.

Malaysia is a signatory to the conventions on the Elimination of All Forms of Discrimination against Women, the Rights of the Child, the Right to Organise and Collective Bargaining, and the Prevention and Prohibition of Genocide.[4]

What these examples show is that Muslim majority countries have signed some but not all of the human rights treaties and which treaties they have signed has varied from country to country.

When entering into international human rights treaties some Muslim majority nations have also entered what are known as reservations, indicating that they will not abide by aspects of the treaty that they believe to be incompatible with Islamic law. This can be seen, for example, in the cases of the conventions on the elimination of discrimination against women (CEDAW) and on the rights of the child (CRC).

In the case of CEDAW, reservations have been entered by, for example, Bangladesh, Kuwait and Libya. In 1984 Bangladesh entered reservations against Article 2 calling for the elimination of all forms of discrimination against women, and against specific provisions in Articles 13 (a) and 16.1 (c) and (f) on equality in family benefits, equal rights and responsibilities during marriage and divorce, and equal rights in matters of guardianship and the adoption of children on the grounds that they 'conflict with Sharia law based on Holy Quran and Sunna.'[5] Also in 1984 Kuwait entered reservations on matters to do with equality between men and women in regard to the nationality of children, guardianship and adoption rights and voting rights, in part due to the provisions of the Kuwait Nationality Act which stipulated 'that a child's nationality shall be determined by that of his father,' but also because in its view the provisions of CEDAW with regard to guardianship and adoption were in conflict 'with the provisions of the Islamic Shariah, Islam being the official religion of the State.' In 1989 Libya became party to CEDAW 'subject to the general reservation that such accession cannot conflict with the laws on personal status derived from the Islamic Shariah.'

In the case of CRC, reservations have been entered by, for example, Syria, Iran and Saudi Arabia. Syria entered reservations in 1993 'on the Convention's provisions which are not in conformity with the Syrian Arab legislations and with the Islamic Sharia's principles, in particular the content of Article (14) related to the Right of the Child to the freedom of religion, and Articles 2 and 21 concerning the adoption.' In 1994 Iran reserved the right 'not to apply any provisions or Articles of the Convention that are incompatible with Islamic Laws and the international legislation in effect.' In 1996 Saudi Arabia similarly entered a general reservation 'with respect to all such Articles as are in conflict with the provisions of Islamic law.'[6]

What all these examples from 1948 onwards show is that Muslim majority nations have had a complex attitude to the development of international rights law. They have neither completely accepted it nor completely rejected it. Instead they have signed up to some treaties and conventions, but not others, and have entered reservations which mean that they accept some, but not all, of the conventions that they have signed up to. Furthermore, not all Muslim majority countries have signed up to the same treaties and conventions and the reservations they have entered have not been identical, even when based on an appeal to Islamic law.

4.4   ISLAMIC DECLARATIONS OF HUMAN RIGHTS

In addition to responding to the Universal Declaration of Human Rights and the various international human rights treaties since, Muslims have also produced three specifically Islamic declarations of human rights designed to provide alternative Islamic statements on human rights.

The first of these is the *Universal Islamic Declaration of Human Rights*,[7] issued in 1981 by the 'Islamic Council of Europe', a group established in 1973 which brought together Islamic statesmen and scholars to discuss contemporary issues facing Muslims living in the West.

This declaration consists of a preamble setting out the theological basis for human rights in Islam and twenty-three Articles, loosely based on the Universal Declaration of Human Rights, which set out a series of specific rights possessed by all human beings. The rights that are covered are:

1. Right to Life
2. Right to Freedom
3. Right to Equality and Prohibition Against Impermissible Discrimination
4. Right to Justice
5. Right to Fair Trial
6. Right to Protection Against Abuse of Power
7. Right to Protection Against Torture
8. Right to Protection of Honour and Reputation
9. Right to Asylum
10. Rights of Minorities
11. Right and Obligation to Participate in the Conduct and Management of Public Affairs
12. Right to Freedom of Belief, Thought and Speech
13. Right to Freedom of Religion
14. Right to Free Association
15. The Economic Order and the Rights Evolving Therefrom
16. Right to Protection of Property
17. Status and Dignity of Workers
18. Right to Social Security
19. Right to Found a Family and Related Matters

20. Rights of Married Women
21. Right to Education
22. Right of Privacy
23. Right to Freedom of Movement and Residence

At the end of the declaration there is a reference section which gives a series of references from the Quran and Sunna (the traditions about the life of Muhammad) to support each of these rights.

What is notable about this declaration is the way in which it places statements about human rights within an Islamic framework. It does this through the way in which the preamble places rights within the context of Islamic theology, by the linking of each right to quotations from the Quran and the Sunna and by the way in which it places rights under the authority of Islamic law.

This last point can be seen, for example, in the statement on the Right to Freedom of Belief, Thought and Speech. This states:

a) Every person has the right to express his thoughts and beliefs so long as he remains within the limits prescribed by the Law. No one, however, is entitled to disseminate falsehood or to circulate reports which may outrage public decency, or to indulge in slander, innuendo or to cast defamatory aspersions on other persons.

b) Pursuit of knowledge and search after truth is not only a right but a duty of every Muslim.

c) It is the right and duty of every Muslim to protest and strive (within the limits set out by the Law) against oppression even if it involves challenging the highest authority in the state.

d) There shall be no bar on the dissemination of information provided it does not endanger the security of the society or the state and is confined within the limits imposed by the Law.

e) No one shall hold in contempt or ridicule the religious beliefs of others or incite public hostility against them; respect for the religious feelings of others is obligatory on all Muslims.

As the explanatory notes to the declaration explain, 'the term ‹Law› denotes the *Shari'ah*, i.e. the totality of ordinances derived from the Qur'an and the Sunnah and any other laws that are deduced from these two sources by methods considered valid in Islamic jurisprudence.' This means that the Right to Freedom of Belief, Thought and Speech is subject to Islamic law even for non-Muslims and the same is true for all the other rights set out in the declaration.

The second declaration is the *Cairo Declaration of Human Rights in Islam*[8] which was produced by the Nineteenth Islamic Conference of Foreign Ministers in 1990. This Declaration states that:

> ... fundamental rights and freedoms according to Islam are an integral part of the Islamic religion and that no one shall have the right as a matter of principle to abolish them either in whole or in part or to violate or ignore them in as much as they are binding divine commands, which are contained in the Revealed Books of Allah and which were sent through the last of His Prophets to complete the preceding divine messages and that safeguarding those fundamental rights and freedoms is an act of worship whereas the neglect or violation thereof is an abominable sin, and that the safeguarding of those fundamental rights and freedom is an individual responsibility of every person and a collective responsibility of the entire Ummah [the worldwide Islamic Community].

It then goes on to set out these rights and freedoms in a set of twenty-five Articles. The Articles cover:

- The fundamental equality of all human beings as subjects of Allah and descendants of Adam;

- The right to life;

- The protection to be afforded to non-belligerents in time of war;

- The right to protection of good name and honour and of the body and burial place after death;

- The right to marriage and family life;

- The equal dignity of women with men and the responsibility of men for the welfare and maintenance of the family;

- The rights of the child and the right to care of parents and other relatives;

- The right to knowledge and education;

- The right not to be coerced into changing religion;

- The right to freedom from enslavement, oppression and colonialism;

- The right to freedom of movement;

- The right to work and to enjoy the fruits of work;

- The right to own property;

- The right to live in a clean environment, to food, clothing, shelter and other basic rights;

- The right to live in security;

- The right to equality before the law, to a fair trial and to freedom from arbitrary arrest;

- The right to participate in public affairs.

The list overlaps, but is not identical with, the rights contained in the 1981 Declaration. Like the 1981 Declaration, the 1990 Declaration places human rights within an Islamic theological framework and makes the enjoyment of rights and freedoms subject to *Shari'a* law. Thus Articles 24 and 25 state that 'All the rights and freedoms stipulated in this Declaration are subject to the Islamic Shari'ah' and that 'The Islamic Shari'ah is the only source of reference for the explanation or clarification of any of the Articles of this Declaration.'[9]

The third declaration is the *Arab Charter on Human Rights*[10] which was first produced by the League of Arab States in 1994, was revised in 2004 and came into force in 2008 after ratification by seven league members.

According to the preamble to the Charter, it is:

Based on the faith of the Arab nation in the dignity of the human person whom God has exalted ever since the beginning of creation and in the fact that the Arab homeland is the cradle of religions and civilizations whose lofty human values affirm the human right to a decent life based on freedom, justice and equality.

It is also said to be in 'furtherance of the eternal principles of fraternity, equality and tolerance among human beings consecrated by the noble Islamic religion and the other divinely-revealed religions.'

The Charter consists of fifty-three Articles. The first Article explains the purpose of the Charter as being to achieve four aims:

1. To place human rights at the centre of the key national concerns of Arab States, making them lofty and fundamental ideals that shape the will of the individual in Arab States and enable him to improve his life in accordance with noble human values.

2. To teach the human person in the Arab States pride in his identity, loyalty to his country, attachment to his land, history and common interests and to instil in him a culture of human brotherhood, tolerance and openness towards others, in accordance with universal principles and values and with those proclaimed in international human rights instruments.

3. To prepare the new generations in Arab States for a free and responsible life in a civil society that is characterized by solidarity, founded on a balance between awareness of rights and respect for obligations, and governed by the values of equality, tolerance and moderation.

4. To entrench the principle that all human rights are universal, indivisible, interdependent and interrelated.

The remaining Articles set out a series of rights freedoms and prohibitions and a framework for the implementation of the Charter. The rights, freedoms and prohibitions are as follows:

- The right to national self-determination;

- Equality between men and women;

- The right to life, with capital punishment only to be applied in extreme cases and not to be applied to minors or pregnant or nursing women;

- Prohibition of torture and cruel, humiliating or inhumane treatment;

- Protection of people from medical or scientific experimentation;

- Prohibition of slavery, forced labour, and people trafficking;

- The right to equal treatment before courts and tribunals;

- The right to a fair and public trial;

- The right to liberty and security of person;

- No conviction or penalty without prior provision of the law;

- The presumption of innocence before conviction and nobody to be tried twice for the same offence;

- Special protection for children involved in the legal system;

- Prohibition of imprisonment for debt;

- The humane treatment of prisoners;

- The right to recognition as a person before the law;

- The right to participate in civic affairs and freedom of association;

- Protection of the culture and religion of minorities;

- Freedom of movement;

- The right of asylum;

- The right to a nationality and to change nationality;

- Freedom of thought, conscience and religion;

- The right to own property;

- The right to information and freedom of opinion and expression;

- The right to marriage and family life;

- The right to work for both men and women and the protection of children from economic exploitation;

- The right to join a trades union and to strike;
- The right to social security;
- The right to personal development;
- The right to an adequate standard of living for an individual and his family;
- The right to enjoy physical and mental health;
- The right to a decent life of those with disability;
- The elimination of illiteracy;
- The right to participate in cultural life and to enjoy the benefits of scientific progress.[11]

The contents of this list of rights, freedoms and prohibitions overlaps with, but differs from, what is said in the 1981 and 1990 declarations. Although it makes reference to the 'noble Islamic religion', the Charter also differs from these earlier declarations in not seeking to place what it says within an overtly Islamic theological framework and in not making its provisions subject to Sharia law.

What we see in these three declarations are three attempts to produce comprehensive accounts of human rights from a Muslim majority perspective. These declarations overlap and diverge in a variety of different ways and the similarities and differences between them, and between them and other international statements about human rights (such as the Universal Declaration of Human Rights or the European Convention on Human Rights), are a further indication of the complexity of Islamic approaches to human rights. They show that Muslim approaches to human rights neither wholly agree, nor wholly disagree, with wider international human rights thinking and neither wholly agree, nor wholly disagree, with each other.

Muslims are clearly supportive of the basic concept of human rights, so to say Muslims are against human rights would be wrong, but they have developed a variety of specifically Islamic approaches to the concept.

4.5   ISLAMIC HUMAN RIGHTS ORGANISATIONS

Recent years have also seen the emergence of a range of Islamic human rights organisations. Three examples of these are the Independent Permanent Human Rights Commission, the Islamic Human Rights Commission and the Women's Islamic Initiative in Spirituality and Equality.

The Independent Permanent Human Rights Commission was established in 2011 by the Organisation of Islamic Co-operation (the umbrella body for Muslim majority nations) as a permanent international Islamic human rights body. Its objectives include:

- Advising OIC's policy-and-decision-making bodies on all matters in the realm of human rights.

- Undertaking studies and research in the field of human rights.

- Advancing human rights and fundamental freedoms in Member States as well as the fundamental rights of Muslim minorities and communities in non-member states in conformity with the universally recognized human rights norms and standards and with the added value of Islamic principles of justice and equality.

- Promoting and strengthening human rights in Member States by providing 'technical cooperation and assistance in the field of human rights and awareness-raising.'

- Pursuing interfaith and intercultural dialogue as a tool to promote peace and harmony among various civilizations and to promote the true image of Islam.

- Extending support to Member States and their national institutions in the promotion and protection of human rights for all in an independent manner.

- Reviewing OIC's own human rights instruments and recommending ways for their fine-tuning, as and where appropriate, including the option of recommending new mechanisms and covenants.

- Promoting cooperative working relations with relevant bodies of UN and OIC, as well as relevant regional human rights mechanisms.

- Promoting and supporting the role of Member States' accredited civil society organizations.

- Participating in missions for observing elections in Member States.[12]

The Islamic Human Rights Commission describes itself as 'an independent, not-for-profit, campaign, research and advocacy organization based in London UK.'[13] It lists its aims as being:

1. To champion the rights & duties revealed for human beings.

2. To promote a new social & international order, based on truth, justice, righteousness & generosity, rather than selfish interest.

3. To demand virtue & oppose wrongdoing in the exercise of power (from whatever base that power derives – e.g. political, judicial, media, economic, military, personal, etc.).

4. To gather information about, & to publicise, atrocities, oppression, discrimination, & other abuses of divinely-granted rights.

5. To campaign for redress, & to support the victims, of such crimes.

6. To campaign to bring the perpetrators & their accomplices to justice.

7. To cooperate with other groups & individuals where such cooperation is likely to further the achievement of these aims.[14]

The American based Women's Islamic Initiative in Spirituality and Equality (WISE) describes itself as 'a global program, social network and grassroots social justice movement led by Muslim women.' Its statement of belief ('the WISE compact') is as follows:

We, the women of WISE (Women's Islamic Initiative in Spirituality and Equality), declare gender equality to be an intrinsic part of the Islamic faith. As Muslims, we affirm our conviction that the Muslim woman is worthy of respect and dignity, that as a legal individual, spiritual being, social person, responsible agent, free citizen, and servant of God, she holds fundamentally equal rights to exercise her abilities and talents in all areas of human activity. Furthermore, we insist that these

rights are embedded within the Qur'an and six objectives of Shari'a—
the protection and promotion of religion (al-din), life (al-nafs), mind
(al-'aql), family (al-nasl), wealth (al-mal), and dignity (al-'ird).

As WISE women, we embrace our collective and individual
responsibility to work towards building a unified change movement of
Muslim women – driven by compassion and justice – that will enable
Muslim women to realize their full potential as individuals and in
relationship to family, community, nation, and globe.[15]

A comparison of the work of the Islamic Human Rights Commission
and WISE once again highlights the issue of the complexity of Muslim
approaches to human rights. The Islamic Human Rights Commission takes
a generally conservative approach to Islam and focuses on issues such as
attacks on Muslims, discrimination against Muslims and the detention of
Muslims by governments around the world under anti-terrorism legislation.
WISE, by contrast, takes a generally liberal approach to Islam and focuses
on upholding and developing the rights of women within Islam, tackling
issues such as access to healthcare and education, domestic violence, parental
rights, female genital mutilation, dress codes, early marriage, polygamy
and sex trafficking. For the Islamic Human Rights Commission the key
rights issue is the treatment of Muslims by non-Muslims; for WISE it is
the treatment of women within Islam.

4.6   ISLAMIC THEOLOGICAL APPROACHES TO HUMAN RIGHTS
It is common ground among Islamic scholars that the basis for the existence
of human rights from an Islamic perspective is that all human beings
regardless of sex, race or religion have a basic common dignity because they
have been created by God and endowed by God with the ability to obtain
knowledge, to engage in conceptual thinking and to exercise freedom and
responsibility over whether they will believe in God and submit to him.

As Muddathir Abd al-Ramin writes, it is on the basis of this human
dignity:

...that has been graciously and gratuitously conferred by God on
humanity and, at the same time, in order to guard and protect
the divine gift in question itself that the highly sophisticated and

elaborate structure of human rights (and obligations) in Islam has been established. The ultimate objective in Islam is to make it possible for humans to attain self-fulfilment during their lifetimes on earth and salvation thereafter in the eternal life to come.[16]

It is also common ground that there are three basic sources for Islamic reflection on the God-given dignity of human beings and the rights and obligations that flow from this, the Quran, the Sunna and the various traditions of Sharia law. The complexity of Islamic thinking about human rights reflects the fact that Islamic thinkers and writers have interpreted and built on these common sources in a variety of different ways in relation to a variety of different cultural and political settings.

Broadly speaking there have been three theological responses within Islam to the emergence of human rights since World War II, all of which have drawn in different ways on the three basic sources for Islamic theology and ethics. These three responses are the puritan, the apologetic and the reformist.

As El Fadl explains, the puritan tradition within Islam, which has found its main expression in the Wahabbi and Salafist movements within Sunni Islam, and which has provided the ideological basis for the hard line Islamic movements we know today, is based on the rejection of compromise with the modern world. As he puts it:

Puritanism resisted the indeterminacy of the modern age by escaping to a strict literalism in which the text became the sole source of legitimacy. It sought to return to the presumed golden age of Islam, when the Prophet created a perfect, just polity in Medina. According to the puritans, it was imperative to return to a presumed pristine, simple, and straightforward Islam, which was believed to be entirely reclaimable by a literal implementation of the commands and precedents of the Prophet and by a strict adherence to correct ritual practice. The puritan orientation also considered any form of moral thought that was not entirely dependent on the text to be a form of self-idolatry and treated humanistic fields of knowledge, especially philosophy as 'the sciences of the devil'. It also rejected any attempt to interpret the divine law from a historical or contextual perspective, and, in fact, treated the vast majority of Islamic history as a corruption or alteration of the true and authentic Islam. The dialectical and indeterminate hermeneutics of the classical jurisprudential tradition were considered corruptions of the purity of the faith and law, and the puritan movement became very intolerant of the long-established Islamic practice of considering a variety of schools of thought to be equally orthodox and attempted to narrow considerably the range of issues upon which Muslims may legitimately disagree.[17]

El Fadl further notes that according to the puritan tradition the perfection of Islam means that:

...ultimately Islam does not need to reconcile itself or prove itself compatible with any other system of thought. According to this paradigm, Islam is a self-contained and self-sufficient system of belief and laws that ought to shape the world in its image, rather than accommodate human experience in any way.[18]

In relation to the issue of human rights this emphasis on the perfection of Islam meant that for the puritans there is no need to reconcile Islam with contemporary human rights thinking:

...the puritan claim was that whatever rights human beings are entitled to enjoy, they are entirely within the purview of Shari'a law. It is important to realize that the puritans did not deny, in principle, that human beings have rights; they contended that such rights could not exist unless granted by God. Therefore one finds that in puritan literature there is no effort to justify international rights on Islamic terms but simply an effort to set out the divine law on the assumption that such a law, by definition, provides human beings with a just and moral order.[19]

Unlike the puritan tradition, the apologetic tradition has seen it as important to relate Islam to contemporary human rights thinking. The way that it has done this has been to argue that the rights that are affirmed in contemporary thinking about human rights have already been affirmed in the three classical Islamic sources.

This apologetic approach is implicit in the way in which the Universal Islamic Declaration of Human Rights links each of the rights it lists to references in the Quran and the Sunna and it is explicit, for example, in Riffat Hassan's essay 'Are Human Rights Compatible with Islam?'

In this essay Hassan declares that 'Of all the sources of the Islamic tradition, undoubtedly, the most important is the Qur'an which is regarded by Muslims in general, as the primary, and most authoritative, source of normative Islam.'

He then goes on to give an account

...of the Qur'an's affirmation of fundamental rights which all human beings ought to possess because they are so deeply rooted in our humanness that their denial or violation is tantamount to a negation or degradation of that which makes us human. From the perspective of the Qur'an, these rights came into existence when we did; they were created, as we were, by God in order that our human potential could be actualized. Rights created or given by God cannot be abolished by any temporal ruler or human agency. Eternal and immutable, they ought to be exercised since everything that God does is for 'a just purpose.'

Hassan lists twelve of these rights: the right to life; the right to respect; the right to justice; the right to freedom; the right to acquire knowledge; the right to sustenance; the right to work; the right to privacy; the right to protection from slander, backbiting and ritual; the right to develop one's aesthetic sensibilities and enjoy the bounties created by God; the right to leave one's homeland under oppressive conditions, and the right to the 'good life'. For each of these rights he gives an explanation of how they are affirmed in the Quran. Three examples will illustrate this.

On the right to respect he writes:

The Qur'an deems all human beings to be worthy of respect [Surah 17: Al-Isra': 70] because of all creation they alone chose to accept the 'trust' of freedom of the will [Surah 33: Al-Ahzab: 72]. Human beings can exercise freedom of the will because they possess the rational faculty, which is what distinguishes them from all other creatures [Surah 2: Al-Baqarah: 30-34]. Though human beings can become 'the lowest of the lowest', the Qur'an declares that they have been made 'in the best of moulds' [Surah 95: At-Tin: 4-6], having the ability to think, to have knowledge of right and wrong, to do the good and to avoid the evil. Thus, on account of the promise which is contained in being human, namely, the potential to be God's vicegerent on earth, the humanness of all human beings is to be respected and considered to be an end in itself.

On the right to sustenance he declares:

As pointed out by Surah 11: Hud: 6, every living creature depends for its sustenance upon God. A cardinal concept in the Qur'an – which underlies the socio-economic-political system of Islam – is that the ownership of everything belongs, not to any person, but to God. Since God is the universal creator, every creature has the right to partake of what belongs to God [Surah 6: Al-An'am: 165; Surah 67: Al-Mulk:15]. This means that every human being has the right to a means of living and that those who hold economic or political power do not have the right to deprive others of the basic necessities of life by misappropriating or misusing resources which have been created by God for the benefit of humanity in general.

On the right to the 'good life' he states:

The Qur'an upholds the right of the human being not only to life but to 'the good life.' This good life, made up of many elements, becomes possible when a human being is living in a just environment. According to Qur'anic teaching, justice is a prerequisite for peace, and peace is a prerequisite for human development. In a just society, all the earlier-mentioned human rights may be exercised without difficulty. In such a society other basic rights such as the right to a secure place of residence, the right to the protection of one's personal possessions, the right to protection of one's covenants, the right to move freely, the right to social and judicial autonomy for minorities, the right to the protection of one's holy places and the right to return to one's spiritual centre, also exist [Surah 2:Al- Baqarah:229; Surah 3: Al-'Imran: 17,77; Surah 5: Al-Ma'idah:1; 42-48; Surah 9: At-Tawbah: 17; Surah 17: Al-Isra': 34; Surah 67: Al-Mulk:15.][20]

The reformist or 'progressive' tradition within Islam holds that it is not sufficient to simply quote sources from the Quran, the Sunna or Sharia to seek to prove that human rights are supported by Islam. Instead, writers within this tradition argue that what is needed is a systematic rethinking of the Islamic tradition in the light of the challenge presented by contemporary human rights thinking.

Abdullahi An-Na'im writes, for example:

> ...the challenge is how to develop and apply a systematic and effective methodology of reinterpretation of Sharia, instead of arbitrarily selecting sources and historical evidence to support one view or another on an isolated issue or subject. It is easy to find verses of the Quran that apparently support modern human rights principles, such as freedom of religion and equality for women. But one can equally quote verses that seem to support the opposing view. The real issue is to establish a consistent 'framework of interpretation,' and not simply the availability of texts of the Quran that can be understood one way or another.[21]

He goes on to argue that there needs to be a 're-framing' of the debate about Islam and human rights and this re-framing needs to involve the abandoning of the traditional Islamic approach which has seen Sharia as the basis for state law.

In his view, because the purpose of Sharia is to teach people how to live rightly before God it follows that

> ...by its nature and purpose, Sharia can only be freely observed by believers, and its principles lose their religious authority and value when they are enforced by the State. This religious dimension requires free reflection and choice by believers among equally accessible competing interpretations and religious authorities, independently from the coercive authority of the State.[22]

He suggests that instead of being based on Sharia (or any other religious tradition)

> ...the rationale of all public policy and legislation should be based

92

on what might be called 'civic reason.' Muslims and other believers should be able to propose policy and legislative initiatives emanating from their religious beliefs, provided they can support them in free and open debate by giving reasons that are accessible and convincing to the generality of citizens, regardless of their religion or other beliefs. But since such decisions will in practice be made by democratic vote in accordance with democratic principles, all state action must also conform to basic constitutional and human rights safeguards to protect against the tyranny of the majority. Accordingly, the majority would not be able to implement any policy or legislation that violates the fundamental constitutional rights of all citizens, women and men, Muslims and non-Muslims alike.

In this way, both the adoption of human rights norms as well as opposition to them must be founded on civic reason, without reference to the religious beliefs of any community. At the same time, however, since Sharia principles will remain binding on all Muslims in individual and collective practice outside state institutions, the need for reform through internal debate about the meaning of Shariah will continue. [23]

4.7   AREAS OF TENSION OVER ISLAM AND HUMAN RIGHTS

There are a number of specific areas where there is tension in relation to Islamic beliefs and practices and human rights.

4.7.1   Ritual slaughter and Circumcision

As with Judaism, the first of these areas of tension is the issue of the freedom of Muslims to practise their form of the ritual slaughter of animals to produce halal meat and to circumcise male babies. The basic issue here, as in the case of Judaism, is whether the right of Muslims to practise their religion freely should take precedence over what objectors would see as cruelty to animals and an assault on the bodily integrity of babies.

4.7.2   Equality

The second area of tension is over equality between Muslims and non-Muslims, equality between men and women and equality for gay and lesbian people.

On the issue of equality between Muslims and non-Muslims, the traditional *dhimma* system which formally restricted the rights of non-Muslims in a variety of ways may no longer form part of the civil law of Muslim majority countries, but many would argue that in a large number of Muslim majority countries there is still a large degree of discrimination against non-Muslims in a way that means that non-Muslims are effectively second-class citizens.

On the issue of equality between men and women, many Islamic communities, although affirming the basic equality between men and women as human beings, have traditionally had a strong emphasis on male authority and on the differentiation of roles between men and women and have restricted the roles which women can play outside the home, both in civic society and in religious life, in a way which many today would see as discriminatory against women.

Two further issues in this area are polygamy, which is practised in some Muslim communities and which some would see as putting women at a disadvantage over men, and traditional forms of Islamic dress for women such as the hijab or the burqa which are intended to protect female modesty, but which many would now see as dehumanising and as preventing women from exercising freedom of choice over what they wear.

On the issue of equality for gay and lesbian people, the traditional Islamic view has been that sexual activity and marriage should only be between men and women and therefore many Muslims would disapprove of moves towards the social and legal acceptance of same-sex relationships and the introduction of same-sex marriages.

4.7.3   Islamic Punishments

The third area of tension is over the forms of punishment that are practised in a number of Muslim majority countries, including capital punishment not only for murder, but for religious offences such as blasphemy and apostasy and moral offences such as adultery and forms of corporal punishment such as flogging and amputation. Critics of such forms of punishment would see them as coming under the category of cruel, inhuman and degrading forms of punishment.

4.7.4 Freedom of Religion

The fourth area of tension is over freedom of religion. It is accepted as Quranic teaching that 'there shall be no compulsion in matters of faith' (Sura 2:256 Al-Baqarah), and on that basis there has been Islamic acceptance of 'freedom of religion' in statements of human rights. However, there has also been strong resistance to the idea that freedom of religion means freedom to convert from Islam to some other form of religion or to no religion at all. Shariah law forbids apostasy from Islam and makes it a capital offence. Conversion from Islam is forbidden in the civil law of most Muslim states and in many of them it still carries the death penalty.[24]

4.7.5 Diversity within Islam

Returning to the issue of the complexity within Islam, it is important to note, however, that there is a strong diversity within Islam over issues such as equality, forms of punishment and freedom of religion.[25] In all these areas there is an internal debate within Islam itself about how far traditional Islamic beliefs and practices are genuinely rooted in the Quran and the Sunna and how far they reflect interpretations of these sources in cultural contexts that are now past and should therefore not be regarded as normative for today.

The way in which the Women's Islamic Initiative in Spirituality and Equality is challenging traditional views about the role of women within Islam is a good example of this kind of internal debate, as is the debate about whether Islamic teaching really requires the imposition of the death penalty for apostasy or whether the traditional law regarding apostasy is 'inapplicable in contemporary circumstances where a change of faith is not accompanied by disloyalty to the state.'[26]

Notes

[1] Khaled Abou El Fadl, 'The Human Rights Commitment in Modern Islam', in Runzo, Martin and Sharma (eds), op. cit. p. 302.

[2] Ann Mayer, 'Current Muslim Thinking on Human Rights', in Abdullahi Ahmed An-Na'im and Francis M Deng (eds), *Human Rights in Africa: Cross Cultural Perspectives*, Washington DC: Brookings Institute, 1990, p.133.

[3] Bassam Tibi, 'The European Tradition of Human Rights and the Culture of Islam', in An-Na'im and Deng (eds), op. cit. p.124.

[4] The information about Afghanistan, Egypt and Malaysia can be found at the website of the University of Minnesota Human Rights Library at http://www1.umn.edu/humanrts/ research/ratification

[5] The reservations with regard to Articles 13 and 16 were withdrawn in 1997.

[6] For a discussion of these reservations see Ann Mayer, 'Islamic Reservations to Human Rights Conventions – A Critical Assessment', in *Recht Van de Islam*, 1998, pp.25-45.

[7] For the full texts of this Declaration see Appendix 3 to this report.

[8] For the text of this Declaration see Appendix 3 of this report.

[9] Text of the Cairo Declaration from William H Brackney (ed), *Human Rights and the World's Major Religions*, Santa Barbara: Praeger, 2013, pp.432-439.

[10] For the text of this Charter see Appendix 3 of this report.

[11] The text of the Charter is on the website of the University of Minnesota Human Rights library at

http://www1.umn.edu/humanrts/instree/loas2005.html?msource=UNWDEC19001&tr=y&auid=3337655

[12] International Permanent Commission on Human Rights, 'Mission and objectives' at http://www.oic-iphrc.org/en/about/

[13] http://www.ihrc.org.uk/about-ihrc

[14] http://www.ihrc.org.uk/about-ihrc/aims-a-objectives

[15] http://www.wisemuslimwomen.org/resources/

[16] Muddathir 'Abd al-Rabim, 'The Worldview of Islam', in Brackney (ed), op.cit. p. 147.

[17] El Fadl, in Runzo, Martin and Sharma (eds), op. cit. pp.308-309.

[18] Ibid., p.309.

[19] Ibid., p.310.

[20] Rifat Hassan, 'Are Human Rights Compatible with Islam?' at http://religiousconsultation. org/hassan2.htm#six

[21] An-Na'im, 'Islam and Human Rights', in Witte and Green (eds), op. cit. p. 65.

[22] Ibid., p.67.

[23] Ibid.

[24] See Shah A Niaz, 'Freedom of Religion, Koranic and Human Rights Perspectives', *Asia Pacific Journal on Human Rights and the Law*, 6/1.2005, pp.69-88, and http://www.loc. gov/law/help/apostasy/index.php

[25] The 2013 survey by the Pew Research Center on 'The World's Muslims: Religion, Politics and Society' provides a helpful snapshot of the range of Muslim attitudes in the world today. http://www.pewforum.org/2013/04/30/the-worlds-muslims-religion-politics-society-overview/

[26] Michael Nazir-Ali, *Conviction and Conflict, Islam, Christianity and World Order*, London and New York: Continuum, 2006, p.250, and Patrick Sookdheo, *Freedom to Believe: Challenging Islam's Apostasy Law*, McLean, VA: Isaac Publishing, 2009.

Chapter Five

HINDUISM AND HUMAN RIGHTS

5.1   NEGATIVE PERCEPTIONS OF HINDUISM AND HUMAN RIGHTS

Although Islam is now often seen as the chief example of a conflict between religion and human rights, a similar negative view is often taken of the relationship between Hinduism and human rights.

In the words of Arvind Sharma in his article 'The Rights in Hinduism':

It is often maintained, directly or by implication, that Hinduism is antagonistic to human rights, that the only relationship possible between them is one of diametrical opposition, that the hierarchy of the caste system on which Hinduism is based leaves no room for the equality on which human rights are based.[1]

Werner Menski similarly notes in his essay 'Hinduism and Human Rights':

While missionaries eventually softened in their views on Hinduism, other scholars of political science and human rights continue vigorously to denigrate Hindu culture and Hinduism. Not unlike Western missionaries centuries ago, many so-called human rights activists today myopically treat anything Hindu as incapable of addressing human rights concerns. Hindu religion and customs are viewed as tainted by irrationality and adherence to backward customs such as sati (the burning of widows on the husband's funeral pyre, forced marriages, dowry demands, frantic killing of non-believers in communal riots, and, of course, multiple caste-based discriminations.

Recent studies simply start from the presumption that equality is a value per se and that 'the most plainly revealed system of inequality is associated with the Hindu order of castes.' They conclude that the ancient principle of natural inequality, devised by Brahmans, 'continues to define the system till today' and thus defies progress in terms of human rights protection.[2]

In recent years the destruction of the mosque at Avodhya in 1992 by the Hindu Rashtriya Swayamsevak Sangh (National Patriotism Organization), what has been seen as the poor human rights record of India's Hindu Nationalist Bharatiya Janata Party and the increase on attacks on religious minorities in India by Hindu Nationalist groups seeking to create a purified Hindu society has increased the view that there is a conflict between Hinduism and human rights.

On the other hand, the two countries with Hindu majority populations, India and Nepal, are both signatories to the International Bill of Rights and a range of other human rights conventions,[3] a 'Universal Declaration of Human Rights by the Hindus' similar to the Universal Declaration of Human Rights was produced in 1994[4] and scholars of Hinduism such as Sharma, Menski and Nancy Martin have argued that there is no inherent incompatibility between Hinduism and human rights. To quote Sharma again, the view that there is such an incompatibility appears to be so partial as to be erroneous. It may contain some truth in individual instances, but should not obscure the larger reality of Hinduism being entirely hospitable to human rights.[5]

In the remainder of this chapter we shall look at the arguments that have been put forward to show why Hinduism provides support for human rights and explore areas of tension in relation to Hinduism and human rights.

HINDUISM AND HUMAN RIGHTS

5.2   HINDU TEACHING AND SUPPORT FOR HUMAN RIGHTS

5.2.1   The Hindu scriptures and worldview

Hinduism is not something that is easy to define. It is a form of religion that has gradually developed in South Asia over thousands of years and that encompasses a vast range of religious beliefs and practices. However, for the purposes of this report what is important to note is that alongside its diversity there are a set of texts which form the Hindu scriptures and an overall Hindu worldview based on these texts.

The most important of the Hindu scriptures are the Vedas. These are the fundamental texts of Hinduism and are viewed as containing eternal truths revealed to the ancient sages by God. There are four Vedas, the Rigveda, the Samaveda, the Yajurveda and the Atharavaveda. Each of these four Vedas has been sub-classified into four major types of text: the Samhitas (mantras and benedictions), the Aranyakas (texts on rituals, ceremonies, sacrifices and symbolic-sacrifices), the Brahmanas (commentaries on rituals, ceremonies and sacrifices), and the Upanishads (texts discussing meditation, philosophy and spiritual knowledge).

Alongside the Vedas, and regarded as compatible with them, there is a variety of other texts which have helped to shape Hindu belief and practice. These include epic texts such as the *Mahabharata* and the *Ramayana*, the *Puranas*, an encyclopedic collection of texts on a diverse range of topics including cosmogony, cosmology, the genealogies of the gods, goddesses, demigods, kings, heroes and sages, folk tales, pilgrimages, temples, medicine, astronomy, grammar, minerology, humour and love stories, as well as theology and philosophy, and legal texts such as the *Law of Manu*, which has traditionally been regarded as the basis for the Hindu caste system. Part of the *Mahabharata* is the *Bhagavad Gita*, a text which is sometimes regarded as an additional Upanishad because its contents are seen as similar to the *Upanishads* in the *Vedas*.

Based on these texts and others there is an overall Hindu worldview. This holds that there is one supreme God (or for non-theistic Hindus one supreme reality) from which all things emanate and to whom all things will ultimately return. The various gods of the Hindu pantheon are understood as emanating from the supreme deity and representing some aspect of his existence.

Human existence is seen as a cycle of birth, death and rebirth in which the soul passes through various reincarnations. The nature of these reincarnations depends on how the previous life was lived, in line with the principle of karma, the principle that all actions have consequences either in this life or in the next. In order to live well in each successive incarnation one needs to behave in accordance with dharma, the order which governs the cosmos and human behaviour within it. The eventual goal of human existence is to achieve moksha, liberation from the cycle of reincarnation and union with God.[6]

As the three examples below show, those writers who have explored the connection between Hinduism and human rights have built on these texts and this overall worldview in a variety of ways.

5.2.2 Nancy Martin 'Rights, Roles and Reciprocity in Hindu Dharma'

In her 2003 essay 'Rights, Roles and Reciprocity in Hindu Dharma', Nancy M Martin notes that within:

> ...the purview of the wide-ranging beliefs and practices arising in South Asia that are collectively called 'Hinduism', there is a perceived order inherent in the world which is at once natural, social and moral. This principle is dharma.[7]

Dharma, she says, 'encompasses two levels of 'privileges, duties and obligations – those that are common or universal (*sadharana dharma*), i.e. incumbent on all people; and those that are specific, depending on one's gender, caste and life-stage.'[8]

In her view, it is the first of these two forms of dharma which comes closest:

> ...to what we would call 'universal human rights and responsibilities', though in the Hindu view, one begins with duties and obligations, the fulfilment of which then confers privileges (rather than 'rights' per se). According to Gautama's *Dharma* (one of the earliest texts on dharma),

elements of this common or universal dharma include the virtues of 'compassion for all creatures, patience, lack of envy, purification, tranquility, having an auspicious disposition, generosity and lack of greed,' and other texts offer additional listings. Most important of these is the principle of ahimsa or non-injury, from which many of the other virtues flow.

Implied in the type of virtues Gautama lists are basic responsibilities toward others – namely, to cause no injury and to treat them with compassion, patience and generosity, without greed or envy. Therefore, these virtues, if practiced, would clearly offer motivational support for the protection of the basic rights of others – even, one might add, at the expense of one's own rights. Madhu Kishwar, the social activist and editor of the women's journal *Manushi,* recalls a story her mother told her repeatedly as a child when she would want to retaliate for some perceived wrong. The story tells of a saintly man who was bathing in a river. A scorpion had fallen into the water and the man reached in to rescue it from drowning. The scorpion immediately stung him, causing him to drop it again into the water. The man reached out again and again to rescue the scorpion and each time it stung him, causing him to drop it. A curious onlooker asked why he persisted. His response was 'The scorpion's dharm is to sting, my dharm as a human is compassion. How can I forgo my dharm and return injury for injury, when even the scorpion is not willing to leave his own.' Hinduism is replete with similar stories which explore the application of dharmic virtues and obligations and take account of real-life situations as only narrative can.[9]

Underlying the second, specific, form of dharma there is, she writes:

...an organic view of society and a relational understanding of the human person. A person is defined as a member of both a family and a community with particular responsibilities at different stages of his or her life. Roles and responsibilities are further understood to be a function of one's nature as defined by gender, by the kinship group into which one was born – i.e. one's caste – and by one's individual abilities.

Ideally, such an organic understanding of society facilitates the well-being of all through the division of labor and mutual responsibility and reciprocity. The image of society as divided in this manner in terms of roles appears in the earliest Hindu text, the *Rig Veda*. In the hymn to Purusha (*Rig Veda* 10:90) the world is said to be created through the sacrifice of the Cosmic Person. From the mouth the Brahmin priests are made, the Kshatriya rulers and warriors from the arms, the Vaishya merchants and artisans from the thighs, and the Shudras or servants from the feet. This hymn suggests social stratification and role division quite apart from any consideration of heredity.[10]

However, observes Martin, it is nonetheless the case that 'hierarchy seems inherent in such an image of the mutual division of labor, and indeed these divisions seem to be ossified in a hereditary and hierarchically related manner based on an understanding of purity.'[11] The underlying idea is that:

> ...those at the highest level of society are to remain pure in order that they might carry out the necessary ritual interaction with the divine on behalf of society as a whole and preserve and teach the wisdom of the sages. With each descending level impurity increases. The lowest of the Shudras traditionally carried out the most impure functions needed within society, such as the sweeping up of excrement and dealing with the bodies of dead animals in the making of leather goods.[12]

When hierarchy rather than complementarity does become the dominant conception of the relationship between the castes:

> ...the system can become oppressive, particularly so when acceptance of one's low status (and the deprivation that may come with it) is religiously justified in terms of dharma and when a reward for endurance is promised in future lives by way of compensation. For instance, the Bhagavad Gita states unequivocally that it is better to do one's own dharma, even if poorly, than to try to do another's dharma. Emphasis is also sometimes put on one's karma as a justification for the social position of one's caste or gender in any given birth, so that a low status and difficult life becomes a kind of penance for past wrongs, with a promise of improved future lives through the proper fulfilment of one's caste and/or gender duties in this life.[13]

Having acknowledged these difficulties within the Hindu tradition, Martin then argues that they are no reason for simply writing off Hinduism completely:

> ...just as we should not dismiss Christianity as having no resources to support human rights because of the use of Christian texts to reinforce slavery or because there are racists who identify themselves as Christians, so we should not dismiss Hinduism because of caste-based or gender-based oppression, though certainly these actions and prejudices must be challenged in both traditions. Turning our attention to Hinduism, there are other voices coming from within the Hindu tradition which do radically challenge such oppression and uphold the dignity of all.[14]

As an example of such voices Martin turns first of all to the Upanishads. These, she declares:

> ...radically relativized existing notions of caste, suggesting that the true self of all individuals is one with the true self of all that is – Atman – and that this unity, rather than caste, is what ultimately matters. One implication of belief in the oneness of all is a sense of responsibility for all that happens in the world, including human rights abuses, because as the *Chandogya Upanishad* says, 'all that is you.'[15]

As a second example she turns to the devotional, or bhakti, traditions within Hinduism that began to appear in South India from the sixth century onwards. In these traditions there are even more moral radical statements than in the Upanishads:

> ...suggesting that we are all equal in the presence of the one divine reality of which we are all a part, conceived in personalistic terms as God. The particulars of one's current incarnation – including gender and caste – have no relevance before God. Religious authority lies not in heredity but in religious experience and the ability to draw others into relationship with the one divine reality who is loved by and loves the devotee.[16]

To illustrate the bhakti tradition she quotes the words of the ninth-century saint Nammalvar who said in one of his songs:

> The four castes
> Uphold all clans;
> Go down, far down
> To the lowliest outcastes
> Of Outcastes

If they are the servants of God:

> Then even the salves of their slaves
> Are our masters.

Martin comments that in so saying Nammalvar 'does not deny the existence of castes or the complementarity of their roles and responsibilities, but he does deny the ideal of hierarchy that would value and privilege the Brahmin over the outcaste.'[17]

Martin's overall conclusion is that the way forward for Hinduism is to try to find a right balance 'between the hierarchical complementarity of roles and the individualistic egalitarianism of rights in a language and action that will honor both equality and individual rights and mutual responsibilities and complementarity.' In her view:

> To advocate, as Gandhi did, a possible vision of community structured by an egalitarian complementarity (rather than a hierarchical complementarity or an individualistic egalitarianism) is not to advocate the 'separate but equal' understanding of the segregationist southern United States. It is to challenge any hierarchical valuing of human differences radically and to call for the full recognition of the humanity and dignity of all, and in so doing to erase the degradation and oppression of those deemed 'lower' that might result from hierarchical valuing. But to advocate egalitarian complementarity is also to advocate a deep recognition of interrelationship and interdependence in a way that values and cherishes difference as a vital part of the world community. This is the model that Hinduism challenges us to consider, as we seek to uphold human rights worldwide – an egalitarian

complementarity, where roles and differences both find a place without hierarchy and where reciprocity ensures that the rights and dignity of all can be upheld.[18]

5.2.3   Dipti Patel 'The Religious Foundations of Human Rights: A Perspective from the Judeo-Christian Tradition and Hinduism.'

In her 2005 essay 'The Religious Foundations of Human Rights: A Perspective from the Judeo-Christian Tradition and Hinduism', Dipti Patel looks at a Hindu approach to the issues of rights, equality and freedom of religion.

On the issue of rights she notes that in Hinduism (as in Judaism) 'there is no word for rights.'[19] The closest word, she says, 'is adhikara, which relates to the idea of 'just claim'. Such a claim exists: 'in the context where one has performed some act, or performed a duty.'[20]

This idea of a claim based on the performance of a duty is linked, Patel argues, 'to the central concept of Dharma, the central doctrine of Hindu thought.'[21] Dharma, she writes:

...is a comprehensive term, which includes duty, morality, ritual, law, order and justice. For example, it can be used in a ritualistic context to mean the religious duties, or it can be used to mean the duties of the different castes (varna-dharma), or it can refer to those duties that are common to all irrespective of class.

In Hindu thought dharma is:

...a mode of life or a code of conduct, which regulates a man's work and activities as a member of society and as an individual. It is intended to bring about the gradual development of man and to enable him to reach the goal of human existence.[22]

Dharma is also

....the way in which the cosmos, the whole universe, or the balance in the cosmos is maintained. It holds together in a systematic manner the integrity and progression of life in the universe. Hindu thought starts with the cosmos and works its way in to the individual. At the human level, it involves self-regulation and social regulation. It is the duty of society and each individual to maintain this larger cosmic framework of which they are a part.[23]

Patel concedes that within this Hindu worldview in which cosmic order is maintained by each individual performing his or her allotted duty 'it might seem that the concept of human rights is not relevant.'[24] However, she argues, there are a number of ways in which space can be found within Hindu teaching for the idea of rights.

First, rights can be seen as the other sides of duties. For example, Hinduism upholds the duties of 'truthfulness and non-stealing' and 'the duty to tell the truth then means one would have the right to be told the truth.'[25]

Secondly, the ability of human beings to perform duties:

... is a special feature of being human, a sign of human worth and dignity. All humans are to be accorded dignity since they are equally working towards the goal of maintaining the cosmos, whether it is within the socially created caste duties or not. All Hindus are working to achieve spiritual liberation. In addition, human beings are said to be the best poised for salvation and therefore human worth can be signified as truly universal.

Thirdly, in Hindu texts 'the word dharma can be translated into a term meaning "rights" when used in the context of a crisis (apad-dharma).'[26] For example, writes Patel:

... the concept of rights exists if one looks at the duties of the king (raja-dharma). It is the king's duty to protect all and also assist in times of apad-dharma. However, there is no right for the subjects to be ruled over fairly or justly (just like the idea that a neighbour does not have a right to be loved within the Judeo-Christian tradition). As a result they cannot enforce their rights.

However, the Mahabharata, a Hindu religious text, grants the people to 'gird themselves up and kill a cruel king, who does not protect his subjects, who extracts taxes and simply robs them of their wealth.' There is a right (adhikara) to rebel against a king if he does not fulfil his duty to protect the people. This is a clear example of how the concept of human rights can be interpreted within the context of human duties.[27]

Overall, argues Patel, both the Judeo-Christian tradition and Hinduism accept that human beings have both rights and duties. However, they reach this conclusion by different routes:

The concept of human rights as seen in the Judeo-Christian tradition is by virtue of being created in God's image and the state of grace that gives all human beings inherent worth. In human rights language this translates to certain basic rights. However, this is not to be understood as meaning there are no duties within this tradition. This can be seen from the fact that individuals are created to live in communion with others and have a duty to love their neighbours. The Hindu tradition focuses on the whole, that is, the cosmos, and individuals are seen within this cosmos to maintain it. They have duties which, if fulfilled, carry rights. Therefore, human rights are not inherent but rather to be worked towards by the fulfilment of duties. Furthermore, it has been seen how rights can be read into the concept of dharma, especially in times of apad-dharma.

What all this means, according to Patel, is that:

... the idea of rights is not totally redundant within Hindu thought. It is simply that Hindu thought places Article 29 of the UDHR prior to any other Article. This is the main difference between Western rights talk and principles within the Hindu tradition. The approach that international human rights law has taken places the fundamental idea of dignity in a rights-based context. It is submitted that this founding principle can be better recognised in a rights and duty based system. In this regard, a better recognition and interpretation should be given to the concept of duties as found in Article 29 of the UDHR. Mahatma Gandhi expressed that '...all rights to be deserved and preserved came from duty well done. Thus the very right to live accrues to us only when we do the duty of citizenship of the world'. This would mean that all rights in the UDHR would be correlated with duties. Some

Indian scholars have taken the idea of duties further and have said that Article 29 of the UDHR should be the guiding principle and all other Articles should be subordinated to this one. However, one submits that there needs to be a balanced approach in law, an approach whereby both rights and duties find a place. The concept of duty cannot stand alone without the correlative concept of rights, one can only have a binding obligation to do his duty when the other has a right upon him. In this context, if one looks at Hinduism's focus on duties rather than rights, its character can be reformulated as follows: Hinduism tends to accord greater recognition to the rights that others have in relation to us as compared to the rights we have in relation to them. Concern for the common good enhances human rights by teaching those virtues that include respect for the human dignity of each and every person. So, for example, one would have a right to life but would also have a corresponding duty to protect life. Rather than focusing solely on 'I have this right' or 'we have this right' it is time to start thinking about one's duties, 'I have this duty' or 'we have this duty'. It is this kind of thinking which is stressed in both religious traditions, and it is this type of thinking which can contribute to the further development and promotion of human rights on a universal level.[28]

On the issue of equality Patel maintains that 'the fundamental concept of equality identified within the Judeo-Christian tradition may also be found in Hindu thought.'[29]

She begins her argument by looking at the Hindu caste system, a system which many have seen as fundamentally inimical to ideas of human equality. She defines caste as:

> ... a group of persons characterised by hereditary membership which ranks the different groups as relatively superior or inferior to one another. Four castes have been constructed, Brahmans, Ksatriyas, Vaisya and Sudras and can be translated as the priestly, warrior, agriculturalist and trading, and servicing classes respectively. In addition there were the untouchables who formed a separate group at the bottom, and with whom contact was considered polluting.[30]

Within the traditional caste system, she says:

Each caste had a dharma corresponding to its position on the caste scale. The failure to perform one's caste duty would constitute a violation of dharma. Since this thinking draws a sharp moral distinction between human beings in different castes, it seems in stark contrast to the view in the Judeo-Christian tradition with its firm belief in the inherent equality and worth of all simply from being created in the divine image. As an example, upper caste Hindus frequently restricted temple entry so as to keep untouchables out of the temple. As a result of such inequality, many people from the lower castes have turned to alternative religions such as Christianity and Buddhism. This implies that all human beings are not seen as (inherently) equal.[31]

Patel accepts that this shows that the caste system is 'clearly in violation of international human rights law with its emphasis on the inherent equal worth of all human beings' and that 'it is difficult to envision a universal principle of equality when Hindu thought maintains the caste system.'[32] Her solution to this problem is to argue that if we get behind the teaching of later texts such as the *Law of Manu* we find that original teaching of the Vedas was about the equality of all human beings:

The caste system was an idea that was taken out of the religious context and expanded upon in a philosophical context, in particular in The Laws of Manu (or the Manusmriti which translates into the guidelines for man). The Manusmriti is a book which interprets the Vedic scriptures. Since each caste was created to serve a specific purpose or duty, it was an effective system to organise society, a division of labour. The ideas in original Vedic scriptures incorporate the principle of equality. This is demonstrated by a verse in Rigveda, where a poet exclaims, 'I am a reciter of hymns, my father is a physician, and my mother grinds corn with stones.' This means that one can be whatever he desires and is not restricted by his 'caste' as understood by many. Equality of all human beings was reiterated in the Vedic period, no one was superior or inferior, all were considered as equal 'like the spokes of a wheel of the chariot connecting its rim and the hub'. A deeper meaning of equality is found within the Hindu religion. This embraces the idea of harmony and fraternity among all human beings, the equality of all human souls.[33]

According to the teaching of the Vedas, she writes:

... the soul in every human being is the same, therefore, all human beings should be treated as such. This is because God is present in all that exists: 'God covers all that moves in the Universe.' Hinduism believes in universal brotherhood and since God permeates every being, there is unity and equality in diversity: 'A Seer is he who sees the immutable in the body of all mortals; and, realizing that the same being equally exists everywhere, he attains salvation as he does not slay others bringing death to his own self.' This means that there is inherent equality in all human beings, an idea which is also reflected within the Judeo-Christian tradition. It can therefore be said that a religious theory for the principle of equality as expressed in international human rights law can be found. This is so within the Judeo-Christian tradition and Hinduism. The caste system is clearly in violation of international human rights law with its emphasis on the inherent inequality of persons based upon duties of one based on their caste. However, if one adopts the foundational concept of equality, the original idea in religious texts, then the caste system as understood in other texts can be and must be disregarded. The principle of equality as stated in human rights law does also have a foundation within Hinduism.[34]

On the issue of freedom of religion, Patel once again highlights the importance of the concept of dharma. 'Dharma,' she writes, 'means, at the human level, the order inherent in man, the ethical life.' In Hindu thought it is 'the duty of every individual to make out this order in order to bring about unity throughout the world.'[35]

This Hindu approach, what she calls the 'dharmic scheme', gives freedom to every individual to follow their own religious path. In Hinduism, she explains:

The purpose of a human life is to reach the highest spiritual goal, that is, to escape from this cycle of material reality. The only way one can reach liberation from the cycle is for the individual to attain complete realisation of the nature of the self, that is, identity with the Supreme Being. One must be free to experiment and discover the truth in order to find this identity. Therefore religious freedom is identified as an important aspect. The freedom to follow one's own religion necessarily requires tolerance and respect for other religions. The nature of Hindu religion is conducive to religious tolerance. Hinduism recognises that the goal of attaining realisation with the nature of self can be reached through many paths. All traditions which help an individual to lift his soul to the Supreme Being are held up as worthy of adherence.[36]

The theological basis of this tolerant approach is

... the belief that the Supreme or Ultimate Reality is without name, form, personality or qualities. In the Rig Veda, the most ancient of the Sanskrit scriptures, it is written 'The real is one, the learned call it by various names ....' Similar attitudes are also stated in the Bhagavad-Gita, in particular in Chapter 4 it is stated 'Whoever approaches me in whatever manner, I accept him. All paths men are struggling through lead unto Me.' Vedanta philosophy further expounds on this tradition with its insistence upon the one absolute truth expressed through manifold manifestations. The doctrine of having ishta-devata (chosen deity) invites individuals to select from a variety of Gods which satisfy their spiritual learning. Hinduism can therefore be seen to provide for a theory of human rights in the context of religious freedom. Being free to practice religion and discover the truth in order to reach liberation is the primary reason. Furthermore, Hinduism is seen as promoting religious freedom through its liberal tolerant attitude towards other faiths. This conception of one absolute truth expressed through many ways is a prime example of the freedom of thought, conscience and religion under Hinduism.[37]

5.2.4   Arvind Sharma

In his article 'The Rights in Hinduism', referred to at the beginning of this chapter, Sharma gives five examples of the way in which the Hindu tradition can be seen to support human rights.

The first example, somewhat surprisingly perhaps, is the teaching of the

Hindu tradition about the origin of the caste system.

Sharma notes that there are various accounts in the Hindu tradition of the origins of the caste system. The best known of these, he says, is the account in 'the Purushasukta of the Rigveda, which explains that the universe was created out of a single cosmic man (Purusha) when his body was offered at the primordial sacrifice. The four *varnas* or classes came from his mouth (priest), arms (warrior), thighs (peasant) and feet (servant).'[38]

However, he says, there is a lesser known account in the *Brihadaranyaka* Upanishad which contains the idea of individual human rights:

> A lesser known origin of the caste system is found in, the largest of the Upanishads. According to this account, in the beginning there was the One Reality, Brahman. It did not flourish by itself so it created the Brahmins, or priests. Still it did not flourish, so it created the Kshatriyas, warriors. Still it did not flourish, so it created the Vaishyas, peasants. When it still did not flourish it created the Shudras, servants.
>
> Then it reflected. The Kshatriya is to protect them all but the Kshatriya tends to be intrusive. So in order to protect them all, it created Dharma, religion, or precepts and ethics which make the universe thrive. It is on account of Dharma that the weak overcomes the strong. If this is not the concept of individual human rights as a protection against the power of the state, what is? In the West, this right is given legal and moral basis, but in this passage it is identified with truth, and provided with an ontological and therefore even more firm basis, by being rooted in an is-ness rather than an ought-ness.[39]

The second example is the teaching of the *Taittiriya* Upanishad about the fact that human beings are unique in comparison with other forms of life because they are moral agents. In this text, Sharma writes:

> Sankara maintains that a human being differs from say, animals, in that he possesses the capacity for knowledge (Jnana) and action (Kriya). In brief, the uniqueness of a human being consists in his or her being a moral agent.
>
> This moral agency involves entitlement to basic rights and obligations. It then becomes obligatory on the part of society and state

to maintain conditions of life in which the human being can exercise his or her moral agency by being able to claim rights and discharge obligations.[40]

The third example, is the Hindu 'conception of the three debts and its extension in the Mahabharata'. Sharma explains that:

The Hindu law books refer to the debts one owes to the Gods, the sages and ancestors and these are respectively discharged through worship, scriptural study and the memorial service called Shraddha. To these the Mahabharata adds a fourth: The debt we owe to all human beings, which then is a debt which all human beings owe to one another, a concept which lies at the core of human rights, for these rights constitute entitlements of each human being on every human being.[41]

The fourth example is the emphasis on duties with Hinduism. According to Sharma:

A little reflection will reveal that one party's duty often coincides with another party's right. Thus a human being has a right to safety of person, which in turn is the duty of the state to ensure.

It is this convertibility of duties - rights idiom which perhaps explains the easy and swift shift of discourse from duties to rights in the West, for instance in the US civil rights movement, as Cox points out. A similar easy and swift switch is noticeable in India. By the beginning of the 19th century, social and religious reformer Raja Ram Mohan Roy spoke effortlessly of the rights of Indian women.[42]

The fifth example is the teaching contained in the Hindu myths. As an instance of how these function as a resource for thinking about rights Sharma cites the story of King Shibi:

As he sat in the court one day, a sparrow sought refuge in his lap, while being chased by a falcon. The falcon demanded the sparrow from the king as it constituted his means of subsistence. Accepting the falcon's right, the king offered his own flesh in order to fulfill his duty of protecting his subjects.[43]

In Sharma's view, what these examples show is that:

What are now called human rights can be identified in the range of Hindu scriptures from the philosophical to the popular. The cause of promoting human rights is better served by identifying these elements within Hinduism, rather than its wholesale and undiscerning condemnation. This is not to deny that Hinduism may contain elements opposed to human rights, but to challenge the notion that Hinduism is wholly incompatible with human rights.[44]

5.3   AREAS OF TENSION IN RELATION TO HINDUISM AND HUMAN RIGHTS

There are four areas where there can be seen to be tension in relation to Hinduism and human rights.

5.3.1   Equality

In the area of equality the first issue is that of the traditional Hindu caste system. As we have already seen in this chapter, there is a continuing debate about how to reconcile the caste system with a human rights commitment to human equality. The question under debate is whether the concept of caste has to be rejected entirely or whether it can be understood in a less hierarchical and more egalitarian fashion.[45]

A second issue is that of gender equality. As Werner Menski points out, there is an ambivalence about attitudes to women within Hinduism that shows itself in the *Law of Manu*. On the one hand this declares that:

Women must be honoured and adorned by their fathers, brothers, husbands and brothers-in-law; who desire [their own] welfare. Where women are honoured, there the gods are pleased; but where they are not honoured, no sacred rite yields results.[46]

On the other hand it also declares:

Day and night women must be kept in dependence by the males [of] their [families], and, if they attach themselves to sensual enjoyments, they must be kept under one's control. Her father protects [her] in childhood, her husband protects [her] in youth, and her sons protect [her] in old age; a woman is never fit for independence.[47]

As Menski notes:

In social reality, for many traditional Hindus the need to protect female chastity remains a major concern, both in India and in the West, and many Hindu females only reluctantly go out to work. Older girls are under especially strict supervision, and a clear preference for single-sex education is a logical consequence of such attitudes.[48]

As with the issue of the caste system there is an internal debate within Hinduism about how far such traditional attitudes to women are a necessary part of Hinduism or whether Hinduism can (or should) move towards the view of equality between the sexes found in many Western societies.

A third issue is that of gay and lesbian equality. Hinduism has traditionally taken a positive attitude to sex, but has seen the place for sex as within marriage between people of the opposite sex and has linked sex to procreation. This being the case, traditional Hinduism has held that homosexual conduct is contrary to dharma and has had no place for same-sex marriage, but this view is now being challenged by a growing number of voices arguing that Hinduism is compatible with LGBT equality.[49]

5.3.2 Reproductive rights

To quote Menski again:

In the context of Hindu marriage neither abortion nor birth control may be acceptable to many Hindus: one of the major life aims of a Hindu is to procreate, so preserving and promoting life is a central aspect of dharma. The classical texts, therefore, see causing an abortion or miscarriage as a serious crime or sin.[50]

This being the case, many traditional Hindus would continue to be opposed to the idea of reproductive rights in the sense of allowing free access to birth control and abortion. On the other hand, the preference of traditional Hindu families for having sons to continue the family line continues to result in the killing of girl children and a growing trend to abort girl foetuses now that advances in medical technology mean that girl babies can be identified in the womb. Such actions are not supported by traditional Hindu teaching, but are a reality with which Hindus are having to wrestle in India and elsewhere.

5.3.3   Freedom of religion

As has already been noted in the course of this chapter, Hinduism is hospitable to the idea of freedom of religion in the sense that everyone should pursue their own path towards moksha. However, precisely because Hindus see all paths to moksha as having equal validity they are opposed to the idea of conversion from one religion to another. One should pursue dharma in the tradition into which one was born.

For this reason many Hindus have supported anti-conversion laws in India and Nepal. As they would see it, there is no problem about someone born a Hindu deciding, for example, that they want to follow Jesus, but they should do that within the context of Hinduism rather than converting from Hinduism to Christianity and being baptised.

5.3.4   Capital punishment

Although Hinduism opposes killing, violence and revenge, in line with the principle of ahimsa (non-violence), nonetheless the traditional Hindu law codes contained in the *Dharmasastras* allow for the imposition of capital punishment and India still imposes the death penalty. On the other hand, there are Hindu voices that support the arguments of human rights bodies that in today's world capital punishment should now be abolished.[51]

Notes
[1] Arvind Sharma, 'The Rights In Hinduism', *Open Democracy*, 15 April 2014, at https://www.opendemocracy.net/openglobalrights/arvind-sharma/rights-in-hinduism
[2] Werner Menski, in Witte and Green (eds), op.cit, p.79.
[3] See the University of Minnesota Human Rights Library, http://www1.umn.edu/humanrts/research/ratification-index.html
[4] Text in Arvind Sharma, *Hinduism and Human Rights*, New Delhi: OUP, 2003, pp. 166-177. For the text of this declaration see Appendix 4 of this report.
[5] Sharma, art.cit.
[6] For a helpful introduction to the Hindu worldview see S Radhakrishnan, *The Hindu View of Life*, London: George Allen and Unwin, 1954.
[7] Nancy M Martin, 'Rights, Roles and Reciprocity in Hindu Dharma', in Joseph Runzo, Nancy M Martin and Arvind Sharma (eds), op.cit. p. 270.
[8] Ibid., p.270.
[9] Ibid., pp.270-271.
[10] Ibid., pp.271-272.
[11] Ibid., p.272.
[12] Ibid., p.272.
[13] Ibid, p.273.
[14] Ibis., pp.274-275.
[15] Ibid., p.275 quoting *Chandogya Upanishad*, sixth prapathaka.
[16] Ibid., p.275.
[17] Ibid., p.276 quoting A K Ramanujan trans., *Hymns for the Drowning: Poems for Vishnu by Nammalvar*, Delhi: Penguin books, 1993, p.60.
[18] Ibid., p.278.
[19] Dipti Patel, 'The Religious Foundations of Human Rights: A Perspective from the Judeo-Christian Tradition and Hinduism', *The Human Rights Law Commentary*, Vol 1, 2005, p.8.
[20] Ibid., p.8.
[21] Ibid.
[22] Ibid.
[23] Ibid.
[24] Ibid.
[25] Ibid.
[26] Ibid.
[27] Ibid.
[28] Ibid., pp.8-9.
[29] Ibid., pp.11-12.
[30] Ibid., p.12.
[31] Ibid., p.12.
[32] Ibid., p.12.
[33] Ibid., p.12 quoting *Rig-Veda* IX, 112.3.
[34] Ibid., p.13 quoting *Isa Upanishad*, verse 1 and *Bhagavad Gita* 13, verses 27-28.
[35] Ibid., pp.13-14.
[36] Ibid., p.14.
[37] Ibid., p.14 quoting *Rig Veda* and *Bhagavad Gita* 4, verse 11.
[38] Sharma, art.cit.
[39] Ibid.

[40] Ibid.

[41] Ibid.

[42] Ibid.

[43] Ibid.

[44] Ibid. Arvind Sharma offers a more detailed account of the relationship between Hinduism and human rights in his book *Hinduism and Human Rights*.

[45] For a series of recent statements on this subject see 'Statements against Caste-based Discrimination by Today's Leading Hindu Religious and Spiritual Leaders and Organizations', produced under the auspices of the Hindu American Foundation in 2014. http://www.hafsite.org/media/pr/statements-caste-hindu-leaders

[46] *The Law of Manu*, 3:55-56, quoted by Menski, in Morgan and Lawton (eds), op.cit. p.46.

[47] *The Law of Manu*, 9:2-3 in Ibid., pp.46-47.

[48] Menski in Ibid., p.47.

[49] See for instance S Venkataraman and H Voruganti, 'A Hindu Approach to LGBT rights', 4 July 2015, at http://swarajyamag.com/culture/a-hindu-approach-to-lgbt-rights/

[50] Menski, in Morgan and Lawton (eds), op.cit. p.36.

[51] See for example, Mahua Das, 'Capital Punishment: Time to Abandon it?,' *Hinduism Today*, December 2006, at http://www.hinduismtoday.com/modules/smartsection/item.php?itemid=1451

Chapter Six

BUDDHISM AND HUMAN RIGHTS

6.1   THE POPULAR PERCEPTION OF BUDDHISM AND HUMAN RIGHTS

If the popular perception of Islam and Hinduism is that they are opposed to human rights, the popular perception of Buddhism is that it is strongly supportive of human rights. This view of Buddhism has two roots.

The first is that the typical representative of Buddhism is seen, by non-Buddhists at least, as being a Buddhist monk. As Robert Florida writes, when thinking of a Buddhist the popular imagination 'thinks of a Theravada monk in his flowing saffron robes, walking calmly and carefully with downcast eyes, so dedicated to the welfare of all beings that he takes care in order not to harm crawling insects.'[1]

Because human rights are seen as being about ensuring people's welfare, this view of Buddhists as people dedicated to the welfare of all beings is translated into the belief that they are necessarily in favour of human rights.

The second is that the most well-known individual Buddhists at the moment are the Tibetan religious leader the Dalai Lama and the Burmese political leader Aung Sang Suu Kyi, both of whom have publicly stressed their belief in the importance of human rights.

In a speech on 'Human Rights, Democracy and Freedom' given in 2008 to mark the sixtieth anniversary of the Universal Declaration of Human Rights the Dalai Lama declared, for example, that human rights are so important that they have to take precedence over historic traditions:

Internationally, our rich diversity of cultures and religions should help to strengthen fundamental human rights in all communities. Underlying this diversity are basic human principles that bind us all together as members of the same human family. The question of human rights is so fundamentally important that there should be no difference of views about it. We all have common human needs and concerns. We all seek happiness and try to avoid suffering regardless of our race, religion, sex or social status. However, mere maintenance of a diversity of traditions should never justify the violations of human rights. Thus, discrimination against persons of different races, against women, and against weaker sections of society may be traditional in some regions, but if they are inconsistent with universally recognized human rights, these forms of behaviour should change. The universal principle of the equality of all human beings must take precedence.[2]

In similar fashion, in her book *Freedom from Fear* Aung San Suu Kyi rejects the argument of the military leaders in Burma that human rights are a Western idea incompatible with traditional Burmese culture:

It was predictable that as soon as the issue of human rights became an integral part of the movement for democracy the official media should start ridiculing and condemning the whole concept of human rights, dubbing it a western artefact [sic] alien to traditional values. It was also ironic – Buddhism, the foundation of traditional Burmese culture, places the greatest value on man, who alone of all beings can achieve the supreme state of Buddhahood. Each man has in him the potential to realize the truth through his own will and endeavour and to help others to realize it. Human life therefore is infinitely precious. 'Easier it is for a needle dropped from the abode of Brahma to meet a candle stuck in the earth than to be born as a human being.' ...

It is a puzzlement to the Burmese how concepts which recognize the inherent dignity and inalienable rights of human beings, which accept that all men are endowed with reason and conscience and which recommend that universal spirit of brotherhood, can be inimical to indigenous values. It is also difficult for them to understand how any of the rights contained in the thirty articles of the Universal Declaration of Human Rights can be seen as anything but wholesome and good. That the declaration was not drawn up in Burma by the Burmese seems an inadequate reason, to say the least, for rejecting it, especially as Burma was one of the nations which voted for its adoption in 1948. If ideas and beliefs are to be denied validity outside the geographical and cultural bounds of their origin, Buddhism would be confined to north India, Christianity to a narrow tract in the Middle East and Islam to Arabia.[3]

Such statements are taken to be typical of Buddhist thought and thus Buddhism is seen as a staunch ally of human rights. In reality, however, the relationship between Buddhism and human rights is much less straightforward than this popular perception would suggest.

In the last two chapters we have seen that the idea that Islam and Hinduism are necessarily enemies of human rights is misleading. In this chapter we shall go on to see that the idea that Buddhism is necessarily on the side of human rights is also misleading. Once again the truth is far more complex.

6.2 SUPPORT FOR HUMAN RIGHTS AMONG BUDDHISTS

In the quotation given above, Aung San Suu Kyi draws attention to the fact that Burma, a Buddhist majority nation, voted for the Universal Declaration of Human Rights in 1948. In fact, both of the Buddhist majority nations who were members of the United Nations in 1948, Burma (now Myanmar) and Siam (now Thailand) voted for the Declaration.

Since 1948 Buddhist majority nations have varied in the extent to which they have signed up to international human rights treaties and conventions. This can be seen, for example, in the following three examples.

Cambodia is a signatory to the International Bill of Rights, the International Convention on the Elimination of all forms of Racial Discrimination, the Convention on the Elimination of all forms of Discrimination against Women, the Convention against Torture and other Cruel, Inhuman or Degrading Treatment or Punishment, the Convention on the Rights of the Child, the Convention against Discrimination in Education, the Freedom of Association and the Right to Organize Convention, the Convention concerning Forced or Compulsory Labour, the Convention on the Protection of the Rights of all Migrant Workers, the Convention on the Rights of Persons with Disabilities, the Convention relating to the Status of Refugees and the Convention on the Prevention and Punishment of the Crime of Genocide.

Sri Lanka is a signatory to the International Bill of Rights, the International Convention on the Elimination of all Forms of Racial Discrimination, the Convention on the Elimination of all Forms of Discrimination against Women, the Supplementary Convention on the Abolition of Slavery, the Slave Trade and Practices Similar to Slavery, the Convention on the Rights of the Child, the Convention against Discrimination in Education, the Freedom of Association and the Right to Organise Convention, the Convention concerning Forced or Compulsory Labour, and the Convention on the Prevention and Punishment of the Crime of Genocide.

Myanmar is a signatory to the Convention on the Elimination of all Forms of Discrimination against Women, the Convention on the Rights of the Child, the Freedom of Association and the Right to Organise Convention, the Convention concerning Forced or Compulsory Labour, the Convention on the Rights of Persons with Disabilities, and the Convention on the Prevention and Punishment of the Crime of Genocide.

In addition to these actions by the governments of Buddhist majority countries, an increasing number of individual Buddhists have come to view support for human rights as in line with their Buddhist beliefs. We have already seen this in the case of the Dalai Lama and Aung Sang Suu Kyi, but for another example the Sri Lankan Buddhist L P N Perera has produced a Buddhist commentary on the Universal Declaration of Human Rights arguing in detail for the compatibility of the Declaration and Buddhist teaching. In the preface to this commentary another Sri Lankan Buddhist, the diplomat Ananda Guruge, claims that 'every single Article of the Universal Declaration of Human Rights – even the labour rights to fair wages, leisure and welfare – has been adumbrated, cogently upheld and meaningfully incorporated in an overall view of life and society by the Buddha.'[4]

Furthermore there has also been the development of Buddhist groups supportive of human rights, such as the International Network of Engaged Buddhists[5] and the Tibetan Centre for Human Rights and Democracy.[6]

This increasing Buddhist support for human rights has found expression in campaigns for human rights in the face of authoritarian regimes in places such as Myanmar, Sri Lanka, Thailand and South Korea and in the face of the Chinese occupation of Tibet.

In Cambodia Buddhists and secular human rights groups have been working together to try to re-build Cambodian society in the face of the continuing legacy of the self-inflicted genocide of the Khmer Rouge period. As Sallie King explains in her essay 'Buddhism and Human Rights':

The legacy of the Khmer Rouge era has been a significant loss of traditional Buddhist-based morality. Even decades after the fall of the regime, Cambodia remains a country with a high degree of lawlessness and corruption, discredited legal institutions, de facto impunity, and little trust. In an effort to rebuild order and trust, the Buddhist community and secular Cambodian NGOs have combined their efforts to teach basic Buddhist morality together with international human rights. For example, the Cambodian Institute of Human Rights, a secular NGO, has developed their Human Rights Teaching Methodology Project that has trained 25,000 teachers on 'how best to convey messages about human rights, peace, democracy and non-violence.' These teachers teach almost 3 million Cambodian school children every school year. They point out, Buddhism never vanished from the hearts of the Cambodian people during the dark years. There are parallels between modern ideas like democracy, human rights and good governance and the ancient teaching of the Buddha – on treating other people with respect and kindness. The principle of non-violence (*avihimsa*), means less harm is done to others. Besides the initial five Buddhist precepts [the five lay precepts – not to kill, steal, lie, commit sexual immorality or ingest intoxicants] ..., four other Buddhist principles of interpersonal behaviour are relevant [namely, loving-kindness, compassion, sympathetic joy and equanimity].... These ideas, or Buddhism at least, is familiar and acceptable to all Cambodians, including leaders, so they [Buddhist teachings] are much more likely to be received favorably than if we simply talked about the International Covenant on Civil and Political Rights or other complicated documents considered Western and even alien.

For their part, the Cambodian Buddhist leadership readily affirmed that human rights were consistent with Buddhist teachings. Maha Ghosananda, the late beloved Cambodian Buddhist monk called the 'Gandhi of Cambodia,' wrote that the 'Cambodian people must obtain all basic human rights, including rights of self-determination and rights to freely pursue economic, social and cultural development.' Today Buddhist monks are trained in human rights as a part of their preparation to teach and are expected to include instruction in human rights as a regular part of their sermons. It is hoped this will be a powerful approach adding as it does an element of international cachet to the appeal to traditional authority and morality.[7]

These examples show that there has been a growth in Buddhist support for human rights, but as King notes, there continues to be 'debate among Buddhist intellectuals about the extent to which the concept of human rights is compatible with Buddhist culture.'[8]

6.3   BUDDHISM AND ITS WORLDVIEW

To understand this debate it is necessary first of all to understand something about Buddhism and its worldview.

Buddhism is a spiritual tradition that traces its origins to the teaching and practice of the Buddha, Siddhartha Gautama, who lived sometime in the sixth century BC. He was born into a royal family in present-day Nepal and lived a life of privilege and luxury until one day he left the royal enclosure and encountered for the first time, an old man, a sick man, a corpse, and lastly an ascetic holy man who was apparently content and at peace with the world. As a result of these four encounters, he abandoned royal life and entered on a spiritual quest that eventually led him to become enlightened (the term Buddha means 'enlightened one') about how to escape from being trapped in the endless cycle of suffering and re-incarnation.

Following this enlightenment he attracted a band of followers, instituted a monastic order and spent the rest of his life travelling throughout the northeastern part of the Indian subcontinent teaching others about the path of awakening that he had discovered.

There are now numerous schools of Buddhism that seek to follow the path laid down by the Buddha in a variety of different ways. The two largest are Theravada Buddhism, which is most popular in Sri Lanka, Cambodia, Thailand, Laos and Myanmar, and Mahayana Buddhism, which is strongest in Tibet, China, Taiwan, Japan, Korea, and Mongolia.

For most Buddhists the foundations of their belief and practice lie in what are known as the 'three jewels'. These are the Buddha himself, the teachings of Buddha (the Dharma) and the congregations of monastic practitioners (the Sangha) who preserve the authentic teachings of the Buddha and provide further examples of the truth of the Buddha's teaching that enlightenment is attainable. There is no one single text that is regarded as spiritually authoritative by all Buddhists with the Theravada and Mahayana schools of Buddhism each having their own set of texts (the Pali Canon and Mahayana Sutras respectively).

In spite of the diversity within Buddhism it is possible to talk about an overall Buddhist worldview. In this worldview there is no creator God, rather the universe is simply the working out of a cyclical process in which world-systems come into being, exist for a time, are destroyed and are then re-made. Within this cyclical worldview human beings are also seen as being trapped in an endless process of re-incarnation, experiencing suffering through many lives on the basis of their behaviour in previous incarnations (what is known as 'contingent origination'). Only achieving nirvana, or liberation, through enlightenment can lead to freedom from this cycle of death and re-birth.

What is offered by the Buddha and by Buddhism is an understanding of the causes of suffering and the way to achieve nirvana through 'The Eightfold Path' which consists of:

(1) Right understanding (the acceptance of Buddhist teachings);

(2) Right intention (a commitment to cultivate right attitudes);

(3) Right speech (truthful speech that avoids slander, gossip and abuse);

(4) Right action (engaging in peaceful and harmonious behaviour, and refraining from stealing, killing and overindulgence in sensual pleasure;

(5) Right livelihood (avoiding making a living in harmful ways such as exploiting people, killing animals, or trading in intoxicants or weapons;

(6) Right effort (freeing oneself from evil and unwholesome states of mind and preventing them from arising in future);

(7) Right mindfulness (developing an awareness of the body, sensations, feelings and states of mind;

(8) Right concentration (the development of the mental focus necessary for this awareness.

At the basis of Buddhist ethics are what are known as the 'five lay precepts' which are not absolute commands or prohibitions but training rules designed to enable people to live a life in which they are happy, without worries, and can meditate well. These five precepts are not to kill, steal, lie, commit sexual misconduct or take intoxicants. These five basic precepts are expanded to eight for lay people who want to adopt an ascetic way of life, to ten for novice monks and nuns and to more detailed sets of rules for those who have fully embraced a monastic way of life (227 rules in the Theravada tradition).

All these precepts and rules are intended to help people travel the path to nirvana more effectively.

6.4 BUDDHIST CONCERNS ABOUT HUMAN RIGHTS

A number of objections to the idea of human rights have been put forward by Buddhist scholars.

The first objection is that 'there is no concept of rights in classical Buddhism.'[9] Rights are simply not part of the Buddhist tradition.

The second is that the idea of rights is contrary to the basic Buddhist teaching of 'anatman', the idea that as part of the general impermanence of all existence 'there is no soul or fixed self, no entity of any kind, constituting the core or foundation or human identity.' In the light of this teaching the '...key difficulty for...a Buddhist human rights ethic is to define the rights-holder. Without a substance [substantial self] who claims the right?'[10]

The third is that the idea of human rights wrongly privileges humans over other sentient beings to whom in Buddhist teaching compassion is equally due.

The fourth is that the concept of inalienable rights is incompatible with 'The Four Noble Truths' taught by the Buddha (the reality of suffering, the origin of suffering, the cessation of suffering and the path to the cessation of suffering). To quote James Fredericks:

Rights are merely an impermanent mental construction. As is the case with all mental constructions, human rights are dependently arisen... and therefore contingent not absolute. Since rights have no inherent existence, to claim that rights are inalienable is unintelligible for a Buddhist. Therefore clinging to human rights, insisting on the universality of rights, and most of all asserting our own rights is yet another form of thirst which leads to the creation of more suffering, in accordance with the Second Noble Truth's teaching that suffering arises through craving. The pursuit of rights...also entails a denial of the First Noble Truth, which teaches the universality of suffering. Buddhism does not teach that human beings have a right to be secure from suffering or immune from the fact of impermanence (annica). Suffering and impermanence are universal facts, what Buddhism calls a 'mark of existence' and are unavoidable regardless of what 'rights' may be attributed to human beings as 'inalienable'.[11]

The fifth is that the idea of human rights is inadequate to the demand of Buddhist ethics. To quote Fredericks again:

Buddhist ethics is based on the demand for infinite compassion, not the assertion of rights. When rights replace compassion as the moral starting point, too much evil and indifference to suffering is permitted. According to Western Liberalism, society is a contractual construct made up of autonomous and competing individuals. Within such a society, social relations must be regulated by rights. In this understanding of society, compassion is relegated to the realm of private choice, that is, as one of a number of optimal ways of responding to people within the social contract. Liberalism, therefore, is much at odds with the Buddhist understanding of society and social solidarity. The promotion of human rights may not be inimical to Buddhism, but it does not measure up to the demands of Buddhist ethics.[12]

The sixth, which is related to the fifth, is that the idea of rights is based on an adversarial view of human relationships. In the words of the Thai monk Phra Payutto, the concept of human rights as it has developed in Western society:

...is a result of division, struggle and contention. The idea of human rights has been established to ensure self-preservation and the protection

of mutual interests. Human rights are usually obtained by demand....
demands for human rights...are often based or influenced by aversion,
resentment or fear. As long as such feelings are there, it will be difficult
to obtain a truly good result from human rights activities, because the
basic feeling behind them is not truly harmonious. When human rights
activities are motivated by unskilful drives, the resulting behaviour will
be too aggressive to obtain the desired result.[13]

Interestingly, however, Payutto continues to support human rights in
practice precisely because we do live in 'an age of contention'. 'Human
rights are our guarantee of not destroying each other while we are still under
the influence of such divisive thinking.'[14]

6.5   BUDDHIST REASONS FOR SUPPORTING HUMAN RIGHTS

Although Buddhist scholars have raised these objections, other Buddhist
scholars have argued that Buddhism does provide reasons for supporting
human rights. Their arguments are helpfully summarised by King under
five headings.

6.5.1   The preciousness of human rights and human enlightenability

This is the argument we have already seen being appealed to by Aung Sun
Suu Kyi. As King explains:

The idea of human rights is premised in international documents upon
recognition of the inherent dignity of human being. In Buddhism, this
recognition is expressed in teachings of the preciousness of a human
birth and teachings of human enlightenability. Buddhism teaches
that sentient beings are born, die and are reborn again and again and
that this process has been going on for a vast amount of time and will
continue for a vast amount of time. Within these rounds of births,
sentient beings may be born as animal, humans, gods, denizens of hell,
and other sentient life forms. Of all these births, however, a human
birth is considered the 'precious birth' even more precious than as a
god, because it is only as a human that one can obtain enlightenment.

This birth, while precious, is very rare, as there are far more sentient beings born in other life forms than as humans. This enhances the preciousness of human birth. This teaching is common to all forms of Buddhism. Mahayana forms of Buddhism add to this that all sentient beings possess within themselves the Buddha Nature, or fully developed Buddhahood, an immanent reality that, while it may be concealed at present, guarantees future realization (in a human birth) of that innate, but hidden Buddhahood.[15]

6.5.2 The Five Lay Precepts

The argument here is that there is continuity between the Five Lay Precepts and the moral contents of international statements of human rights. King notes that this argument takes two forms.

In some cases:

> ...these moral principles are examined one by one to link them with individual human rights. For example, L.P.N. Perera writes, 'It is little realized that the second precept of the Buddhist *Panca-sila* [Five Lay Precepts] ...dealing as it does with theft, becomes meaningful only if the property rights of every individual are fully recognized.'[16]

In other cases:

> ...an effort is made to look at the precepts as a whole and work out how it might be possible to move from the stance of the precepts, which are expressed in terms of responsibility, to the rights status of human rights principles. Thus Damien Keown writes, 'In the context of the precepts...the right holder is the one who suffers from the breach of Dharmic [moral] duty when the precepts are broken. In the case of the first precept, this would be the person who was unjustly killed. The right the victim has may therefore be defined as a negative claim-right upon the aggressor, namely the right not to be killed. In simple terms, we might say that the victim has the right to life which the aggressor has a duty to respect.'[17]

6.5.3   Human equality

The argument here is that the recognition of human equality which is 'a necessary, though not a sufficient, element in the development of human rights thinking' can be found in the teaching and practice of the Buddha:

> Unlike other important teachers of his time, the Buddha was willing to teach all who would listen to him without imposing restrictions based upon social class (caste), gender, education, or any other characteristics. That the Buddha did not simply step outside of the caste system but rejected it in principle is attested by the Buddha's critique of caste in the *Vasettha Sutta of the Majjhima Nikaya*. In this scriptural text, the Buddha states that unlike the differences between the classes of birds, fish, quadrupeds and snakes, the differences among which are real and innate, class distinction among humans – specifically, the four great classes of the Hindu caste system – which are based upon occupation are not real but merely conventional. On many occasions recorded in the Buddhist scriptures, the Buddha states that a person's place in society should be determined by his actions, not by the class assigned to him at birth. Moreover, persons of all classes, both genders, and varying social backgrounds were, in fact, confirmed as having attained the fruits of liberation by the Buddha.[18]

6.5.4   Nonviolence

The argument here is that the fundamental Buddhist value of non-violence provides a basis for human rights. King notes that:

> ...the philosopher Charles Taylor has come to the conclusion that human rights in Buddhism are best grounded in the fundamental Buddhist value of nonviolence. He sees nonviolence as calling for 'a respect for the autonomy of each person, demanding a minimal use of coercion in human affairs.' The first of the five lay precepts is non-harmfulness. If, as Keown suggests, we can read from precept to right, it does imply at least a right to life and a right not to be harmed.[19]

6.5.5   Human freedom

The argument here is that one can build support for human rights on the affirmation of the importance of freedom in Buddhism.

As evidence for this line of thought King begins by citing the work of the Thai Buddhist Saneh Chamarik:

Sameh Chamarik writes that 'there is no need at all to search for a place of human rights in the Buddhist tradition. Freedom is indeed the essence of Buddhism....' He develops this notion by referring, first, to the Buddha's advice to the villagers of Kalama in which he urged them to make decisions on what spiritual path to follow by relying on their own experiential knowledge, not upon anyone or anything external to themselves. Secondly, he refers to the dying words of the Buddha: 'Be islands unto yourselves.... Be a refuge to yourselves, do not take any other refuge.... Work out your own salvation with diligence.' These ideas emphasize self-reliance in achieving the task of the human life: working towards enlightenment. 'In the Buddhist view, then, the individual is not merely a means. One can sense a subtle meaning of equality here. Although men may not be born "free" they are equal in dignity and rights, that is to say, dignity and rights to their own salvation and freedom.'[20]

She then notes that Chamarik's ideas are confirmed and extended by Phra Payutto:

He writes: 'Man is the best of trainable or educable beings. He has the potentiality of self-perfection by which a life of freedom and happiness can be realized. In order to attain this perfection, man has to develop himself physically, morally, psycho-spiritually and intellectually...[T]he law of the Dharma [i.e. Buddhism]...entails that every individual should be left free, if not provided with the opportunity, to develop himself so that his potentiality can unfold itself and work its way to perfection.' To be left alone to pursue self-development, then, is a must and therefore a right. Ideally, Payutto continues, all conditions should be made to support the individual's effort at self-development. Thus, 'freedom of self-development and the encouragement of opportunities for it' are a 'foundation of Buddhist ethics.' '[E]very individual has the right to self-development... [The Buddha] teaches the goal of freedom that is to be reached by means of freedom and a happy means that leads to a happy end.'[21]

In these words, writes King, we see: '... one of the most thoroughly Buddhist of all potential Buddhist justifications for human rights: the freedom to pursue Buddhahood, or self-perfection.' She describes this as: 'our innate right as human beings, based upon the deepest level of our identity as human beings.' She continues:

'Certain internationally recognized rights are directly entailed in this end: freedom of thought, conscience and religion. Other rights are essential to it: the right to life, liberty and personal security; the freedoms of speech, assembly and movement. Potentially, one could develop a full list of human rights, including the right to self-determination, freedom from want, the collective rights of peoples to the protection of their culture and more, on the basis of the recognition that they are important supports for the pursuit of spiritual self-development.'[22]

6.6   RIGHTS LANGUAGE AS 'SKILFUL MEANS'

Although, for the sorts of reasons just outlined, there are Buddhists who see the concept of human rights as being compatible with Buddhism this does not necessarily mean that Buddhists necessarily mean the same thing as Western Liberals when they talk about human rights. As Fredericks observes:

A final theme which runs through the current conversations among Buddhists about human rights has to do with the need to distinguish between Buddhist human rights and secular human rights.[23]

Fredericks notes that while King sees an 'implicit doctrine of human rights' within Buddhist tradition, nevertheless she sees 'fundamental differences between Buddhist rights and Liberal rights.' Fredericks highlights six such differences:

1. For Buddhism, human rights have to do with whole communities. They do not presume or promote the illusion of the autonomous individual. In practice, Buddhist human rights are not about protecting individual autonomy; rather, they are about securing the well-being of all.

2. For this reason, Buddhist human rights language conscientiously avoids the rhetoric of self-assertion in favour of a rhetoric of selfless compassion. Rights are realized when self-assertion is renounced.

3. Therefore, Buddhist human rights, in contrast to human rights as understood by Western Liberalism, are non-adversarial.

4. Moreover, Buddhist rights do in fact recognize value in the individual, but not in the same way that Western Liberalism does. Instead of asserting the immunities and entitlements of autonomous individuals, Buddhism roots the value of each and every individual in the potential, enjoyed by every human being, for Buddhahood.

5. Additionally, human rights, in the Buddhist perspective, are not fundamentally suspicious of governmental and political structures. Rather, Buddhist human rights reflect the true interconnectedness of all sentient beings by recognizing the potential of all social institutions to contribute to the enlightenment of all.

6. And finally, Buddhist understanding of human rights never pits the human good against the good of other sentient beings, in contrast to the anthropocentrism of Western Liberal notions of *human* rights.[24]

Given these differences between Western and Buddhist views of rights the question that naturally arises is why Buddhists would want to make use of the rights language that has originated in the West. One answer that has been given to this question by a number of scholars is that the use of human rights language is an example of the Buddhist concept of 'skilful means'. As Robert Florida explains:

One of the key concepts in Buddhism, especially Mahayana Buddhism, is *upaya* (skilful or expedient means). It refers to the skills that a Buddha or Buddhist practitioner brings to bear in presenting *dharma* [the truth about the nature of things] to people of varying levels of intelligence and accomplishment to help them along the path that leads to the cessation of suffering. Both compassion and wisdom are necessary for the exercise of skilful means. Compassion for the suffering of others provides the motivation, and the wisdom and insight of the teacher enables him or her to find ways to present the dharma that are appropriate to the temperament, needs, and social situation of the hearers.[25]

In similar fashion, it is argued, the use of rights language by Buddhists can be justified as a way of alleviating suffering and furthering the acceptance of Buddhist values. For example, Florida notes that the engaged Buddhist David Chappell:

...argues for the practicality of adopting rights language in spite of the fact that, technically speaking, there is no Buddhist doctrine of human rights. He makes the point that the Buddhist metaphysics that undercuts any doctrine of a permanent self [and thus undercuts any support for a notion of individual rights] also allows the Buddhist to make use of human rights language without the danger of reifying rights into absolutes. As he puts it, 'the Buddha warned not to take doctrines too seriously'. As long as it is kept in mind that human rights are man-made constructs, they can safely be used to advance Buddhist values.

Human rights may not be inherent in people in a metaphysical sense, but they are strongly supported by Buddhist leaders as a negotiated social contract based on fairness and respect since everyone wants freedom from arbitrary arrest and imprisonment, health, food, self-esteem, and education. Chappell explicitly makes this point in the light of what is going on in Burma, Tibet, Vietnam and other Buddhist societies. Although he does not use the terminology, Chappell is actually making a very clever argument for human rights as a skilful device, or *upaya*. He acknowledges that human rights approaches are not found in traditional Buddhist thought and practices, but takes them up in order to alleviate the real suffering caused by oppression.[26]

The use of human rights language by supporters of the Tibetan cause

134

provides a helpful illustration of the use of 'skilful means' in practice. Human rights are not a part of traditional Tibetan Buddhist thought or culture, but the Dalai Lama and other advocates of the Tibetan cause have used the language of human rights to draw the attention of the international community to what is going on in Tibet in ways that make sense to those who are not Tibetan Buddhists. By so doing they are seeking to act with wisdom and compassion in order to alleviate the sufferings of the Tibetan people.

6.7 TENSIONS BETWEEN BUDDHISM AND HUMAN RIGHTS IN PRACTICE

As well as the tensions between the Buddhist worldview and human rights thinking that we have explored already in this chapter there are also a number of areas where there can be seen to be tensions between Buddhism and human rights in practice.

6.7.1 Buddhism and nationalism

The most serious area of tension is the linkage between Buddhism and nationalism in parts of Asia.

The following report by David Mathieson on developments in Burma posted on the website of the human rights campaign group Human Rights Watch on 4 October 2015 highlights the problem by drawing attention to the participation of Buddhists in stirring up anti-Muslim sentiment in Burma:

> In Burma's rapidly intensifying election campaign, last Sunday's mass rally at Rangoon's Thuwannu Stadium heralded the coming-out party of a new political force, the Association for the Protection of Race and Religion, known as Ma Ba Tha. Thousands of Buddhist monks and nuns packed the arena, with thousands more lay supporters outside to hear speeches from some of this country's most well-known and outspoken abbots – many of whom are also notorious for their racist and anti-Muslim rhetoric and campaigning. Preceding formal speeches was dancing by ethnic Arakanese, Pa-O and Shan dancers, and even Padaung "long-neck" women were in attendance.
>
> The event was the culmination of a nationwide celebration for

the national parliament's passing of four so-called "race and religion protection" laws championed by the Ma Ba Tha. President Thein Sein signed them into law in May and August. These laws, addressing monogamy, religious conversion, population control, and interfaith marriage, have elicited domestic and international criticism for their anti-Muslim bias and threats to women's rights. A speech by famous screen actor Nay Aung, who jubilantly heralded the passing of the laws aimed at protecting Buddhist women from Muslim men, was greeted by widespread audience applause and jubilant thumbs-up from the demagogue monk U Wirathu, who has gained notoriety by making threats against both Burmese Muslims and United Nations officials.

The speeches by the movement's leaders – especially the movement's founder Insein Ywa Ma Sayadaw – espoused Buddhist nationalism that has championed growing anti-Muslim rhetoric throughout Burma, reflecting a sense of "threat" following communal violence between Muslims and Buddhists in Arakan State in 2012, and throughout central Burma in 2013 in towns like Meiktila. In signing the race and religion laws, the military-installed government and the ruling Union Solidarity and Development Party are pandering to Ma Ba Tha leaders in hopes of gaining the votes of extremists in November's parliamentary election.

To register their rising concern, nine embassies in Rangoon recently took the unusual step of issuing a public statement expressing concern at 'the prospect of religion being used as a tool of division and conflict during the campaign season.' Ma Ba Tha may have arrived on the national stage, but so too has increased concern over their support of laws that threaten fundamental rights.[27]

Similar examples of a linkage between Buddhism and campaigns against religious and ethnic minorities can be found in Thailand where Buddhists have been involved in campaigns against the Muslim minority, and Sri Lanka where Buddhists have been involved in violence not only against the Hindu Tamil community, but also against Muslims and Christians.

Many Buddhists not only in the West, but also in the countries concerned, have drawn attention to the tension between this sort of activity and not only human rights laws and principles, but also the basic Buddhist precept against harming other sentient beings, but at the moment this is a serious problem that shows no signs of resolution.

6.7.2   Equality

A second area of tension lies in the area of equality. Here there are two main issues.

The first has to do with equality between men and women in monastic life with the tradition being that 'women obeyed more monastic rules than the men and that they were under the authority of the men' and with the full ordination of women into monastic orders being forbidden within the Theravada tradition of Buddhism.[28]

The second has to do with acceptance of homosexual practice in view of the fact that homosexual relationships have traditionally been seen as 'unwise and unnatural in traditional Buddhism which identified only two types of straightforward sexuality: that of celibate monks and nuns and that of married householders engaged in heterosexual family life, mainly for the procreation of children.'[29]

In both these areas traditional attitudes remain strong, but there is also pressure for change with the Dalai Lama, for example supporting the cause of female Buddhist ordination and affirming the dignity and rights of homosexual people.

6.7.3   Capital Punishment

In spite of the precept against harming other sentient beings Buddhist ethics has traditionally accepted that it is right for rulers to impose capital punishment just as it is right for them to go to war. Indeed there are Buddhist majority countries such as Thailand that still maintain the death penalty.

However, there is a debate within Buddhism about the issue with a growing number of voices suggesting that 'capital punishment can never be approved, as nothing can excuse the taking of life.'[30]

Notes

[1] Robert Florida, 'State, Society and the Buddhist Order', in Brackney (ed), op. cit., p.331.

[2] Tenzin Gyatso, XIV Dalai Lama, 'Human Rights, Democracy and Freedom', at http://www.dalailama.com/messages/world-peace/human-rights-democracy-and-freedom

[3] Michel Aris (ed), Aung San Suu Kyi, *Freedom from Fear and Other Writings*, New York: Penguin, 1991, pp.174-175.

[4] L P N Perera, *Buddhism and Human Rights: A Buddhist Commentary on the Universal Declaration of Human Rights*, Colombo: Karunaratne and Sons, 1991, p.xi.

[5] For details see their website at http://inebnetwork.org/ and Sallie B King, *Being Benevolence: The Social Ethics of Engaged Buddhism*, Honolulu: University of Hawaii Press, 2005.

[6] For details see their website at http://www.tchrd.org/

[7] Sallie B King, 'Buddhism and Human Rights', in Witte and Green (eds), op. cit., p.p.104-105.

[8] Ibid., pp. 103.

[9] Craig Ihara, 'Why there are no rights in Buddhism', in Damien Keown, Carles Prebish and Wayne Husted (eds), *Buddhism and Human Rights*, Richmond: Curzon, 1998, p.44.

[10] Derek S Jeffreys, 'Does Buddhism need human rights?', in Christopher Queen, Charles Prebish and Damien Keown (eds), *Action Dharma: New Studies in Engaged Buddhism*, London: Routledge Curzon, 2003, p.276.

[11] James Fredericks, 'Buddhism and Human Rights', in Runzo, Martin and Sharma, op.cit. p.253.

[12] Ibid., p. 252.

[13] Pra Payutto, *Buddhist Solutions for the Twenty-First Century*, Bangkok: Buddhadhamma Foundation, n.d, p. 71.

[14] Ibid., p.70.

[15] King, in Witte and Green (eds), op.cit. p. 107.

[16] Ibid., p. 107, quoting Perera, op. cit, p.50.

[17] Ibid., pp. 107-108, quoting Damien Keown, 'Are there human rights in Buddhism?', in Keown, Prebish and Husted (eds) op.cit.p. 32.

[18] Ibid., p.108.

[19] Ibid., p.108, quoting Charles Taylor, 'Conditions of an Unforced Consensus on Human Rights', in Joanne Bauer and Daniel A Bell (eds), *The East Asian Challenge for Human Rights*, Cambridge: CUP, 1999, p.134.

[20] Ibid., pp.108-109, quoting Saneh Chamarik, *Buddhism and Human Rights*, Bangkok: Thai Khadi Research Institute, Thammasat University, 1982, pp.5, 22 and 23.

[21] Ibid., p.109, quoting Payutto in the Preamble to Chamarik, op.cit.

[22] Ibid., p.109.

[23] Fredericks in Runzo, Martin and Sharma (eds), op.cit. p. 254.

[24] Ibid., p.255, referring to Sallie King, 'Human Rights in Contemporary Engaged Buddhism', in Roger R Jackson and John J MaKransky (eds), *Buddhist Theology: Critical Reflections by Contemporary Buddhist Scholars*, Richmond: Curzon, 2000, p.300.

[25] Robert Florida, 'Human Rights as Skillful Means,' in Brackney (ed), op.cit. p.316.

[26] Ibid., pp.319-320.

[27] David Mathieson, 'Dispatches: Burma's Pageant of Bigotry', 4 October 2015, at https://www.hrw.org/news/2015/10/08/dispatches-burmas-pageant-bigotry

[28] Peggy Morgan, 'Buddhism', in Morgan and Lawton (eds), op.cit. p.99.

[29] Ibid., p.71.

[30] Ibid., p.94. For a detailed discussion see Leanne Alarid and Hsiao-Ming Wang, 'Mercy and Punishment: Buddhism and the Death Penalty', *Social Justice*, Vol.28, No.1, 2001.

Chapter Seven

SIKHISM AND HUMAN RIGHTS

7.1   SIKHISM AND ITS WORLDVIEW

Sikhism is the smallest and youngest of the world's major religions. There are approximately twenty million Sikhs in the world, the majority of whom live in the province of Punjab in North West India, although there is now a worldwide Sikh diaspora.

Sikhism began to develop in the fifteenth century in the Punjab district of what is now India and Pakistan (the district was divided between the two at the Partition of India in 1947). It was founded by Guru Nanak and is based on his teachings and that of the nine Gurus who followed him.[1]

The fundamental belief of Sikhs is in the 'Ik Onkar', the 'one constant', which in Western religious terms translates into belief in one God who creates and sustains all things. What Sikhs believe about God is set out in the opening line of the Sikh Scriptures, the *Adi Granth*. This declares:

> There is but one all pervading spirit, and truth is its name! It exists in all creation; it does not fear; it does not hate; it is timeless and universal and self-existent.

All human beings, regardless, of sex, race or religion, are the creation of this one God and as such have equal value and dignity.

Like Hinduism and Buddhism, Sikhism believes that human souls exist in an endless cycle of life, death and rebirth and that the quality of existence in each new life depends on the operation of the law of karma which determines the quality of that life in accordance with how the soul behaved in its previous life. Again like Hinduism and Buddhism, the central question to which Sikhism provides an answer is how to escape from this cycle.

The answer that Sikhism provides is that the way of escape (which is called mukti or liberation) is through achieving total knowledge of, and union with, God. In order to achieve this a person has to switch the focus of their attention from themselves to God and live accordingly. This is something that happens through the grace of God at work in a person and takes place as God shows them the best way to get close to him through their own personal religious experience and through the teaching of holy books and holy people.

The way of life that Sikhs see as forming the path to liberation involves avoiding five vices and performing three basic duties.

The fives vices are lust, covetousness and greed, the attachment to the things of this world, anger and pride. The three duties or 'pillars' are:

- Nam japna, 'meditation on God through reciting, chanting, singing and constant remembrance followed by deep study and comprehension of God's Name and virtues';
- Kirt Karna, 'to honestly earn by one's physical and mental effort while accepting both pains and pleasures as God's gifts and blessings';
- Vand Chhakna, 'To share the fruits of one's labor with others before considering oneself.'[2]

The ultimate theological authority within Sikhism that provides along the path to mukti is the teaching of the eleven Gurus.

In Sikh belief there are ten human Gurus: Guru Nanak and his nine successors and a written Guru, the Sikh holy book, the *Adi Granth*. As Eleanor Nesbitt explains, 'In Sikh belief all are the physical embodiments of the same Guru. One Sikh analogy for Guru-ship is a flame that lights a succession of torches.'[3] As the entry on the *Adi Granth* in the online Sikh encyclopaedia SikhWiki notes:

Guru Granth Sahib or Adi Sri Granth Sahib Ji ... (also called the Adi Granth or Adi Guru Darbar) is more than just a scripture of the Sikhs, for the Sikhs treat this Granth (*holy book*) as their living Guru. The holy text spans 1430 pages and contains the actual words spoken by the founders of the Sikh religion (the Ten Gurus of Sikhism) and the words of various other Saints from other religions including Hinduism and Islam.

Guru Granth Sahib was given the Guruship by the last of the living Sikh Masters, Guru Gobind Singh Ji in 1708. Guru Gobind Singh said before his demise that the Sikhs were to treat the Granth Sahib as their next Guru. Guru Ji said – 'Sab Sikhan ko hokam hai Guru Manyo Granth,' meaning, 'All Sikhs are commanded to take the Granth as Guru.' So today, if asked, the Sikhs will tell you that they have a total of 11 Gurus (10 in human form and the SGGS).[4]

Alongside the *Adi Granth* there are two other texts which are also important for Sikh belief and practice. The first of these is the *Dasam Granth* which contains texts attributed to the tenth Guru. These texts are important to many Sikhs, but the *Dasam Granth* does not have the same authority as the *Adi Granth*. The second are the *Janamsākhīs* (literally 'birth stories'), writings which provide accounts of the life of Guru Nanak and the foundations of the Sikh religion.

The most well-known symbols of Sikh identity, and what most people think of when they think of Sikhism, are what are known as the 'five ks'.

These are five physical symbols worn by male Sikhs who have undergone the Sikh initiation ritual or 'amrit' as a sign of their dedication to God. These symbols are:

- Kesh (uncut hair)
- Kara (a steel bracelet)
- Kanga (a wooden comb)
- Kaccha - also spelt, Kachh, Kachera (cotton underwear)
- Kirpan (steel sword)

As well as keeping their hair uncut Sikh men (and increasingly women as well) wear a turban as a further sign of their dedication to God. As the article 'Why do Sikhs wear turbans?' on the SikhNet website puts it:

The turban tells others that we are different. By having a distinct appearance, Sikhs become accountable for their actions. Our distinct Sikh appearance not only makes us think more often about our conduct and its reflection upon a wider society, it also makes us reflect upon our own ideals and how they reflect the teachings of the Siri Guru Granth Sahib.

The turban is there to remind us of our connection to God. It frames us as devotees of God and gives us a way to live in gratitude for this gift of recognition. This responsibility of being recognized is also a way of keeping ourselves from self-destructive habits, such as smoking, drinking, etc.

The thing is, in our religion our identity goes hand in hand with the turban. There is no other religion in the world that wears a turban as a daily Badge of Identity. The turban of a Sikh is his or her primary identifying feature. It is a statement of belonging to the Guru, and it is a statement of the inner commitment of the one who wears it.[5]

7.2 SIKH ENGAGEMENT WITH HUMAN RIGHTS

Unlike in the cases of the other religions we have looked at in this report, there is no Sikh state or Sikh majority country.[6] This means that there is no Sikh country that is signatory to international human rights treaties or conventions.

In addition there do not appear to have been any statements in support of human rights from representative Sikh bodies, any Sikh equivalent to the Jewish, Islamic and Hindu statements of human rights, or any commentaries on the Universal Declaration of Human Rights.

Furthermore, although Sikhism has begun to be the subject of academic study, there do not as yet appear to have been any scholarly articles or books written on the subject of human rights.

However, there are three ways in which there has been a Sikh engagement with human rights. First of all, individual Sikhs such as Lord Indarjit Singh have spoken out on human rights matters. For example, at an address given in 2001 at an event to launch a joint booklet between the Network of Sikh Organisations and the Department for International Development on reducing world poverty, Lord Singh stressed the importance of human rights from a Sikh perspective:

It was Guru Nanak's birthday last week, and, as Sikhs like to stretch their festivals, we are still celebrating. As you know, today is also Human Rights Day, and there could be no better time to launch this Sikh booklet on combating poverty, than on the birth anniversary of one of the most perceptive teachers the world has ever known, who, 500 years ago, taught that the way to true peace lay in respect for others and concern for the deprived.

If I were asked to sum up Sikh teachings in a single sentence, it would be 'a total commitment to working for human rights, as a way to serving the one God of us all.'

Perhaps the most important of these rights, is the need for tolerance and respect for other ways of life. Guru Nanak, who lived at a time of bitter conflict between Hindus and Muslims on the Indian subcontinent and similar excesses in Europe, referred to this in his very first sermon when he said Na koi Hindu, na koi Mussalman – that is, in God's eyes there is neither Hindu nor Muslim, and by today's extension, neither Christian, Sikh nor Jew. That God isn't the least bit interested in our different labels, but in how we conduct ourselves. All religions were attempts to understand the ultimate reality and all should be respected.[7]

Secondly, there are now Sikh human rights groups. Examples of these are the Khalsa[8] Rights Group, which is the human rights arm of the United Kingdom Sikh Federation, the Sikh Human Rights Group, and the Sikh Welfare Research Trust.

The Sikh Human Rights Group describes itself as:

...a group of volunteers, professionals, activists and Non-Government Organisations with a mutual interest in the protection and promotion of human rights, the peaceful resolution of conflicts, diversity, sustainable development, good governance, pluralism and reform of international agencies to be more responsive to people and their cultures and civilisations. It bases its aims, approach and concepts on the humanitarian and plural philosophical basis of Sikhi which are consistent with principles of the UN Charter and Conventions but sometimes more progressive in areas such as pluralism and diversity.

SHRG offers a platform to individuals and organisations that share its aims and is not restricted to Sikhs.[9]

The Sikh Welfare Research Trust was:

...established in 1997 to nurture, support and fund organisations and individuals involved in voluntary sector activities, research and human rights work regardless of their religion, race or nationality.

SWRT supports a broad range of activities based on the principles of Sikh philosophy which include alleviation of poverty, hunger and homelessness, social and economic housing, enjoyment and coexistence of different cultures, religions and people, principles and enjoyment of human rights, principles and enjoyment of economic and social rights and development, principles and advancement of social and political coexistence and pluralistic societies, advice on civil rights and general welfare, voluntary work action in social, legal and economic welfare.[10]

Secondly, material has been produced that explains how the Sikh religion provides a basis for supporting human rights. The following three examples illustrate this.

First, in an unpublished address given to a conference of Amnesty International on 'Religion and Human Rights' in 1989 Indarjit Singh makes four points about 'Sikhs and Rights':

1. Sikh theology means that Sikhs believe in freedom of religion and respect for those of other faiths:

Sikhism is some 500 years old. Guru Nanak, the founder, was born at a particularly difficult time in Indian history. The majority Hindu community had become debilitated by the cruel rigidities of caste. The country had been invaded by the Moguls, Islam-professing descendants of Gengiz Khan, who, forgetting the true teachings of their faith, were bent on conquest and conversion. Each community viewed the other with contempt in the belief that it alone was the one true faith.

It was against this background that Guru Nanak preached his first sermon 'Na koi Hindu, Na koi Mussalman'. 'In God's eyes there is neither Hindu nor Muslim, only man.' He taught that God was not interested in religious labels but in conduct and action. Sikhism stresses that no one faith has a monopoly of truth. A natural corollary to this belief is Sikh emphasis on respect for other faiths and a total commitment to freedom of belief and worship, one of the most fundamental of all human rights.

2. Sikh theology is also committed to the equality of all human beings:

Sikhs believe in one God, the ultimate reality behind the Universe, a God without birth, without enmity of favourites. Sikhs believe that God does not divide people into high or low and Sikhism is very critical of any notion of caste or race.

> Call everyone high, none low
> God the one potter has fashioned all alike
> His light alone pervades all creation.
>
> (G.G.S p62) [11]

In much the same way, Guru Nanak was appalled at the lowly position accorded to women in society. Women were not only considered inferior and unclean but were also forbidden to participate in religious worship. The Guru underlined the absurdity of describing as inferior those who give birth to kings. Sikhism teaches the full equality of women who not only participate in Sikh worship, but also often lead it. While all male Sikhs are given the common name Singh, literally 'lion' to underline the ideal of courage, all Sikh women are given the title 'Kaur', literally princess, to emphasise their dignity and status in society.

3. Guru Nanak refused to accept the idea that 'religion is something to be divorced from social and moral responsibility (politics).' According to Indarjit Singh:

He taught that Sikhs should live in society, work constantly for its improvement (politics?), and yet always be above its meanness and pettiness. It is this positive attitude of voicing concern on social issues and working to alleviate injustice that has so frequently brought

Sikhs into conflict with secular authority who respond with smears of 'extremist' influence in politics. Sikhs are duty bound to protest against injustice or the cruel or arbitrary behaviour of those in authority.

4. Although the use of armed force by Sikhs down the centuries has given them a warlike reputation they are in fact committed to using violence only as a last resort and in a just cause:

… the correct Sikh response to personal injustice is forgiveness, or as our Scriptures put it 'to kiss the feet of he who would harm you,' a sentiment similar to the Christian teaching of turning the other cheek. Sikhs are forbidden to use violence either to further religious or political following, or to acquire an inch of territory. On the other hand, they are duty bound to defend the weak and innocent, if necessary by the sword. A close examination of the UN declaration of human rights reveals similar sentiments.

While Sikhism, like the UN Declaration of Human Rights, recognises the use of force as a last resort, torture, or cold-blooded killing, judicial or otherwise, of those in captivity, is clearly contrary to Sikh sentiment. In its opposition to the death penalty, and its dedicated stand on human rights, Sikhs applaud and support the work of Amnesty International.

Secondly, the entry 'Guardian of Human Rights' in SikhWiki sets out how human rights are supported by Sikh teaching.

The entry begins by outlining three aspects of the 'primary message' of Guru Nanak that support human rights, the existence of one creator God, the equality of all human beings, and the need to take responsibility for others:

The central message of Guru Nanak is that there is only one God – Ek Onkar and that this one God is the sole creator, sustainer and destroyer of all existence. We all belong to the one and the same Supreme Creator; there is no other.

The second message is one that stresses the equality of all human beings; to see God in all and hence to respect every person in the same way irrespective of their gender, race, caste, social status, nationality, ethnicity, class, ability, level of talent, etc.

The third message as outlined in Guru Nanak's teaching is that we should live the life of a householder (gristi) and embrace all of the responsibilities of family and community life, meditating on God while carrying out our duties to our families and to our society, as we serve and support our communities; making sure that we offer security to all within society. The well-being of everyone in society is a joint responsibility of all.[12]

It then goes on to quote the words of the fifth Guru, Guru Arjan, from the *Adi Granth*, 'The One God is our father; we are the children of the One God. You are our Guru', and then comments:

There is only one God; he is the father of all; we are all His children. So it is important that we treat every other human being as an equal and as a brother or sister; a father or mother; a daughter or son depending on their age relative to ours. If we fail to do so, we have turned our face away from God – we cannot be called Gurmukh – *one who is with the Guru*; one who listens to the wise saints. Instead we will live our lives, this precious, brief existence on Earth as Manmukh or *self-centred* or *ego-centric* men and women.[13]

It is leaders afflicted by Manmukh, the entry says, who have been the cause of war:

Because of Manmukh (self-centred or ego-centric) leaders, many wars have been fought between nations, either to protect one's own nation or to conquer other nations. In most of these wars one nation would fight against its neighbour to gain dominance, national pride, territory, wealth or other material gain. Most wars are as a result of discrimination and victimisation on the part of the aggressor against its opposite party. When a group considers its neighbour low or inferior; a source of easy wealth or territory, the result has, all too often, become a war.[14]

However, the ninth Sikh Guru, Guru Tegh Bahadur, pointed to a different and better way by giving the world 'an important lesson in responsibility and in sacrifice. He showed the world how one should care for their neighbour and protect their rights.'[15]

In 1675, the entry says, the Kashmiri Pandits (high caste Hindu religious leaders) asked for his help in preserving their community from the threat of either forced conversion or annihilation by the Muslim Mughal Empire. Even though he was a Sikh he chose to help them at the cost of his own life:

> To Guru Tegh Bahadur, a quiet man of peace, like Guru Nanak, it was clear that the Kashmiri Pandits, long the most respected priests, scholars, cooks and medical men of Hinduism, were in a dire situation. The Guru was aware of the important role that these Pandits played in the structure of Hindu society. He knew that Hinduism itself would probably not survive the loss of its most venerated Pandits if they did not get help; their community would suffer mass forced conversion to Islam. There were only two choices: either to offer to help them or to ignore their plight and turn away from the path of righteousness (Dharam).

From 1665 when Guru Ji became the ninth master, Sikhism had flourished in northern India and the name of the Guru was known throughout most of India. The Guru had travelled to the East as far as present-day Bangladesh and to Assam to spread the word of Nanak and to bring his message of peace and unity to all. So by 1675, the Guru was a well-known figure in Northern India. The Guru chose to shock the nation and awaken the masses. He knew that the Mughal invaders could only be defeated by awakening the whole of the nation; they could only be defeated by a concerted effort by all the communities of India.

And so on 24 November 1675 at Chandni Chowk, Delhi, India, the Guru who had dared Aurangzeb to attempt his conversion, staying true to his religion and his pledge to the Kashmiri Pandits sacrificing his life to end Aurangzeb's threats to the Hindus. He gave his life for the right of people to practice their religion freely without interference from the state.

This action by the Guru shook the nation as it showed the commitment of the Guru to stand against tyranny even at the cost of his own life. Soon his son would follow his path and create the Khalsa by asking 5 men to make such a sacrifice themselves. With the

SIKHISM AND HUMAN RIGHTS

Khalsa, a whole nation was created that would stand against tyranny and suppression of the weak.

The Guru gave his life so that it would awaken the nation to the need to unite against their Mughal overlords. The sacrifice of the Guru was the beginning of the end of the Mughal Empire. The Guru by his action established a clear message for the Sikhs – to stand firm to protect the rights of the weak or needy at any cost. The Guru is now fondly called *Hind-dee-chader – the protector of Hindustan (India).*[16]

The entry does not make explicit the connection between what it says and current international statements of human rights, but the implicit point is clear. Sikhs should support human rights because of the equality of all human beings before the one God and the need to take responsibility for the welfare of others, even if they belong to another religion.

Thirdly, the 2005 article by Gurmukh Singh on 'Sikhism and Human Rights' posted on the website of the Sikh Missionary Society argues that:

... the human rights enshrined in the constitution of the United Nations Organisation, when looked at in the light of the standards set by the Guru, show that the provisions for universal human rights by the modern progressive society fall well short of those provided for in Gurbani and lived in the Sikh historical tradition.[17]

Gurbani means the teaching contained in the *Adi Granth.* Three points are made to support this claim.

1. There is a long history of Sikhs acting to defend the human rights of everyone regardless of race, caste or religion: Guru Nanak, the founder of the Sikh religion, raised his voice in defence of human rights and the Sikh chronicle is mainly a long list of martyrs who laid down their lives in the defence of human rights without distinction between religion, caste or creed. Guru Tegh Bahadhur's martyrdom for the defence of another religion and culture (Hinduism in that case) also laid the foundation stone of the modern human rights movement. Never before had the history of mankind witnessed such a sacrifice. The Sikhs followed the example of the Guru and the Sikh history of the 18th century is full of examples of Sikh sacrifices for

the protection of non-Sikhs. (I invite young Sikhs world-wide to read this most interesting and adventurous part of Sikh history.) Jo saran aai, tis kanth lai (Those who seek protection [from the Khalsa] shall be warmly received) became the famous motto of the Guru's Khalsa. All communities could depend on the Khalsa for protection of their just rights. Thus there are numerous episodes in Sikh history when Muslims and Hindus alike came to the Khalsa for protection and help. The distinct Sikh identity ensured that a Guru's Sikh could not deny his Guru or shirk his religious duty to stand up for the defence of the weak and the downtrodden.[18]

2. Guru Nanak taught the importance of freedom from fear in a way that went beyond the concept of rights in modern societies:

The Guru preached that man's desire for ultimate salvation could only be achieved through freedom from fear. Fear none and frighten none is a central theme of Gurbani. The Lord is fearless and one reaches Him through total freedom from fear. Struggle for the freedom of all mankind without distinction is a Sikh ideal. However, for universal freedom, high ideals alone are not enough; it is important to play an active part in life to obtain freedom from the fear of oppression, injustice, superstition, insecurity, ignorance and ultimately even death itself. Thus the human rights concept as enshrined in Sikhee goes further than that which is currently accepted by civilised societies.[19]

3. Sikh convictions mean that when Sikhs have taken up arms it has always been a response of last resort to the abuse of human rights:

That response has always been specific and objective and aimed directly at the evil or oppression which has confronted the Sikhs from time to time. Sikh history and more recent events have clearly shown that Sikhs are not capable of communal violence despite provocation e.g. there was no communal Sikh backlash against the Hindus in Punjab or abroad even when over three thousand Sikhs had been slaughtered in Delhi in November 1984. It is not in the Sikh psyche to attack a community or religious group per se. How can they, for the teachings of Hindu and Muslim Bhagats (saints) are included in Guru Granth

Sahib and the foundation stone of Harimandar (Golden Temple) is reputed to have been laid by a Muslim saint. Hindus and Muslims alike have fought injustice side by side with the Sikhs. Indeed at times there were more Muslims fighting tyranny side by side with Guru Govind Singh than his own Sikhs e.g. when Pir Budhu Shah came to the Guru's help with his seven hundred mureeds (followers) when the Guru was suddenly attacked by hill rajahs at Paunta Sahib. Pir Budhu Shah lost two sons in that battle.[20]

The third point made by Gurmukh Singh in this article has as its background the specific issue of the violence that took place in Punjab in the 1980s and 1990s.

During the 1970s and 1980s the movement for the creation of an independent Sikh homeland of Khalistan flourished in Punjab with its Sikh majority population. In the 1980s some of the proponents of Khalistan turned to armed militancy to try to achieve their aim. This in turn led to counter insurgency operations by the Indian security forces and in June 1984 Operation Blue Star took place.

In this operation units of the Indian army led by the Sikh General Kuldip Singh Brar forcibly entered the Golden Temple at Amritsar, the holiest Sikh shrine, in order to overpower armed militants led by the Sikh religious leader Jarnail Singh Bhindranwale who had occupied the site. The subsequent fighting led to the destruction of the Golden Temple and the loss of hundreds (possibly thousands) of lives with casualties being suffered on both sides.

In retaliation for what many Sikhs saw as the desecration of the Golden Temple the Indian Prime Minister Indira Gandhi was subsequently assassinated by two Sikh bodyguards. This in turn led to anti-Sikh riots in Delhi stirred up by Hindu nationalists which resulted in the deaths of thousands of Sikhs in what many Sikhs view as an act of genocide.

In January 1986, the Golden Temple was occupied by militants belonging to the All India Sikh Students Federation and the Damdami Taksal (a Sikh educational organisation) and on 26 January the gathering passed a resolution in favour of the creation of Khalistan. Subsequently, a number of rebel militant groups in favour of Khalistan waged a major insurgency against the government of India. This insurgency was suppressed by the Indian security forces in the 1990s and Sikh political movements such as the Khalsa Raj Party now pursue the goal of an independent Khalistan through non-violent means.

However, the memory of the insurgency is still a live issue both in India and among the Sikh community worldwide. Sikhs argue that the Sikh community continues to suffer discrimination and violence both from Hindu nationalists and from the Indian authorities and that this is a major human rights issue that is largely ignored by the outside world.[21]

The Sikh commitment to the fundamental human rights value of equality emphasised in the first two of the articles above is further emphasised in the FAQ section of the RealSikhism website. In response to the question 'Do Sikhs believe in equality of all Humanity?' the answer that is given is 'Yes, Sikhs believe that all humans are equal.'

In support of this answer the section goes on to declare:

One of the major principles of Sikhism is to consider all human races equal, regardless of caste, colour, class, culture, gender, wealth, and religion. In the fourteenth century, the Hindu caste system was at its peak in India. Many Hindu priests (Brahmins) believed in the caste system and perpetuated it as much as possible by segregating individuals of lower castes and labelling them as untouchables. People in India, who considered themselves of a high-class society wouldn't even touch a person who they considered as being part of any lower caste. If touched accidentally, they would take a shower to clean themselves. They also would serve food to their servants and workers on the floor and would themselves eat while sitting higher on some sort of chair or table.

Sikh Gurus preached to 'Recognize the Lord's Light (Spirit) within all, and do not consider social class or status; there are no classes or castes in the world hereafter' (Guru Granth Sahib Ji, 349). Guru Nanak Dev Ji, the first Guru established Langar, a free community kitchen. Langar is free food served in all Gurdwara Sahib, which is prepared by a Sikh congregation and then consumed by them and their guests while sitting at the same level on the floor next to each other since there is nothing lower than the floor. The purpose of the Langar is to both feed the needy and to eliminate any type of caste system. While eating Langar together, there remains no difference between rich and poor, superior or inferior, for all present are eating the same food at the same level. Langar is served in all Gurdwara Sahib around the globe twenty-four hours a day.

Furthermore, by knowing the last name one could distinguish which caste the person is from, Guru Gobind Singh Ji gave all Sikh men the last name 'Singh' and all Sikh women the last name 'Kaur' so that no one can distinguish anyone's caste. Everyone is considered equal in Sikhism.

Sikhism states that 'All beings and creatures are His; He belongs to all' (Guru Granth Sahib Ji, 425). God does not love based on one's caste or color, He loves all, He belongs to all. In addition, 'Sing the Praise of the Immaculate Lord; He is within all. The Almighty Lord controls everything; whatever He wills, comes to pass. He establishes and disestablishes everything in an instant; there is no other except Him. He pervades the continents, universe, islands and all worlds. He alone understands to whom God Himself provides wisdom; He becomes a pure and unstained being' (Guru Granth Sahib Ji, 706). Bhai Gurdas Ji writes 'The special feature of the Sikh of the Guru is that he goes beyond the framework of caste-classification and moves in humility. Then his labor becomes acceptable at the door of God' (The Vaars of Bhai Gurdas Ji, 1).

7.3   TENSIONS IN RELATION TO HUMAN RIGHTS ISSUES

As in the cases of the other religious traditions examined in this report there are a number of areas where there continue to be tensions in relation to Sikhism and human rights.

In the past one major area of tension was the question of the right of Sikh men to wear the Turban in public and to carry the Kirpan. This was partly a simple matter of race discrimination (as when Sikh bus drivers were forbidden to wear the turban at work in Manchester and Wolverhampton in the 1960s), but more recently the issue has been about health and safety concerns such as whether Sikhs should be allowed to wear a turban rather than a motorcycle helmet or Sikh students should be allowed to take a Kirpan into school. These issues still occasionally arise, but for the most part successful compromise solutions have been found.

For example, in the United Kingdom the Motor-Cycle Crash-Helmets

(Religious Exemption) Act of 1976 permitted Sikhs to wear turbans rather than crash helmets and a European Community Directive in 1993 said that Sikhs must wear safety helmets rather than turbans in warehouses, but could wear turbans on building sites.[22]

Two areas of tension which still exist, however, are reproductive rights and equality.

7.3.1   Reproductive rights

On the basis of the teaching of the Adi Granth most Sikhs have traditionally held that life begins at conception and therefore abortion has generally been forbidden in Sikhism. In the words of Gobindsingh Mansukhani, 'Abortion is taboo as is an interference in the creative work of God. If the conception has taken place it would be a sin to destroy life.'[23]

However, some Westernised Sikhs would accept the legitimacy of abortion if the mother's life was in danger and in the Sikh community in India abortions sometimes occur to defend family honour when an unmarried girl has become pregnant and, as in the Hindu community, there is also a major issue about the abortion of female babies.

As Nesbitt explains, 'Abortions frequently occur because, despite Sikh teaching, sons are more prized than daughters as they carry on the family name, look after their parents and do not require dowries.' As she goes on to say, the result of the increase of the ultrasound screening of pregnant women has been an increase in such abortions. 'In Punjab the Census shows the accelerated decrease in the number of female births between 1991 and 2001 and at the time of writing [2007] the ratio of female to male births is less than eight to ten.'[24] Although the major incidence of such abortions is in Punjab there is also evidence of it happening in the Sikh diaspora as well.

This issue is increasingly being seen as a major human rights concern by the Sikh community and it is the focus of a current campaign by the Sikh Human Rights Group.[25]

7.3.2   Equality

The existence of 'female foeticide' is an indication that the equality between men and women which is a feature of Sikh theology is not always translated into Sikh practice. In many traditional Sikh communities there are still traditional demarcations of gender roles and expectations about how women should dress in order to preserve modesty that can be seen as in tension with a Western rights emphasis on individual choice.

In addition, it is still men who tend to take leadership roles in the Sikh community, including the leading of worship at the Sikh temple or Gurdwara and there is a continuing issue about women being allowed to serve in the Golden Temple in Amritsar on an equal basis with men.

Another area where there is tension between theory and practice is the continuing existence of caste distinctions within the Sikh community in spite of the denunciation by the Gurus of the caste system. To quote Nesbitt again:

> ...caste-based prejudice persists in many Sikh families, and not least in the diaspora. In fact in the UK the titles of some gurdwaras include the names 'Bhastra,' 'Ramgarhia' and 'Ravidasi' which denote the zat [caste] of the committee and of most, if not all, of the congregation. Moreover most marriages continue to be between Sikhs of the same zat and families seeking a spouse for their son or daughter usually indicate their zat.[26]

A final area of tension in relation to equality is the issue of same-sex relationships. As the entry on homosexuality on the RealSikh site indicates, for example, traditional Sikh teaching would be opposed to homosexual practice on the basis that sexual activity should only take place within heterosexual marriage:

> Sikhism has no specific teachings about homosexuality. The holy scripture of Sikhs, Guru Granth Sahib Ji, does not explicitly mention homosexuality; however, married life is encouraged time and time again in Guru Granth Sahib Ji. Whenever marriage is mentioned, it is always in reference to a man and a woman.
>
> Guru Granth Sahib Ji is the complete guide to life and salvation. Some Sikhs believe that if a marriage between two of the same sexes is not mentioned, it is therefore not right. The counterargument is that, marriage is mentioned as a spiritual unity and since the soul does not have a gender, homosexuality should be permitted. The counterargument again arises that spiritual unity in marriage is only

mentioned between a man and a woman. Since sexuality with the same gender is not directly mentioned in Guru Granth Sahib Ji, Sikhism's stand on homosexuality is derived from other beliefs such as marriage and sex.

Since marriage is only mentioned as a spiritual relationship between a man and a woman in Guru Granth Sahib Ji, same sex marriages are not conducted in Gurdwara Sahib. Only the services that are clearly permitted are conducted in the Gurdwara Sahib.

Sikh Gurus introduced a lifestyle with which one remains focused in life in order to be one with God. Homosexuality is not a part of the lifestyle instructed by Sikh Gurus. And nor is having premarital sex or having multiple sex partners if you are a heterosexual. According to Sikh Lifestyle, sexual relationship is to only exist between a man and a woman married in the Gurdwara Sahib.

Since sexual relationship can only be after marriage and marriage can only be between a man and a woman, homosexual lifestyle is logically not accepted by Sikh beliefs.[27]

Furthermore, as the entry on Homosexuality on the Sikhwiki notes:

The supreme Sikh religious body, the Akal Takht, has issued an edict condemning gay marriage, and Vedanti's words were echoed by Manjit Singh Kalkatta, another highly respected Sikh preacher who sits on the governing body of the Golden Temple, the Shiromani Gurdwara Parbandhak Committee. 'The advice given by the highest Sikh temporal authority to every Sikh is saying that it is unnatural and ungodly, and the Sikh religion cannot support it.'[28]

This negative view of homosexual practice means that many Sikhs would continue to be opposed to social acceptance of such practice and to gay marriage. However as the Sikhwiki also notes, there are Sikhs who 'believe that Guru Nanak's emphasis on universal equality and brotherhood is fundamentally in support of the human rights of homosexuals',[29] and particularly in the Sikh diaspora there are Sikhs who would be affirming of lesbian and gay relationships. For example in this country there is Sarbat – LGBT Sikhs which describes itself as:

... a social and support group for LGBT Sikhs. We offer a platform for like-minded Sikhs from all walks of life and aim to promote the LGBT Sikh cause in a fair and courteous manner. We also strongly believe that there is no room for discrimination within our communities for being who we are. We would also like LGBT issues to be discussed openly within our communities without the taboo or any awkwardness attached to it.[30]

Notes

[1] For an accessible introduction to the emergence and development of Sikhism see Eleanor Nesbitt, *Sikhism: a Very Short Introduction*, Oxford: OUP, 2005, Chs 2-5.

[2] Definition of the three pillars from Sikhwiki at http://www.sikhiwiki.org/index.php/Three Pillars

[3] Nesbitt, op.cit. Kindle edition, Ch.2.

[4] Guru Granth Sahib at http://www.sikhiwiki.org/index.php/Guru_Granth_Sahib. In saying that the *Adi Granth* is the eleventh Guru what is meant is that Sikhs follow its teaching as they would the teaching of a living Guru.

[5] 'Why do Sikhs wear turbans?' at http://fateh.sikhnet.com/s/WhyTurbans#Men%20Women%20Hair

[6] Many Sikhs would like to see the establishment of a Sikh state (Kalistan) in the current Indian state of Punjab where Sikhs are a majority of the population. However many other Sikhs do not support this idea and there seems little likelihood of it happening in the near future. See note on this issue below.

[7] 'On target for reducing poverty' at http://www.sikhspirit.com/khalsa/nso011210.htm

[8] Khalsa literally refers to men who have undergone amrit, but it is used here as a description for the whole Sikh community.

[9] Sikh Human Rights Group, 'We Are' at http://shrg.net/intro/

[10] 'Sikh Welfare Research Trust' at http://shrg.net/affiliates/sikh-welfare-research-trust/

[11] The reference is to p.62 of the Guru Granth Sahib or Adi Granth.

[12] 'Guardian of Rights' at http://www.sikhiwiki.org/index.php/Guardian_of_human_rights

[13] Ibid.

[14] Ibid.

[15] Ibid.

[16] Ibid.

[17] 'Sikhism and Human Rights' at http://www.sikhmissionarysociety.org/sms/smsarticles/advisorypanel/gurmukhsinghsewauk/sikhismandhumanrights.html

[18] Ibid.

[19] Ibid.

[20] Ibid.

[21] For a good introduction to what happened in 1984 see Mark Tully, *Amritsar: Mrs Gandhi's Last Battle*, Rupa; New Delhi, 2011. For an account from a Sikh perspective see Jarnail Singh, *I accuse: the Anti-Sikh Violence of 1984*, Harmondsworth: Penguin, 2011.

[22] See Nesbitt, op.cit. Ch.6.

[23] G.S. Mansukhani, *Introduction to Sikhism*, Delhi: Hemkunt Press, 1986, p.183.

[24] Nesbitt, 'Sikhism', in Morgan and Lawton (eds), op.cit. p.143.

[25] See the SHRG report 'Where have all the girls gone?' at http://shrg.net/gender-foeticide/

[26] Nesbitt, in Morgan and Lawton (eds), op.cit. p. 148.

[27] 'What are Sikhism's beliefs on homosexuality?' at http://realsikhism.com/index.php?subaction=showfull&id=1250025034&ucat=7

[28] 'Homosexuality and Sikhism' at http://www.sikhiwiki.org/index.php/HomosexualityandSikhism

[29] Ibid.

[30] 'About us' at http://www.sarbat.net/faqs/

Chapter Eight

RELIGION AND HUMAN RIGHTS
IN TODAY'S WORLD

8.1   RIGHTS AND THE LIBERAL ATTACK ON RELIGION

In a recent speech the columnist and social commentator Brendan O'Neill highlights the way in which religion has come under attack in contemporary Europe. He begins his article by noting that:

> Last year, a Baptist Church in Norfolk in England put up a poster suggesting that if you didn't believe in God you would go to hell. The poster said, 'If you think there is no God, you had better be right', and underneath there was a picture of flames, hellfire, the suggestion being that if you don't believe you will suffer. Suffer in eternal damnation, no less.
>
> Now, to some people, certainly to those who don't believe in God, that may seem like a shocking message. But to me, the most shocking thing was what happened next. Which is that passersby complained about the poster, not to each other, which is par for the course when you're walking down the street and see something you don't like: you moan to your friends about it. No, they complained to the police.
>
> The police registered the poster as a 'hate incident'. They launched an investigation. But in order to avoid embarrassment — because it would undoubtedly be very embarrassing for the police in modern Britain to investigate a church for expressing its religious views — the police went to the church, spoke to the pastor, suggested he take the poster down, and so he took the poster down.

I found this really disturbing. For what we had here, in Britain in the 21st century, was a situation where the armed wing of the state put pressure on a church, a private religious association, to take down a public expression of its deeply held beliefs.[1]

He then goes on to observe that such an incident is not a one off:

This was not a weird, rash incident. There have been numerous incidents in Britain where people have been arrested, charged or punished in some way for expressing their religious beliefs. I want to give you a few quick examples.

— Last year in Dundee in Scotland, a street preacher was arrested by the police, taken to a police station, put in a cell, and later questioned. Why? Because he said, as part of his street-preaching, that homosexuality is a sin. For expressing what many Christians believe to be true, he was taken in by the cops.

— In Northern Ireland, a Christian pastor was taken to court in August, charged with "improper use of a public electronic communications network" — i.e. the internet — and charged with making a 'grossly offensive' message. He had said, during an internet sermon, that Islam is a 'Satanic' faith. Many people will find that offensive; Muslims certainly will. But that is his deeply held conviction. He was arrested and hauled before the courts for saying what he believes to be true.

— Some people, including politicians, are campaigning to force Catholic schools in Britain to teach children about homosexual sex and that gay marriage is equal to traditional marriage. Well, newsflash: Catholics don't believe that. They believe traditional marriage is superior to gay marriage. Some believe gay marriage is not real marriage. They are facing great pressure to teach their children something that they do not believe, which goes against 'the dictates of their conscience'.

— Ofsted, Britain's education regulator, now regularly denounces certain Christian schools. Last year it denounced a whole bunch of them as 'inadequate' because they 'fail to teach respect for other faiths, or develop their pupils' awareness of other [belief systems]'. In other words, they teach their own faith. They elevate their own beliefs over others. They teach their children to live by and understand the world through a particular faith, and for doing that they are denounced by a wing of the state.

— Also, there are no explicitly Catholic adoption agencies left in Britain. They've either been closed down or have changed their names and values. Why? Because under equality legislation, if you refuse to adopt children to homosexual couples, as most Catholic adoption agencies do, then the state can judge you a practitioner of inequality and punish you. So these religious agencies were pressured out of existence for the crime of acting on 'the dictates of their conscience'.[2]

He further notes that this is a Europe-wide issue:

And on it goes. Across Europe we're seeing attacks on people of faith, on their right to exercise their freedom of conscience. Swedish pastors arrested for denouncing homosexuality; bakers taken to court for refusing to serve gay weddings; a small Jewish sect threatened with state action because of its rules regarding women's roles in its community life; Islamic schools obsessively investigated in search of radicalism. Religious groups, especially smaller, pretty hardcore one, face a level of state or official investigation that should alarm anyone who, like [Thomas] Paine, believes people must be free to live according to the dictates of their conscience.

What we're witnessing is a silent war on religion. In the 21st century, there is the creeping criminalisation of certain religious views and an undermining of religious groups' right to organise themselves, and those who are voluntarily part of their community of faith, in what they consider to be the most fitting way. Religious people's ability to express themselves publicly is being undermined, and their ability to organise themselves around their faith — such as by having schools and other agencies to propagate their views among their followers — is being undermined too.[3]

The assault on religious freedom outlined by O'Neill has been charted in detail by Rex Adhar and Ian Leigh in their important academic study *Religious Freedom in the Liberal State*,[4] and it is not confined to Europe as indicated by the recent imprisonment of Kim Davies, the Pentecostal Kentucky County Court Clerk, for refusing to issue marriage licences to same-sex couples or the case of the Oregon bakers fined $135,000 for refusing to bake a cake for a lesbian wedding.

If we ask what is driving this assault on the free exercise of religious conviction, the answer is that it is in large part driven by a human rights agenda. Specifically, it is driven by the belief that people have a right not to be offended by statements of religious faith made by other people and by the belief that gay and lesbian people have the right not to have the moral status of their relationships called into question explicitly or implicitly by the words or actions of those who disapprove of them.

Underlying these specific concerns about the perceived incompatibility lies a deeper issue which is the fact that for many people human rights and religion are seen to be antithetical not simply on specific issues, but across the board. As the legal scholar Louis Herkin puts it: 'The human rights ideology is a fully secular and rational ideology whose very promise of success as a universal ideology depends on its secularity and rationality.'[5]

In addition, there is also deep-seated fear about religiously inspired violence. The growing threat of terrorist activity driven by an Islamist ideology has led many governments across the world, including the government in this country, to conclude that religion can be dangerous and that the best way to counteract this danger is to seek to suppress the dissemination of 'extremist' religious ideas.

This approach can be seen for example in the report *Tackling Extremism in the UK* published by the Prime Minister's Task Force on Tackling Radicalisation and Extremism in December 2013. This report declares:

> The UK deplores and will fight terrorism of every kind, whether based on Islamist, extreme right-wing or any other extremist ideology. We will not tolerate extremist activity of any sort, which creates an environment for radicalising individuals and could lead them on a pathway towards terrorism.[6]

It goes on to say:

> Extremists take advantage of institutions to share their poisonous narrative with others, particularly with individuals vulnerable to

their messages. The government must do more to address extremism in locations where it can exert control, such as prisons, and increase oversight where it is needed, such as some independent and religious schools.[7]

In addition it also argues that universities need to control who they allow to speak:

Extremist preachers use some higher education institutions as a platform for spreading their messages. Universities must take seriously their responsibility to deny extremist speakers a platform. This is not about the government restricting freedom of speech – it is about universities taking account of the interests of all their students and their own reputations when deciding who they allow to use their institution as a platform.[8]

Most people would agree that the authorities have a duty to act when individuals or groups advocate the use of illegal violence or the overthrow of the state (what used to be called 'sedition').

However, as numerous commentators have pointed out, the term 'extremism' has not been restricted to those advocating violence or sedition. Fear of being seen to target solely the Muslim community, or particular groups within that community, has meant that the Government has come out against all forms of 'extreme' religion and this has meant that Muslim, Christian and Jewish groups and institutions have fallen foul of the anti-extremism agenda because of, for example, their opposition to same-sex relationships or their advocacy of a 'creationist' view of the origins of the world.[9]

What this combination of a secular rights ideology and fear of Islamic terrorism is in danger of leading to, if indeed it has not led to it already, is the undermining of the very rights that human rights advocates and Western governments say that they support.

At the heart of the 1948 Universal Declaration of Human Rights is Article 18 which declares:

Everyone has the right to freedom of thought, conscience and religion; this right includes freedom to change his religion or belief, and freedom, either alone or in community with others and in public or private, to manifest his religion or belief in teaching, practice, worship and observance.[10]

This right to freedom of religion and belief is included verbatim in Article 9 on the European Convention on Human Rights. Article 9, however, qualifies this right by the inclusion of an additional paragraph which states that this right shall be subject:

> ...to such limitations as are prescribed by law and are necessary in a democratic society in the interests of public safety, for the protection of public order, health or morals, or for the protection of the rights and freedoms of others.[11]

As John Finnis writes in a forthcoming essay 'Equality and Religious Diversity: Oppressing Conscientious Diversity in England', the qualification in paragraph two of Article 9 of the European Convention is undoubtedly justified. As he says, 'there can be no doubt that claims of religious liberty are properly subject to considerations of public order and public morality, as well as to the genuine rights of others.'[12] If, for example, someone speaking in a church, mosque or gurdwara advocates planting a bomb in a restaurant or abusing children or vulnerable adults then that is incitement to murder and abuse and cannot rightly be defended on the basis of an appeal to freedom and belief.

However, as Finnis goes on to argue, it is also important when considering how and when to apply this qualification to give due weight to the particular importance for society of respect for religious conscience and for behaviour flowing from this. As he puts it:

> The ground for treating religious conscience as specially important is that it is really of great importance that people should seek and form a responsible judgment about an issue of unsurpassed importance: the truth about the origin, significance and destiny of the entire universe and of human beings as the only beings, within our experience, who are capable of engaging with reality in this uniquely profound way. Indeed, people have a moral duty to interest themselves in that issue, and to seriously seek the truth about it. A society which fails

to acknowledge that duty, at least indirectly, is to that extent both frivolous and truncated, and in a deep, implicit way is under-cutting its own claim to be taken seriously and defended (at the defenders' peril) against its enemies.[13]

Where this quotation from Finnis is particularly helpful is that it moves the discussion on from a mere assertion that the provision of freedom of religion is contained in the Universal Declaration of Human Rights and the European Convention of Human Rights to an explanation of why such a provision is there in the first place. What it suggests is that the pursuit of religious truth should be protected because it is one of the key things that it is good for human beings to do.

This is turn points us to the fact that if we want to make sense of the whole human rights project and the place of religion within it the best way to do this is to think of it in terms of an attempt to promote what is good for human beings. To put it another way, human rights is really about enabling human beings to flourish by giving them the opportunity to fulfil their human potential. In the next section of this chapter we shall look at this point in more detail.

8.2   HUMAN RIGHTS AND HUMAN FLOURISHING

As we have seen, one of the criticisms of the language of human rights that is made by Buddhist thinkers is that it encourages an adversarial view of human society. It encourages individuals and groups to claim and assert their rights in opposition to other individuals and groups who are perceived to be denying them and in so doing it encourages division and conflict rather than dialogue and co-operation.

A similar criticism of the result of the use of the language of rights is made from a Christian perspective by Mary Glendon in her 1991 study *Rights Talk – The Impoverishment of Political Discourse* in which she explores the impact that the use of the language of rights has on American politics and society. Her conclusion is that:

Our stark, simple rights dialect put a damper on the processes of public justification, communication, and deliberation upon which the continuing vitality of a democratic regime depends. It contributes to the erosion of the habits, practices and attitudes of respect for others that are the ultimate and surest guarantors of human rights. It impedes creative long-range thinking about our most pressing social problems. Our rights-laden public discourse easily accommodates the economic, the immediate, and the personal dimensions of a problem, while it regularly neglects the moral, the long-term, and the social implications.

Rights talk in its current form has been the thin end of a wedge that is turning American political discourse into a parody of itself and challenging the very notion that politics can be conducted through reasoned discussion and compromise. For the new rhetoric of rights is less about human dignity and freedom than about insistent, unending desires. Its legitimation of individual and group egoism is in flat opposition to the great purposes set forth in the Preamble to the Constitution; 'to form a more perfect Union, establish Justice, promote the general Welfare, and secure the Blessings of Liberty to ourselves and our Posterity.'[14]

A recent example of the sort of impoverishment of discourse to which Glendon refers is the way in which the argument about the introduction of same-sex 'marriage' both in the United States and this country has been dominated by the argument that the right to equality of gay and lesbian people necessitates the right to 'equal marriage', an argument which has cut short a proper debate about the nature and purposes of marriage and how marriage contributes to the well-being of individuals and wider society.[15]

What is clear, however, was that it was not the intention of the authors of the Universal Declaration of Human Rights in 1948 to promote such an impoverishment of discourse or to encourage individual and group egotism. From their own accounts of what they were seeking to achieve it is clear that their intention was to try to promote human flourishing (what the preamble to the Universal Declaration describes in terms of 'social progress and better standards of life in larger freedom')[16] in the face of the continuing threat to this from political tyranny and that the use of rights language was a tool to try to bring this about.

Seen in this light, the apparent dichotomy between rights language and the language of duty and responsibility which is more common in religion disappears. Identifying rights in certain specific areas was intended to be a way of highlighting the duty and responsibility of all human beings to help all other human beings to flourish in those particular areas.

In his book *Natural Law and Natural Rights*, John Finnis writes that:

> The modern vocabulary and grammar of rights is a many-faceted instrument for reporting and asserting the requirements or other implications of a relationship of justice from the point of view of the person(s) who benefit(s). It provides a way of talking about 'what is just' from a special angle, the viewpoint of [one] to whom something...is owed and who would be wronged if denied that something.[17]

If we substitute 'human flourishing' for 'justice' this quotation helps us to understand what rights language is actually meant to be about. It provides a way of reporting and asserting what is required for human flourishing from the viewpoint of someone to whom the opportunity to flourish is owed and who would be wronged if they were denied such opportunity.

Viewing the matter in this way helps to understand better what is meant by statements of rights. We can see this, for example, if we look at three of the articles from the Universal Declaration of Human Rights. Article 3 declares: 'Everyone has the right to life, liberty and the security of person.'[18]

The conviction underlying this article is that human beings require life, liberty and security of person in order to flourish. In consequence people have the individual and collective duty to uphold the life, liberty and security of others.

Article 5 states: 'No one shall be subjected to torture or to cruel, inhuman or degrading treatment or punishment.'[19] The conviction underlying this article is that torture, or cruel, inhuman or degrading punishment prevents human beings from flourishing. In consequence people have the individual and collective duty to ensure that people do not undergo such treatment.

Article 23 says:

(1) Everyone has the right to work, to free choice of employment, to just and favorable conditions of work and to protection against unemployment.

(2) Everyone, without any discrimination, has the right to equal pay for equal work.

(3) Everyone who works has the right to just and favorable remuneration ensuring for himself and his family an existence worthy of human dignity,

and supplemented, if necessary, by other means of social protection.
(4) Everyone has the right to form and to join trade unions for the protection of his interests.[20]

The conviction underlying this article is that human flourishing requires that each individual has the opportunity to work, to receive adequate provision to sustain family life through wages and other forms of social provision and to engage in trade union activity to protect their interests. In consequence people have the individual and collective duty to ensure as far as possible that people can work, do receive adequate provision and can freely engage in trade union activity.

Each of the rights contained in the Universal Declaration of Human Rights can be analysed in similar terms and the subsequent human rights treaties and conventions have been attempts to either extend the list of rights contained in the Universal Declaration in order to provide a more comprehensive account of what human flourishing requires or to give legal force to the duties required for human beings to flourish.

Thus the 2006 United Nations Convention on the Rights of Persons with Disabilities which we looked at in chapter one of this report is based on the conviction that people with disabilities have certain needs that need to be met if they are to flourish, it specifies what these needs are and commits signatory nations to undertake the duty of meeting these needs as far as possible.

All this means that, far from being a licence for the selfish assertion of our own interests, human rights, when properly understood, are in fact a summons to recognise the duties and responsibilities we have individually and collectively to ensure that other people flourish and reach their full human potential.

8.3   HOW DO WE DECIDE WHAT MAKES FOR HUMAN FLOURISHING?

If human rights are, as has just been argued, about the promotion of human flourishing then the question that this raises is how we decide what makes for human flourishing and hence what 'rights' people should have. The answer is that this is an issue that each individual or group of individuals has to decide for themselves on the basis of their religious or philosophical convictions.

In his book *The Open Secret* the Christian theologian Lesslie Newbigin writes about the basis on which we can evaluate the claims made by the various world religions. He explains that we have to accept

> ...the simple truth that no standpoint is available to any man except the point where he stands; that there is no platform from which one can claim to have an 'objective' view which supersedes the 'subjective' faith-commitment of the world's faiths; that every man must take his stand on the floor of the arena, on the same level with every other, and there engage in the real encounter of ultimate commitment with those who, like him, have staked their lives on their vision of the truth.[21]

What Newbigin says about the evaluation of the claims of the various world religions applies just as much to claims concerning what makes for human flourishing. There is no neutral standpoint which stands outside the particular worldview that a person or group of people possesses. In Newbigin's words, when discussing what makes for human flourishing every individual or group has to take their 'stand on the floor of the arena, on the same level with every other' and engage in a 'real encounter' with those whose perspective is different from their own.

This sort of real encounter between people with different perspectives is what led to the production of the Universal Declaration of Human Rights in 1948 and is what has been involved in the production of the series of statements about human rights that have been produced since then.

It needs to be noted in this connection that a secular humanist conviction is no more neutral than a conviction based on belief in one of the world's religions. Indeed, it can be argued that although secular and religious viewpoints are conventionally distinguished from one another, secular humanism is in fact simply another form of religion.

This is because the term 'religion' cannot be used simply to refer to systems of belief and practice that involve belief in God, because this would exclude Buddhism and also Confucianism, both of which are generally recognised as religions. It is better, for this reason, to follow Newbigin and to use the term 'religion':

> ...to refer to that which has final authority for a believer or society, both in the sense that it determines his scale of values and in the sense that

it provides the models, the basic patterns through which the believer grasps and organizes his experience.[22]

For secular humanists the tenets of secular humanism are what determines their scale of values and provide the models and basic patterns through which they grasp and organise their experiences. Secular humanism is thus their religion.

If this argument is accepted it follows that secular humanism has no greater *a priori* claim to acceptance as a viewpoint on the basis of which to determine what makes for human flourishing than any of the other six religions we have been considering in this report. It too has to stand on the floor of the arena and make out its case in encounter with those who hold to other religious viewpoints.

It also follows that a society in which the governing belief system expressed in its laws and practices was secular humanism would be no more and no less of a society organised on the basis of religion than a society in which Christianity, Islam or Buddhism fulfilled this role. This is a point to which we shall return later in this chapter.

8.4 HUMAN RIGHTS AS A VARIEGATED CONSENSUS

The fact that each of the world's religions approaches the issue of human flourishing on the basis of their own existing pattern of belief and practice does not mean that a consensus about human rights is impossible. What has taken place since 1948 shows that this is the case.

The Buddhist writer Sallie King, whose work we looked at in chapter 6, helpfully draws attention to the argument of the ethicist Sumner Twiss:

> ... who urges us to recognize that when human rights are affirmed at the international, inter-cultural level, two kinds of justification are present: on the global level, an international 'practical moral consensus' has formed that certain behaviors are necessary and some must be prohibited; on the level of individual traditions, each tradition, says Twiss, must look to 'its own set of moral categories as appropriate to its particular philosophical or religious vision' in order to justify and articulate its participation in this consensus.[23]

Charles Taylor offers a similar approach when he talks about an 'overlapping consensus' on human rights. Taylor argues that we may distinguish between a human right as a norm of conduct and the justification of that norm. There can be agreement on norms even if there is a significant disagreement on how that norm is to be justified.[24]

What we have seen in the previous chapters of this report supports the points made by Twiss and Taylor. All of the six religious traditions we have looked at have accepted the concept of human rights as set out in the United Nations Declaration of Human Rights and subsequent human rights documents as the basis for a 'practical moral consensus' about what makes for human flourishing and what people should do and should not do in consequence. However this consensus is an 'overlapping consensus' in the sense that (a) participation in this consensus has been justified on the basis of radically different religious beliefs and (b) not all rights are accepted by the adherents of all religions. As we have seen, in spite of the overall consensus, there is continuing disagreement over issues such as freedom of religion, reproductive rights, gender equality, equality for gay and lesbian people and appropriate forms of punishment.

These continuing disagreements need to be taken seriously, but they should not obscure the significance of what has been achieved since 1948. An overall consensus about what makes for human flourishing has emerged and has been increasingly accepted among the major world religions. Groups such as Islamic State who have no regard for human rights are the exception rather than the rule.

Furthermore, Twiss' language about a 'practical moral consensus' needs qualification. The consensus is certainly about what should happen in practice, but this reflects an overlapping theoretical understanding of how human beings should relate to each other.

That this is the case will not cause surprise to anyone who has taken the time to look at the history of mainstream human thinking about moral behaviour as this has been reflected in the religions and philosophies of humankind.

In his 1944 essay *The Abolition of Man*, C S Lewis draws attention to what he calls 'The Tao', which he says 'others may call Natural Law or Traditional Morality or the First Principles of Practical Reason or the First Platitudes.'[25] By this he means 'a set of objective values that have been shared, with minor differences, by every culture ... the traditional moralities of East and West, the Christian, the Pagan, and the Jew'.[26]

In the appendix to this work Lewis supports his argument for the existence of the Tao by giving examples of agreement of a basic moral consensus drawn from a variety of sources from across human history and from all parts of the globe. He organises these illustrations under eight headings:

1. The law of general beneficence
2. The law of special beneficence
3. Duties to parents, elders and ancestors
4. Duties to children and posterity
5. The law of justice
6. The law of good faith and veracity
7. The law of mercy
8. The law of magnanimity.[27]

The quotations he gives under headings 1 and 7 will serve to show the point he is making.

The Law of General Beneficence

(a) Negative

'I have not slain men.' (Ancient Egyptian. From the Confession of the Righteous Soul, 'Book of the Dead', v. Encyclopedia of Religion and Ethics [= ERE], vol. V, p. 478)

'Do not murder.' (Ancient Jewish. Exodus 20:13)

'Terrify not men or God will terrify thee.' (Ancient Egyptian. Precepts of Ptahhetep. H. R. Hall, *Ancient History of the Near East*, p. 133n)

'In Nastrond (= Hell) I saw... murderers.' (Old Norse. Volospa 38, 39)

'I have not brought misery upon my fellows. I have not made the beginning of every day laborious in the sight of him who worked for me.' (Ancient Egyptian. Confession of the Righteous Soul. ERE v. 478)

'I have not been grasping.' (Ancient Egyptian. Ibid.) 'Who meditates oppression, his dwelling is overturned.' (Babylonian. *Hymn to Samas.* ERE v. 445)

'He who is cruel and calumnious has the character of a cat.' (Hindu. Laws of Manu. Janet, Histoire de la Science Politique, vol. i, p. 6)

'Slander not.' (Babylonian. Hymn to Samas. ERE v. 445)

'Thou shall not bear false witness against thy neighbour.' (Ancient Jewish. Exodus 20:16)

'Utter not a word by which anyone could be wounded.' (Hindu. Janet, p. 7)

'Has he ... driven an honest man from his family? broken up a well cemented clan?' (Babylonian. List of Sins from incantation tablets. ERE v. 446)

'I have not caused hunger. I have not caused weeping.' (Ancient Egyptian. ERE v. 478)

'Never do to others what you would not like them to do to you.' (Ancient Chinese. Analects of Confucius, trans. A. Waley, xv. 23; cf. xii. 2)

'Thou shalt not hate thy brother in thy heart.' (Ancient Jewish. Leviticus 19:17)

'He whose heart is in the smallest degree set upon goodness will dislike no one.' (Ancient Chinese. Analects, iv. 4)

(b) Positive

'Nature urges that a man should wish human society to exist and should wish to enter it.' (Roman. Cicero, De Officiis, i. iv)

'By the fundamental Law of Nature Man [is] to be preserved as much as possible.' (Locke, Treatises of Civil Govt. ii. 3)

'When the people have multiplied, what next should be done for them? The Master said, 'Enrich them.' Jan Ch'iu said, 'When one has enriched them, what next should be done for them?' The Master said, 'Instruct them.' (Ancient Chinese. Analects, xiii. 9)

'Speak kindness ... show good will.' (Babylonian. Hymn to Samas. ERE v. 445)

'Men were brought into existence for the sake of men that they might do one another good.' (Roman. Cicero. De Off. i. vii)

'Man is man's delight.' (Old Norse. Havamal 47)

'He who is asked for alms should always give.' (Hindu. Janet, i. 7)

'What good man regards any misfortune as no concern of his?' (Roman. Juvenal xv. 140)

'I am a man: nothing human is alien to me.' (Roman. Terence, Heaut. Tim.)

'Love thy neighbour as thyself.' (Ancient Jewish. Leviticus 19:18)

'Love the stranger as thyself.' (Ancient Jewish. Ibid. 33, 34)

'Do to men what you wish men to do to you.' (Christian. Matthew 7:12)

The Law of Mercy

'The poor and the sick should be regarded as lords of the atmosphere.' (Hindu. Janet, i. 8)

'Whoso makes intercession for the weak, well pleasing is this to Samas.' (Babylonian. ERE v. 445)

'Has he failed to set a prisoner free?' (Babylonian. List of Sins. ERE v. 446)

'I have given bread to the hungry, water to the thirsty, clothes to the naked, a ferry boat to the boatless.' (Ancient Egyptian. ERE v. 446)

'One should never strike a woman; not even with a flower.' (Hindu. Janet, i. 8)

'There, Thor, you got disgrace, when you beat women.' (Old Norse. Harbarthsljoth 38)

'In the Dalebura tribe a woman, a cripple from birth, was carried about by the tribes-people in turn until her death at the age of sixty-six.'... 'They never desert the sick.' (Australian Aborigines. ERE v. 443)

'You will see them take care of ... widows, orphans, and old men, never reproaching them.' (Redskin. ERE v. 439)

'Nature confesses that she has given to the human race the tenderest hearts, by giving us the power to weep. This is the best part of us.' (Roman. Juvenal, xv. 131)

'They said that he had been the mildest and gentlest of the kings of the world.' (Anglo-Saxon. Praise of the hero in Beowulf, 3180)

'When thou cuttest down thine harvest ... and hast forgot a sheaf ... thou shalt not go again to fetch it: it shall be for the stranger, for the fatherless, and for the widow.' (Ancient Jewish. Deuteronomy 24:19).[28]

These examples (which could be multiplied many times over from other sources) show a basic human awareness across a whole variety of religious and philosophical traditions of what sort of behaviour is required in order for human beings and human society to flourish. It is because this sort of basic awareness exists (something that from a Christian perspective reflects the creation of human beings in the image of God) that the six religious traditions that we have looked at in this report have been able to accept an overall consensus view of human rights on the basis of what their tradition already teaches.

It is certainly true to say that the impetus for the development of the idea of human rights came from the Christian and Jewish traditions, but this development has not been a case of Christian and Jewish ideas simply being adopted by other faiths. It has instead been a case of these other faiths being stimulated to look again at the resources provided by their own tradition and finding there a basis for making a parallel affirmation about what human flourishing involves.

Another way of looking at this would be to say that the production of the Universal Declaration of Human Rights in 1948 stimulated a global interfaith conversation about human flourishing and the duty to support this with each faith making its own distinctive contribution to the conversation.

We have looked at the evidence for this conversation having produced an overall consensus about human rights in the course of this report and further illustrations of this consensus can be seen in the documents from different religious traditions contained in the appendices. However, a good way to sum up the consensus is to say that there is general agreement that in order to flourish in this world and to prepare themselves to flourish in the world to come human beings need:

- Protection of life and person

- Basic necessities such as food, drink, shelter and clothing

- A secure place to live

- Education and health care

- The opportunity to earn a living

- The opportunity to marry and have a family

- Freedom of religion and belief

- Freedom of conscience and speech

Because these eight elements are required to enable human flourishing, religious believers, along with all other human beings, have a responsibility both individually and working with others to see that they are provided.

All the other rights that have been specified in the various human rights documents that have been produced since 1948 can be seen as involving extrapolations from these eight basic needs or saying how they apply in the case of specific groups within society such as migrants, children, or people with disabilities. The idea behind the concept of equality is that because all human beings have these basic needs they should be provided for all without discrimination on the basis of characteristics such as race, gender or religion.

The consensus is a variegated one. As we have seen in the course of this report, there are still differences about human rights both between and within the six religious traditions we have looked at. However, these continuing differences do not negate the consensus that already exists. They simply indicate that the conversation about human flourishing is a continuing one.

Furthermore, the consensus has not just involved a theoretical acceptance of human rights. Religious believers from across the six traditions have sought to respond to the duty to support human rights in a whole variety of practical ways, whether it has been Christians campaigning against torture, Jewish human rights activists seeking to ensure that Israel lives up to its fundamental values, Cambodian Buddhist monks working with a secular human rights NGO to repair the damage done to Cambodian society by the Khmer Rouge, or Sikh human rights activists working to prevent female foeticide in Punjab.

It is also true that there is a dark side to each of the six traditions. People from the Christian, Jewish, Muslim, Hindu, Buddhist and Sikh traditions have been, and still are, engaged in violations of human rights. They have failed to act in ways that make for human flourishing. However, none of the traditions would find this fact surprising. Each of them in their own way is aware that human beings, including human beings who profess religion, have a huge capacity for evil and they would say that it is precisely because such a capacity exists that religion is needed to provide a path of spiritual discipline to enable people to counteract this tendency.

What the existence of the dark side of religion shows, they would say, is not that human beings need to abandon religion, but that they need to receive better religious instruction and need to be more consistent in their religious practice.

8.5 THE HUMAN RIGHTS IMPLICATIONS OF MODELS OF THE RELATIONSHIP BETWEEN RELIGION AND THE STATE

In every society there has to be some kind of relationship between religion and the state. There has been a huge variety of approaches during the course of human history, but four main models can be identified.

1. A state in which only one religion is permitted

There have been many examples of this kind of state down the centuries and from a perspective of a concern with human rights it has both a strength and a weakness. The strength of this model is that the state religion can provide a strong, coherent and universally accepted moral framework which will encourage the citizens of that country to observe the demands of the Tao and so promote human flourishing. The big weakness is that it does not allow any place for freedom of religion and belief.

2. A secular state

In this model the state promotes a purely secular ideology and allows religion either no place, or a highly restricted place, in the public square.

From a religious perspective this model has three big weaknesses. First, it is a dishonest model. It may claim to promote a religiously neutral ideology, but since secular humanism is, as we have seem, itself a form of religion it is not in fact neutral at all. This model is in fact a strong form of religious establishment under another guise.

Secondly, it is a model which can tend to be oppressive towards other forms of religion. As Adhar and Leigh write:

> The secular state model carries with it certain dangers. Separationism in a purely structural sense – where the state and religious bodies qua institutions are kept apart is not so problematic. The 'wall' may serve religion well by protecting it from the tentacles of state interference. Separationism in its ideological form – a strict quarantining of religious ideas and influences from all public institutions and political life – is a different matter. The state here is not so much remaining neutral as adopting a philosophy of its own, namely secularism. Whilst it

is conceivable that secularism can take benign, even-handed forms which welcome religious contributions to the public sphere, the more prevalent tendency, in practice, is for secularism to be hostile to religion. Secularism seldom remains for long as a straightforward state refusal to align itself with, or establish, a particular faith; rather, experience suggests it inexorably develops a commitment to actively pursue a policy of established unbelief. A thoroughgoing privatization of religion by the state, compounded by official endorsement of secular beliefs, denies many faiths the public witness they desire, and indeed are obliged, to make. [29]

Thirdly, a secular ideology which denies the existence of God and/or an objective transcendent moral law fails to provide a strong and coherent basis for identifying what is good for human beings and hence what needs to be done in order to promote human flourishing. In a famous statement in his book *River Out of Eden* the atheist author Richard Dawkins declares:

> The universe we observe has precisely the properties we should expect if there is, at bottom, no design, no purpose, no evil and no good, nothing but blind, pitiless indifference. As that unhappy poet A.E. Housman put it:
> 'For Nature, heartless, witless
> Nature will neither know nor care.'
> DNA neither knows nor cares.
> DNA just is.
> And we dance to its music.[30]

If this view of the universe is accepted then there is no coherent basis for the collective affirmation of human rights or any other vision of human flourishing. As Arthur Leff argues in his celebrated paper 'Unspeakable Ethics, Unnatural Law', in the absence of any transcendent moral authority, any objective standard of good or evil, what is left is the arbitrary choice of either the individual or the state.

Leff's argument is helpfully summarised by Andy Bannister as follows:

> ... [Leff] points out that any moral claims (e.g. 'You *ought* to help old ladies across the road'; 'You *ought not* to poke badgers with a stick';

'Generosity *is* good'; 'Paris Hilton *is* bad') – are authority claims, and to any authority claim we can respond like the school bully or the town drunk and cry, 'Yeah? Sez *who?*' In the absence of God, says Leff, there are but two options: you can turn every individual person into a little godlet, able to decide good and evil for themselves. But then who evaluates between them when there are clashes between godlet claims. Alternatively, you can turn the state into God and let it determine good and evil, but then might becomes right and you have sheer, naked brutality (and what's wrong with government-sponsored brutality, if the state is the only moral authority?). In short, if you try this latter route, morality becomes *meaningless.* If you go down the former route, morality becomes *impossible.* And in either case, whenever another godlet, or the state, tells you that anything is good, right, or the Proper Thing To Do, you can look them squarely in the eye and sneer: 'Really, sez *who?*' Leff ends his essay by pointing out that there is only one solution to this – and that would be if goodness were something *bigger* than us, something outside us. Only then could ethics, morality, and law actually work.

Only if ethics were something unspeakable by us, could law be unnatural and therefore unchallengeable. As things now stand, everything is up for grabs.

Nevertheless:

Napalming babies is bad.
Starving the poor is wicked.
Buying and selling each other is depraved.
Those who stood up to and died resisting Hitler, Stalin, Amin, and Pol Pot – and General Custer too –have earned salvation.
Those who acquiesced deserve to be damned.
There is in the world such a thing as evil.
[All together now:] Sez who?
God help us.[31]

Furthermore, because a secular vision is limited to this world only, it cannot deal with the problem of what we might call the 'deficit of judgement'. What this means is that we live in a world in which the good is never fully achieved and in which those who do evil are often not brought to satisfactory account for the evil they have done (particularly if they are rich and powerful). What the six religions we have looked at in this report can offer is an incentive to nevertheless keep working for the good and rejecting evil on the basis that, if not in this world then in a future state, the judgement of God, or the outworking of Karma, will ensure that the wicked will not escape the consequences of their actions and that good actions will be met with a just reward. In short, they offer hope.

3. A state gives general encouragement to religion, but does not endorse any one particular religious approach

This is the approach traditionally taken in the United States where the First Amendment to the constitution 'Congress shall make no law respecting an establishment of religion' was originally intended, and understood until after World War II, to mean that there would be no national established Church on the European model, not that the state had no interest in encouraging the exercise of religion or that there should be a 'wall of separation' between religion and the state.[32]

This model gives space, and indeed encouragement for the free exercise of religion and belief, but in order to provide the state with a coherent ethos there would need to be a general agreement among the various religious groups as to what makes for human flourishing. However, the history of the United States and the evidence we have looked at in this report show that this general consensus is something that it is not impossible to obtain.

4. One religion is established, but freedom is given for the exercise of other religions and for unbelief

This is the model of modified establishment that developed in Europe and elsewhere from the 19th century with antecedents in earlier periods. This model provides the state with a clear and coherent overall account of what makes for human flourishing while allowing space for dissent and for the free exercise of religion and belief.

This is, of course, the model that we have in England with the establishment of the Church of England. As the author of this report has noted elsewhere, the objection is frequently made that 'in an ecumenical age and in a pluralist society it is wrong for a particular Church and a particular religion to be given a special place in the life of the state.'

However these objections are not persuasive for two reasons. First:

> ...in a divided Church the establishment of the Christian religion necessarily involves the establishment of a particular form or forms of the Christian religion which in this country, for historical reasons, is the Church of England.
>
> Furthermore, aware of its ecumenical obligations, the Church of England seeks to ensure that it undertakes its established role in a way that supports other Christian churches; and in fact the leaders of the other churches often acknowledge that the established status of the Church of England is helpful in lending Christianity a degree of visibility in the public arena that it might not otherwise possess.

Secondly,

> ....England has historically been a Christian nation and ... a large majority of people in this country who are not necessarily regular church attenders nevertheless still see themselves as having an inherited Christian identity. It therefore makes sense for the importance of religion in the life of the nation to be marked by a Christian establishment (in this case, for reasons already noted, the establishment of the Church of England).
>
> In relation to this second response it is important to note that, just as the Church of England exercises its established role on behalf of other churches, it also exercises it on behalf of members of other religions by acting in a way that is helpful to the interests of religion in general as well as Christianity in particular. This is something that is acknowledged by the leaders of other religions who see the establishment of the Church of England as acting as a bulwark against the advent of a secular society in which the importance of religion is no longer given public recognition.[33]

As Michael Nazir Ali has written, 'It is certainly possible for Britain to be both a plural society and a society that acknowledges its Christian basis.'[34] As the example of the Queen's recent Christmas Messages has shown, it is perfectly possible to draw inspiration from the Christian faith for a coherent vision of human flourishing, and to be open about sharing this inspiration with others while at the same time acknowledging and welcoming the contribution made by those of all faiths and none for the development of the common good.

What all this means is that if the Government is really serious about fostering a shared sense of 'British values' and a shared sense of duty and responsibility it should call an end to the attack on religion noted at the beginning of this chapter. Instead it should publicly celebrate this nation's Christian heritage and the way in which this provides a coherent and inspiring vision of human flourishing and work together with the Church of England, other churches, and other faiths to strengthen a common commitment to duties and responsibilities based on the consensus about human rights that has developed since 1948.

In the second half of the eighteenth century and the first half of the nineteenth century the revival of the Christian religion (the Evangelical Revival) was responsible for transforming the face of British society and laying a strong foundation for human flourishing from which we continue to benefit today. Given the opportunity, a revival of religious commitment could have a similar beneficial and transformative effect today and is therefore something that politicians should seek to encourage.

Notes

[1] Brendan O'Neill, 'The New Inquisition', 11.11.2013 at http://brendanoneill.co.uk/post/132996389494/the-new-inquisition.

[2] Ibid.

[3] Ibid.

[4] Rex Adhar and Ian Leigh, *Religious Freedom in the Liberal State*, 2ed, Oxford: OUP, 2015.

[5] See Louis Herkin, 'Religion, Religions and Human Rights', *The Journal of Religious Ethics*, Vol 26, No.2, Fall 1998, pp. 229-239.

[6] *Tackling Extremism in the UK,* London: The Cabinet Office, 2013, p.1.

[7] Ibid., p.5.

[8] Ibid., p.6.

[9] For examples of the concern about these kinds of developments see John Charmley, 'David Cameron's British values agenda is Anti-Christian', *The Catholic Herald*, 13 August 2015, and "UK Christians see danger in Gov'ts 'British Values' Agenda", *Christian Institute*, 28 August 2015 at http://www.christian.org.uk/news/uk-christians-see-danger-in-govts-british-values-agenda/

[10] The Universal Declaration of Human Rights, in Micheline Ishay (ed), *The Human Rights Reader*, New York and London: Routledge, 1997, p.410.

[11] European Convention on Human Rights, Article 9.2, in ibid, p.315.

[12] John Finnis, *Equality and Religious Diversity: Oppressing Conscientious Diversity in England*, p.18.

[13] Ibid., 15-16.

[14] Mary Anne Glendon, *Rights Talk*, New York: Free Press, 1991, pp.171-172.

[15] For this point see Ryan T Anderson, *Truth Overruled: the Future of Marriage and Religious Freedom*, New Jersey: Regnery Publishing, 2015.

[16] Universal Declaration of Human Rights, Preamble, in Ishay (ed), op.cit. p.408.

[17] J M Finnis, *Natural Law and Natural Rights*, Oxford: OUP, 1980, p.205.

[18] Universal Declaration of Human Rights, Article 3, in Ishay (ed), op.cit, p.408.

[19] Article 5, in ibid., p.409.

[20] Article 23, in ibid., p.411.

[21] Lesslie Newbigin, *The Open Secret*, Grand Rapids: Eerdmans, 1978, p.190.

[22] Ibid., p.181.

[23] King, in Witte and Green (eds), op.cit. p.105 quoting Sumner B Twiss, 'A Constructive Framework for Discussing Confucianism and Human Rights', in Theodore de Bary and Tu Weiming, *Confucianism and Human Rights*, New York: Columbia University Press, 1998, pp.35-36.

[24] Charles Taylor, 'Conditions of an Unforced Consensus on Human Rights', in Bauer and Bell, op.cit. pp.124-144.

[25] C S Lewis, *The Abolition of Man*, London: Harper Collins, e-edition, 2009, chapter 2.

[26] Ibid.

[27] Ibid., Appendix, 'Illustrations of the Tao'.

[28] Ibid., Appendix, Sections 1 and 7.

[29] Adhar and Leigh, op.cit. p.123.

[30] Richard Dawkins, *River Out of Eden: A Darwinian View of Life*, New York: Basic Books, 1995, p.133.

[31] Andy Bannister, *The Atheist Who Didn't Exist*, Oxford and Grand Rapids: Monarch, 2015, e-edition, chapter 8, quoting Arthur A Leff, 'Unspeakable Ethics, Unnatural Law', *Duke*

Law Journal, Vol.6, 1979, p.1249. Leff's full essay can be found online at http://bit.ly/leff.

[32] For this point see Michael Novak, *On Two Wings: Humble Faith and Common Sense at the American Founding*, New York and London: Encounter Books 2002.

[33] Martin Davie, *A Guide to the Church of England*, London and New York: Mowbray, 2008, pp.67-68.

[34] Michael Nazir Ali, *The Unique and Universal Christ*, Milton Keynes: Paternoster, 2008, p.16.

APPENDIX 1

World Council of Churches' Statement on Human Rights,
Harare 1998
TOGETHER ON THE WAY[1]

INTRODUCTION

The World Council of Churches has a long history of involvement in the development of international norms and standards, and in the struggle for advancement of human rights. Through its Commission of the Churches on International Affairs, the Council participated in the drafting of the United Nations Declaration on Human Rights, and contributed the text of article 18 on freedom of thought, conscience and religion. The WCC has since been active in promoting the Declaration's implementation.

In preparation for its fifth assembly, the WCC engaged in a global process of consultation to review its fundamental policy on human rights. That review led to a consultation on "Human Rights and Christian Responsibility" in St Pöten, Austria, 1974, which provided guidelines for the policy statement adopted in Nairobi, 1975, placed human rights at the centre of struggles for liberation from poverty, colonial rule, institutionalized racism and military dictatorships, and formulated a comprehensive new ecumenical agenda for action on human rights.

Churches in many parts of the world took up the Nairobi assembly's challenge, addressing human-rights needs in their respective societies more intentionally, engaging often at great risk in costly struggles for human rights under military dictatorships, establishing a global ecumenical network of human-rights solidarity and new forms of active cooperation with the United Nations' Commission on Human Rights and other national and international human-rights organizations. These strategies significantly increased the effectiveness of the ecumenical witness on human rights and had a substantial impact on the development of new international standards.

Anticipating the eighth assembly, the WCC central committee in 1993 called for a new global review of ecumenical human-rights policy and practice to draw lessons from two decades of intensive engagement, to assess emerging challenges arising from the radical changes which had occurred in the world since the Nairobi assembly, and as a means to stimulate new action in churches where human rights had been given a lower priority. Regional consultations and seminars were held, and their reports were drawn together by an international consultation on "Human Rights and the Churches: New Challenges" in Morges, Switzerland, June 1998.

Previous assemblies and ecumenical consultations have developed a theological basis for the churches' engagement in the promotion and defence of human rights:

As Christians, we are called to share in God's mission of justice, peace and respect for all creation and to seek for all humanity the abundant life which God intends. Within scripture, through tradition, and from the many ways in which the spirit illumines our hearts today, we discern God's gift of dignity for each person and their inherent right to acceptance and participation within the community. From this flows the responsibility of the Church, as the body of Christ, to work for universal respect and implementation of human rights (consultation on "Human Rights and the Churches: New Challenges," Morges, Switzerland, June 1998).

Our concern for human rights is based on our conviction that God wills a society in which all can exercise full human rights. All human beings are created in the image of God, equal, and infinitely precious in God's sight and ours. Jesus Christ has bound us to one another by his life, death and resurrection, so that what concerns one concerns us all, (fifth assembly, Nairobi, 1975).

All human beings, regardless of race, sex or belief, have been created by God as individuals and in the human community. Yet, the world has been corrupted by sin, which results in the destruction of human relationships. In reconciling human kind and creation with God, Jesus Christ has also reconciled human beings with each other. Love of our neighbour is the essence of obedience to God (sixth assembly, Vancouver, 1983).

The spirit of freedom and truth moves us to witness to the justice of the kingdom of God and to resist injustice in the world. We manifest the life of the Spirit by striving for the release of those who are captive to sin by standing with the oppressed in their struggle for liberation, justice and peace. Liberated by the Spirit, we are empowered to understand the world from the perspective of the poor and vulnerable and to give ourselves to mission, service and the sharing of resources (seventh assembly, Canberra, 1991).

The eighth assembly of the World Council of Churches, meeting in Harare, Zimbabwe, 3-14 December 1998 therefore adopts the following statement on human rights:

1. We give thanks to God for the gift of life and for the dignity God has bestowed on all in creation.

2. Costly witness

2.1. We recall the engagements and achievements of the churches, ecumenical bodies, and of human-rights defence groups to uphold the sanctity of life, and especially for the costly witness of those who suffered and lost their lives in this struggle.

2.2. The theme of this assembly, "Turn to God - Rejoice in Hope", reinforces our belief in the three-fold structure of Christian faith and life: God turns to us in grace; we respond in faith, acting in love; and we anticipate the coming, final fullness of God's presence in all of creation. We have newly experienced God's call to jubilee, and this leads us to reaffirm our commitment to human rights, to the dignity and worth of the human person created in God's image and infinitely precious in God's sight, and to the equal rights of women and men, of young and old, of all nations and peoples. Deep theological, liturgical and mystical experience of the broad family of Christian traditions teaches us to develop understanding of human rights and freedom in the spirit of faithfulness to God and responsibility before and for the people of God.

2.3. This we do in a spirit of repentance and humility. We are aware of the many shortcomings of the churches' actions for human rights; of our unwillingness or inability to act when people were threatened or suffered; of our failure to stand up for people who have experienced violence and discrimination; of our complicity with the principalities, powers and structures of our time responsible for massive violations of human rights; and of the withdrawal of many churches from work on human rights as a priority of Christian witness. We ask for God to empower us to face the new challenges.

3. Facing the new challenges

3.1. We thank God for the substantial improvements in international standards achieved since the WCC fifth assembly (1975) in such areas as the rights of the child, of women, of Indigenous Peoples, of minorities, of the uprooted; against discrimination, racial violence, persecution, torture, violence against women, including rape as a weapon of war, forced disappearance, extra-judicial executions and the death penalty; in developing new, "third-generation" rights to peace, development, and sustainable communities; and the new recognition of human rights as a component of peace and conflict resolution. In spite of these provisions, major obstacles still exist, hampering the implementation of human-rights standards.

3.2. We recognize the vital importance of the international norms, but we reiterate the conviction of the WCC sixth assembly (1983) that the most pressing need is for the implementation of these standards. Therefore once again, we urge governments to ratify international covenants and conventions on human rights, to include their provisions in national and regional legal standards, and to develop effective mechanisms to implement them at all levels. At the same time we call upon the churches to overcome exclusion and marginalization in their own midst and to provide for full participation in their lives and governance.

3.3. *Globalization and human rights.* This assembly has addressed the pressing new challenges to human rights of peoples, communities and individuals resulting from globalization of the economy, culture and means of communication, including the erosion of the power of the state to defend the rights of persons and groups under its jurisdiction, and the weakening of the authority of the United Nations as a guarantor and promoter of collective approaches to human rights. Globalization threatens the destruction of human community through economic, racial and other forms of exploitation and repression; and to weaken national sovereignty and peoples' right to self-determination. It preys especially on the most vulnerable members of society. Children's rights are often the first to suffer, as seen in the proliferation today of child labourers and the sexual exploitation of minors.

3.4. Globalization also has within it elements which, if effectively used, can counteract its worst effects and provide new opportunities in many spheres of human experience. We urge churches to encourage and participate in strengthened global alliances of people joined in the struggle for human rights as a way to resist and counter the negative trends of globalization. The right of workers to form trade unions, to collective bargaining and to withhold their labour in defence of their interests must be fully guaranteed. Through such means people can forge a future based on respect for human rights, international law and democratic participation.

3.5. *The indivisibility of human rights*. The process of globalization has once again re-emphasized civil and political rights, dividing them from economic, social and cultural rights. We reaffirm the position taken by the WCC fifth assembly that human rights are indivisible. No rights are possible without the basic guarantees for life, including the right to work, to participate in decision-making, to adequate food, to health care, to decent housing, to education for the full development of the human potential, and to a safe environment and the conservation of the earth's resources. At the same time, we reiterate our conviction that the effectiveness of work for collective human rights is to be measured in terms of the relief it gives both to communities and to individual victims of violations, and of the measure of freedom and improvement of the quality of life it offers every person.

3.6. *The politicization of human rights*. We deplore the re-politicization of the international human-rights discourse, especially by the dominant major powers. This practice, common in the East-West confrontation during the cold war, has now extended to engage nations in a global "clash of cultures" between North and South and between East and West. It is marked by selective indignation, and the application of double standards which denigrate the fundamental principles of human rights and threaten the competence, neutrality and credibility of international bodies created under the UN Charter to enforce agreed standards.

3.7. *The universality of human rights.* We reaffirm the universality of human rights as enunciated in the International Bill of Human Rights and the duty of all states, irrespective of national culture or economic and political system, to promote and defend them. These rights are rooted in the histories of many cultures, religion, and traditions, not just those whose role in the UN was dominant when the Universal Declaration was adopted. We recognize that this declaration was accepted as a "standard of achievement", and the application of its principles needs to take into account different historical, cultural and economic contexts. At the same time we reject any attempt by states, national or ethnic groups, to justify the abrogation of, or derogation from, the full range of human rights on the basis of culture, religion, tradition, special socio-economic or security interests.

3.8. *Global ethics and values related to human rights.* Reaffirming our stance that the church cannot surrender the values of the gospel to the ambiguities of progress and technology, we welcome the renewed calls from humanistic and religious circles for the elaboration of shared global principles of social ethics and values. Shared principles must be based on a diversity of experiences and convictions that transcend religious beliefs and work towards a greater solidarity for justice and peace.

3.9. *Human rights and human accountability.* We reaffirm the right and duty of the international community to hold all state and non-state actors accountable for violations of human rights which occur within their jurisdiction or control, or for which they are directly responsible. Corrupt practices are a major evil in our societies. We uphold the right of every person to be protected under the law against corrupt practices. We reiterate our appeal for governments and non-governmental bodies to exercise objectivity in addressing human-rights concerns, to promote and utilize improved international procedures and multilateral mechanisms for promotion and protection of human rights, and where possible, to pursue a non-confrontational, dialogical approach to the universal realization of human rights.

3.10. *Impunity for violations of human rights.* An essential part of post-conflict healing is the pursuit of truth, justice for victims, forgiveness and reconciliation in societies which have suffered systematic violations of human rights. We support the efforts of churches and human-rights groups in such societies in their struggle to overcome impunity for past crimes whose authors have been given official protection from prosecution. Impunity perpetuates injustice, which in turn generates acts of revenge and endless violence, to the extent of genocide, as we have experienced on different occasions throughout this century.

3.11. We support and encourage the churches to engage in further theological reflection and action on the relationship between truth, justice, reconciliation and forgiveness from the perspective of the victims, and to endeavour to replace cultures of impunity with cultures of accountability and justice. Justice for victims must include provisions for reparation, restitution, and for compensation for their losses. In this connection we welcome the agreement to establish the International Criminal Court, which should help the international community in its enforcement of human rights. We urge the churches to promote their governments' prompt ratification of the Rome agreement, and to incorporate acceptance of its jurisdiction in national legislation.

3.12. *Elimination of the death penalty.* The WCC has long stood against the use of the death penalty, but recourse to this ultimate form of punishment is often sought by victims in societies ridden by crime and violence. The churches have a responsibility to inform society at large of the alternatives to such harsh and irreversible penalties, such as rehabilitation of offenders, and of the need for strict adherence to the international rule of law and international human-rights standards related to the treatment of offenders.

3.13. *Human rights and peace-making.* Human rights are the essential basis for a just and durable peace. Failure to respect them often leads to conflict and warfare, and several times during this century it has led to genocide as a result of uncontrolled ethnic, racial or religious hatred. The international community has time and again shown itself incapable of stopping genocide once it has begun. There is an urgent need to learn the lessons of the past, and to set up mechanisms of early intervention when the danger signs appear. The churches are often most well placed to see the impending danger, but they can only help when they themselves are inclusive communities responding to the gospel message of love for one's neighbour, even when the neighbour is one's enemy.

3.14. The inclusion of human rights in efforts to prevent or resolve conflict through peace missions, under UN and other multilateral auspices, is a welcome development. Once conflict has been brought to an end, social and legal structures should be reformed to promote pluralism and peace-building measures among the people. Peace agreements themselves should incorporate standards of international human rights and humanitarian law and their application to such special groups as military forces, law enforcement personnel and security forces should be ensured.

3.15. ***Human rights and human responsibility.*** Human rights and human responsibility go together. The second WCC assembly, Evanston, 1954, stated that God's love for humans "lays upon the Christian conscience a special measure of responsibility for the care of those who are victims of world disorder".

3.16. The first obligation of churches and others concerned about human rights, including states, is to address violations and to improve protections in their own societies. This is the fundamental basis of ecumenical solidarity which moves beyond one's own situation to offer active support for churches and others engaged in the struggle for human rights in their own countries and regions. An essential form of support is to address the root causes of violations which reside in unjust national and international structures or result from external support for repressive regimes.

3.17. *Religious intolerance.* Religion, in our contemporary world, increasingly influences socio-political processes. Many churches actively participate in peace-making activities and calls for justice, bringing a moral dimension to politics. Yet, religion has also become a major contributor to repression and human-rights violations, both within and between nations. Religious symbols and idioms have been manipulated to promote narrow nationalist and sectarian interests and objectives, creating divisions and polarized societies. Powers increasingly tend to appeal to churches and other religious groups to support narrow national, racial or ethnic aims, and to support discriminatory legislation which formalizes religious intolerance. We urge the churches, once again, to give evidence of the universality of the gospel, and to provide a model of tolerance to their own societies and to the world. Religion can and must be a positive force for justice, harmony, peace and reconciliation in human society.

3.18. *Religious freedom as a human right.* We reaffirm the centrality of religious freedom as a fundamental human right. By religious freedom we mean the freedom to have or to adopt a religion or belief of one's choice and freedom, either individually or in community with others, and in public or private to manifest one's religion or belief in worship, observance, practice and teaching.

3.19. This right should never be seen as belonging exclusively to the church. The right to religious liberty is inseparable from other fundamental human rights. No religious community should plead for its own religious liberty without active respect for the faith and basic human rights of others. Religious liberty should never be used to claim privileges. For the church this right is essential so that it can fulfil its responsibility which arises out of the Christian faith. Central to these responsibilities is the obligation to serve the whole community. Religious freedom should also include the right and duty of religious bodies to criticize and confront the ruling powers when necessary on the basis of their religious convictions.

3.20. Religious intolerance and persecution is widespread today, causing serious violations of human rights, and often leading to conflict and massive human suffering. Churches must offer prayers and solidarity in all practical ways to Christians and all other victims of religious persecution.

3.21. *Religious freedom and proselytism.* There can be no derogation from the fundamental human right to religious freedom, but neither is religion a "commodity" to be regulated according to the rules of an unrestricted free market. We affirm the necessity of ecumenical discipline, particularly with reference to countries in difficult transition to democracy, as they experience the invasion of exogenous religious movements and proselytism. We reiterate the opposition of the WCC to the practice of proselytism, and urge member churches to respect the faith and the integrity of sister churches, and to strengthen them in ecumenical fellowship.

3.22. *The rights of women.* Despite the persistent work by national, regional and international women's groups and churches, especially during the Ecumenical Decade of Churches in Solidarity with Women, progress towards effective protection of women's human rights is slow and often inadequate, both within and outside the churches. The defence and promotion of women's rights is not a matter for women alone, but continually requires the active participation of the whole church.

3.23. We affirm that women's rights are human rights, based on our firm conviction that all human beings are made in the image of God and deserve equal rights, protection and care. Aware that violence against women is on the increase all over the world and ranges from racial, economic, cultural, social and political discrimination and sexual harassment, to genital mutilation, rape, trafficking and other inhuman treatment, we call on governments, judicial systems, religious and other institutions to respond with concrete actions to ensure the basic rights of women. The proposed Optional Protocol to the UN Convention on the Elimination of All Forms of Discrimination against Women would provide a mechanism, at the international level, where individual complaints of women's human-rights violations could be received. We urge churches to press their governments for ratification of the protocol.

3.24. *The rights of uprooted people*. Among the chief victims of economic globalization and of the proliferation of conflicts around the world today are the uprooted: refugees, migrants and the internally displaced. The WCC and its member churches have long been at the forefront of advocacy for improved international standards for the protection of the human rights of refugees, asylum-seekers and migrants, and should continue to share resources and to provide global, regional and local networking to show vital solidarity. We urge the churches to continue their cooperation with the UN High Commissioner for Refugees, and to seek further improvements in international standards and their implementation, particularly in respect of the protection of the rights of internally displaced persons, where few enforceable norms currently exist.

3.25. We welcome the launching of the global campaign for entry into force of the International Convention on the Protection of Rights for All Migrant Workers and Members of their Families, and urge the churches to participate in advocacy with their governments for ratification of the convention.

3.26. *Rights of Indigenous Peoples*. We urge the churches to support Indigenous Peoples' right to self-determination with regard to their political and economic future, culture, land rights, spirituality, language, tradition and forms of organization, and to the protection of Indigenous Peoples' knowledge including intellectual property rights.

3.27. *Racism as a violation of human rights*. We acknowledge that racism is a violation of human rights, and recommit ourselves to the struggle to combat racism both individually and institutionally. We urge member churches to strengthen their efforts to remove the scourge of racism from church and society.

3.28. *Rights of people with disabilities*. We reaffirm the right of persons who have special needs because of physical or mental disabilities to equal opportunity in all aspects of the life and service of the church. The cause of such persons is a human-rights issue and should not be understated as charity or a social or health problem, as has often been done. All members and leaders of the churches should respect fully the human rights of persons living with disabilities. This includes full integration into religious activities at all levels and the eradication of physical and psychological barriers which block the way to righteous living. Governments at all levels must also eliminate all barriers to free access and full participation of people with disabilities to public facilities and public life. We welcome the creation of the new network of ecumenical disability advocates and encourage churches to support it.

3.29. *Interfaith cooperation for human rights.* Violations of human rights and injustice cannot be resolved by Christians alone. Collective interfaith efforts are needed to explore shared or complementary spiritual values and traditions that transcend religious and cultural boundaries in the interests of justice and peace in society. We welcome the progress made by the WCC to pursue such a path through interfaith dialogue in a way which respects the specificity of the Christian witness for human rights and encourages the churches, each in their own place, to continue and deepen interfaith dialogue and cooperation for the promotion and protection of human rights.

4. Safeguarding the rights of future generations. Out of concern for the future of all creation, we call for the improvement of international norms and standards with regard to the rights of future generations.

4.1. *Human-rights education.* Churches have more often reacted to the situations of human-rights violations than to be pro-active agents of prevention. We urge the churches to engage more emphatically in preventive measures by initiating and implementing formal and systematic programmes of awareness-building and human-rights education.

4.2. *Peace-building and Human-rights.* Similarly, we urge churches to participate in processes of peace-building through public monitoring, discernment of early signs of violations of human rights and by addressing the root causes.

4.3. *The future.* Central to the WCC's recommitment to the Universal Declaration of Human Rights is a vision of sustainable communities, of a just, moral and ecologically responsible economy. As we look to the future, we recognize that the accomplishment of human rights is only possible through accepting our God-given responsibility to care for one another and the totality of God's creation (Ps. 24).

4.4. We affirm the emphasis of the gospel on the value of all human beings in the sight of God, on the atoning and redeeming work of Christ that has given every person true dignity, on love as the motive for action, and on love for one's neighbour as the practical expression of active faith in Christ. We are members one of another, and when one suffers all are hurt. This is the responsibility Christians bear to ensure the human rights of every person.

Note
[1] Text taken from http://www.wcc-coe.org/wcc/assembly/hr-e.html

APPENDIX 2

Jewish Declaration of Human Rights

McGill International Colloquium on Judaism and Human Rights

Declaration on Judaism and Human Rights[1]

Adopted in Montreal on April 23, 1974

By

- **The Jacob Blaustein Institute for the Advancement of Human Rights of the American Jewish Committee**

- **Canadian Jewish Congress**

- **Consultative Council of Jewish Organizations**

We, the undersigned, gathered in Montreal at the McGill International Colloquium on Judaism and Human Rights, have adopted the declaration that follows.

I.

In the light of the contributions Judaism and the Jewish experience have made to human rights, we affirm:

Human rights are an integral part of the faith and tradition of Judaism. The beliefs that man was created in the divine image, that the human family is one, and that every person is obliged to deal justly with every other person are basic sources of the Jewish commitment to human rights.

The struggles of Jews for freedom from oppression and discrimination in the modern era have helped advance the cause of human rights for all.

Jews and Jewish organizations have significantly aided efforts to secure national and international protection of human rights and freedoms.

We accordingly reaffirm our long-standing dedication to the advancement and protection of fundamental rights and freedoms for all persons.

II.

To all governments and peoples, we commend the following principles and goals:

The Universal Declaration of Human Rights

Brought into being by a joint effort of the nations and reflecting the varied cultures of the world, the Universal Declaration of Human Rights affirms the human rights and fundamental freedoms of all persons. However much nations may vary in their values, needs and priorities, the Declaration remains a universally applicable standard for the conduct of persons and nations.

The Interdependence of Human Rights

Civil and political rights are interdependent with, and indivisible from economic, social and cultural rights. Difficult though it may be to preserve individual civil and political rights under conditions of poverty and deprivation, it must be done; for abandoning or subordinating them will only exacerbate inequality and injustice, without ensuring economic betterment.

The War Against Poverty

Conversely, a reasonable degree of economic well-being is a precondition for the enjoyment of civic and political rights. On these as well as on humanitarian grounds, the distressing disparities in living standards, income distribution and availability of social services within and among nations, and the dire poverty and famine afflicting vast areas of Africa,

Asia and Latin America, oblige all governments to promote, jointly as well as separately, the economic welfare of their people. Affluent nations must help less fortunate peoples through bilateral and multilateral aid programs and equitable trade arrangements.

Progress in Human Rights Law

Continuing development of effective international law is essential to further just relationships between individuals and their governments, among groups within a nation and among the countries of the world.

All nations should adopt bills of rights and make them effective.

All states which have not yet done so should ratify the Convention on the Prevention of Genocide, the Covenants on civil and Political Rights and on Economic, Social and Cultural Rights, the International Convention on the Elimination of Racial Discrimination, and other human rights agreements inspired by the Universal Declaration.

Effective international institutions and procedures should be set up to implement the international law of human rights.

All nations should make the furtherance of human rights an integral element of their foreign policies.

The Integrity of Human Rights Law

Human rights laws should be interpreted in good faith to further the rights they seek to promote. They must be applied impartially, with a single standard for all, and any tendency to apply them restrictively so as to thwart their true purpose, directly or indirectly, must be resisted. Human rights issues should be treated on their merits; they should never be exploited for the extraneous political purposes.

Elimination of Racial, Ethnic and Religious Discrimination

Racism is an evil wherever or by whomever promoted or maintained, and all forms of racial discrimination and hatred deserve condemnation.

The same applies to ethnic hatred, as is recognized by the International

Convention on the Elimination of Racial Discrimination, which outlaws invidious distinctions based on descent and ethnic origins as well as on color and race, and which obligates all states to take immediate measures to eradicate discrimination and hatreds based on such distinctions.

By the same token, discrimination on the basis of religion should be uprooted. An effective human rights instrument against all forms of religious intolerance should be promptly adopted. Attempts to thwart promulgation of such a document should not be allowed to succeed.

United Nations bodies and agencies, Member States of the UN and non-governmental organizations should accelerate their efforts toward eradicating all manifestations of group discrimination and hatred, and should apply a single standard of disapproval to all such violations.

Governments, nongovernmental organizations and educational institutions should support the goals of the Decade of Action to Combat Racism and Racial Discrimination, proclaimed by the United Nations on December 10, 1973. They should cooperate to the best of their ability with this program, so as to help eliminate all forms of injustice based on race or ethnic origin.

The Struggle Against Anti-Semitism

The current manifestation of anti-Semitism in various parts of the world, whether open or under one or another guise, are to be condemned and combated, in keeping with the International Conventions on the Elimination of Racial Discrimination. Vicious libels about Jews and Judaism are being disseminated in some countries, including certain Arab states and the Soviet Union. It is incumbent on all governments, citizen groups and private persons to desist from any anti-Semitic activity and to do all they can to curb it.

The Preservation of Cultures

Many agreements between two or more nations, including the International Covenant on Civil and Political Rights, confirm the right of each of the world as religious, ethnic and linguistic groups to preserve its unique cultural heritage; but this right is often denied in practice. Jewish minorities in particular have suffered grievously from such denials in some countries. All states should undertake or intensify action to safeguard the rights of all groups to their cultures, according to the existing commitments.

III.

We call on the international community to take a stand against the deprivation of rights currently suffered by Jews; deprivation they have undergone again and again in their history.

Today the Soviet Union denies vast numbers of Jews the right to leave, and harasses, abuses or imprisons those who seek to exercise that right. Soviet Jews also are prevented from freely teaching, practicing and preserving their religion and culture. In Syria, Jews are denied the right to leave, discriminated against and cruelly persecuted.

Silence or inaction in the face of such human rights violations is complicity in injustice. The international community must vigorously condemn and combat these violations.

IV.

We call on Jewish communities to preserve and sharpen the traditional sensitivity of the Jewish conscience to the plight of the downtrodden, whoever and wherever they may be. We reaffirm our faith in study, teaching and education as means to advance human rights throughout the world. More than that, we pledge to be advocates and activists for human rights.

We recognize the commitment and the contributions of other religions and peoples to human rights and recall our many joint efforts in that cause. We look forward to continued partnership in seeking to bring the blessings of human rights, fundamental freedoms and human dignity to all mankind.

Nobel Laureate Rene Cassin has eloquently recalled how Jewish leaders throughout the gages and in our own time have upheld the dignity of human beings and championed human rights. We respect and honor their example; we call upon our generation and our children to emulate them.

To labor for the human rights of all peoples has been an integral part of commitment to Judaism throughout our long past. We shall remain faithful to it in the future.

Note
[1] Text from http://hrusa.org/advocacy/community-faith/judaism1.shtm

APPENDIX 3
ISLAMIC DECLARATIONS OF HUMAN RIGHTS

a. The Universal Islamic Declaration of Human Rights[1]

Universal Islamic Declaration of Human Rights
21 Dhul Qaidah 1401 19 September 1981

Contents
Foreword
Preamble
I Right to Life
II Right to Freedom
III Right to Equality and Prohibition Against Impermissible Discrimination
IV Right to Justice
V Right to Fair Trial
VI Right to Protection Against Abuse of Power
VII Right to Protection Against Torture
VIII Right to Protection of Honour and Reputation
IX Right to Asylum
X Rights of Minorities
XI Right and Obligation to Participate in the Conduct and Management of Public Affairs
XII Right to Freedom of Belief, Thought and Speech
XIII Right to Freedom of Religion
XIV Right to Free Association
XV The Economic Order and the Rights Evolving Therefrom
XVI Right to Protection of Property
XVII   Status and Dignity of Workers
XVIII   Right to Social Security
XIX Right to Found a Family and Related Matters
XX Rights of Married Women
XXI Right to Education
XXII Right of Privacy
XXIII Right to Freedom of Movement and Residence
Explanatory Notes
Glossary of Arabic Terms
References

*This is a declaration for mankind, a guidance and instruction to those
who fear God.*
(Al Qur'an, Al-Imran 3:138)

Foreword

Islam gave to mankind an ideal code of human rights fourteen centuries
ago. These rights aim at conferring honour and dignity on mankind and
eliminating exploitation, oppression and injustice.

Human rights in Islam are firmly rooted in the belief that God, and God
alone, is the Law Giver and the Source of all human rights. Due to their
Divine origin, no ruler, government, assembly or authority can curtail or
violate in any way the human rights conferred by God, nor can they be
surrendered.

Human rights in Islam are an integral part of the overall Islamic order
and it is obligatory on all Muslim governments and organs of society to
implement them in letter and in spirit within the framework of that order.

It is unfortunate that human rights are being trampled upon with
impunity in many countries of the world, including some Muslim countries.
Such violations are a matter of serious concern and are arousing the
conscience of more and more people throughout the world.

I sincerely hope that this *Declaration of Human Rights* will give a powerful
impetus to the Muslim peoples to stand firm and defend resolutely and
courageously the rights conferred on them by God.

This *Declaration of Human Rights* is the second fundamental document
proclaimed by the Islamic Council to mark the beginning of the 15th
Century of the Islamic era, the first being the *Universal Islamic Declaration*
announced at the International Conference on The Prophet Muhammad
(peace and blessings be upon him) and his Message, held in London from
12 to 15 April 1980.

The *Universal Islamic Declaration of Human Rights* is based on the Qur'an
and the Sunnah and has been compiled by eminent Muslim scholars, jurists
and representatives of Islamic movements and thought. May God reward
them all for their efforts and guide us along the right path.

Paris 21 Dhul Qaidah 1401 Salem Azzam
19th September 1981 *Secretary General*

O men! Behold, We have created you all out of a male and a female, and have made you into nations and tribes, so that you might come to know one another. Verily, the noblest of you in the sight of God is the one who is most deeply conscious of Him. Behold, God is all-knowing, all aware.
(Al Qur'an, Al-Hujurat 49:13)

Preamble

WHEREAS the age-old human aspiration for a just world order wherein people could live, develop and prosper in an environment free from fear, oppression, exploitation and deprivation, remains largely unfulfilled;

WHEREAS the Divine Mercy unto mankind reflected in its having been endowed with super-abundant economic sustenance is being wasted, or unfairly or unjustly withheld from the inhabitants of the earth;

WHEREAS Allah (God) has given mankind through His revelations in the Holy Qur'an and the Sunnah of His Blessed Prophet Muhammad an abiding legal and moral framework within which to establish and regulate human institutions and relationships;

WHEREAS the human rights decreed by the Divine Law aim at conferring dignity and honour on mankind and are designed to eliminate oppression and injustice;

WHEREAS by virtue of their Divine source and sanction these rights can neither be curtailed, abrogated or disregarded by authorities, assemblies or other institutions, nor can they be surrendered or alienated;

Therefore we, as Muslims, who believe

a) in God, the Beneficent and Merciful, the Creator, the Sustainer, the Sovereign, the sole Guide of mankind and the Source of all Law;

b) in the Vicegerency (Khilafah) of man who has been created to fulfill the Will of God on earth;

c) in the wisdom of Divine guidance brought by the Prophets, whose mission found its culmination in the final Divine message that was conveyed by the Prophet Muhammad (Peace be upon him) to all mankind;

d) that rationality by itself without the light of revelation from God can neither be a sure guide in the affairs of mankind nor provide spiritual nourishment to the human soul, and, knowing that the teachings of Islam represent the quintessence of Divine guidance in its final and perfect form, feel duty-bound to remind man of the high status and dignity bestowed on him by God;

e) in inviting all mankind to the message of Islam;

f) that by the terms of our primeval covenant with God our duties and obligations have priority over our rights, and that each one of us is under a bounden duty to spread the teachings of Islam by word, deed, and indeed in all gentle ways, and to make them effective not only in our individual lives but also in the society around us;

g) in our obligation to establish an Islamic order:

i) wherein all human beings shall be equal and none shall enjoy a privilege or suffer a disadvantage or discrimination by reason of race, colour, sex, origin or language;

ii) wherein all human beings are born free;

iii) wherein slavery and forced labour are abhorred;

iv) wherein conditions shall be established such that the institution of family shall be preserved, protected and honoured as the basis of all social life;

v) wherein the rulers and the ruled alike are subject to, and equal before, the Law;

vi) wherein obedience shall be rendered only to those commands that are in consonance with the Law;

vii) wherein all worldly power shall be considered as a sacred trust, to be exercised within the limits prescribed by the Law and in a manner approved by it, and with due regard for the priorities fixed by it;

viii) wherein all economic resources shall be treated as Divine blessings bestowed upon mankind, to be enjoyed by all in accordance with the rules and the values set out in the Qur'an and the Sunnah;

ix) wherein all public affairs shall be determined and conducted, and the authority to administer them shall be exercised after mutual consultation *(Shura)* between the believers qualified to contribute to a decision which would accord well with the Law and the public good;

x) wherein everyone shall undertake obligations proportionate to his capacity and shall be held responsible pro rata for his deeds;

xi) wherein everyone shall, in case of an infringement of his rights, be assured of appropriate remedial measures in accordance with the Law;

xii) wherein no one shall be deprived of the rights assured to him by the Law except by its authority and to the extent permitted by it;

xiii) wherein every individual shall have the right to bring legal action against anyone who commits a crime against society as a whole or against any of its members;

xiv) wherein every effort shall be made to

(a) secure unto mankind deliverance from every type of exploitation, injustice and oppression,

(b) ensure to everyone security, dignity and liberty in terms set out and by methods approved and within the limits set by the Law;

Do hereby, as servants of Allah and as members of the Universal Brotherhood of Islam, at the beginning of the Fifteenth Century of the Islamic Era, affirm our commitment to uphold the following inviolable and inalienable human rights that we consider are enjoined by Islam.

I Right to Life

a) Human life is sacred and inviolable and every effort shall be made to protect it. In particular no one shall be exposed to injury or death, except under the authority of the Law.

b) Just as in life, so also after death, the sanctity of a person's body shall be inviolable. It is the obligation of believers to see that a deceased person's body is handled with due solemnity.

II Right to Freedom

a) Man is born free. No inroads shall be made on his right to liberty except under the authority and in due process of the Law.

b) Every individual and every people has the inalienable right to freedom in all its forms¾ physical, cultural, economic and political — and shall be entitled to struggle by all available means against any infringement or abrogation of this right; and every oppressed individual or people has a legitimate claim to the support of other individuals and/ or peoples in such a struggle.

III Right to Equality and Prohibition Against Impermissible Discrimination

a) All persons are equal before the Law and are entitled to equal opportunities and protection of the Law.

b) All persons shall be entitled to equal wage for equal work.

c) No person shall be denied the opportunity to work or be discriminated against in any manner or exposed to greater physical risk by reason of religious belief, colour, race, origin, sex or language.

IV Right to Justice

a) Every person has the right to be treated in accordance with the Law, and only in accordance with the Law.

b) Every person has not only the right but also the obligation to protest against injustice; to recourse to remedies provided by the Law in respect of any unwarranted personal injury or loss; to self-defence against any charges that are preferred against him and to obtain fair adjudication before an independent judicial tribunal in any dispute with public authorities or any other person.

c) It is the right and duty of every person to defend the rights of any other person and the community in general *(Hisbah)*.

d) No person shall be discriminated against while seeking to defend private and public rights.

e) It is the right and duty of every Muslim to refuse to obey any command which is contrary to the Law, no matter by whom it may be issued.

V Right to Fair Trial

a) No person shall be adjudged guilty of an offence and made liable to punishment except after proof of his guilt before an independent judicial tribunal.

b) No person shall be adjudged guilty except after a fair trial and after reasonable opportunity for defence has been provided to him.

c) Punishment shall be awarded in accordance with the Law, in proportion to the seriousness of the offence and with due consideration of the circumstances under which it was committed.

d) No act shall be considered a crime unless it is stipulated as such in the clear wording of the Law.

e) Every individual is responsible for his actions. Responsibility for a crime cannot be vicariously extended to other members of his family or group, who are not otherwise directly or indirectly involved in the commission of the crime in question.

VI Right to Protection Against Abuse of Power

Every person has the right to protection against harassment by official agencies. He is not liable to account for himself except for making a defence to the charges made against him or where he is found in a situation wherein a question regarding suspicion of his involvement in a crime could be *reasonably* raised

VII Right to Protection Against Torture

No person shall be subjected to torture in mind or body, or degraded, or threatened with injury either to himself or to anyone related to or held dear by him, or forcibly made to confess to the commission of a crime, or forced to consent to an act which is injurious to his interests.

VIII Right to Protection of Honour and Reputation

Every person has the right to protect his honour and reputation against calumnies, groundless charges or deliberate attempts at defamation and blackmail.

IX Right to Asylum

a) Every persecuted or oppressed person has the right to seek refuge and asylum. This right is guaranteed to every human being irrespective of race, religion, colour and sex.

b) Al Masjid Al Haram (the sacred house of Allah) in Mecca is a sanctuary for all Muslims.

X Rights of Minorities

a) The Qur'anic principle "There is no compulsion in religion" shall govern the religious rights of non-Muslim minorities.

b) In a Muslim country religious minorities shall have the choice to be governed in respect of their civil and personal matters by Islamic Law, or by their own laws.

XI Right and Obligation to Participate in the Conduct and Management of Public Affairs

a) Subject to the Law, every individual in the community *(Ummah)* is entitled to assume public office.

b) Process of free consultation *(Shura)* is the basis of the administrative relationship between the government and the people. People also have the right to choose and remove their rulers in accordance with this principle.

XII Right to Freedom of Belief, Thought and Speech

a) Every person has the right to express his thoughts and beliefs so long as he remains within the limits prescribed by the Law. No one, however, is entitled to disseminate falsehood or to circulate reports which may outrage public decency, or to indulge in slander, innuendo or to cast defamatory aspersions on other persons.

b) Pursuit of knowledge and search after truth is not only a right but a duty of every Muslim.

c) It is the right and duty of every Muslim to protest and strive (within the limits set out by the Law) against oppression even if it involves challenging the highest authority in the state.

d) There shall be no bar on the dissemination of information provided it does not endanger the security of the society or the state and is confined within the limits imposed by the Law.

e) No one shall hold in contempt or ridicule the religious beliefs of others or incite public hostility against them; respect for the religious feelings of others is obligatory on all Muslims.

XIII Right to Freedom of Religion

Every person has the right to freedom of conscience and worship in accordance with his religious beliefs.

XIV Right to Free Association

a) Every person is entitled to participate individually and collectively in the religious, social, cultural and political life of his community and to establish institutions and agencies meant to enjoin what is right *(ma'roof)* and to prevent what is wrong *(munkar).*

b) Every person is entitled to strive for the establishment of institutions whereunder an enjoyment of these rights would be made possible. Collectively, the community is obliged to establish conditions so as to allow its members full development of their personalities.

XV The Economic Order and the Rights Evolving Therefrom

a) In their economic pursuits, all persons are entitled to the full benefits of nature and all its resources. These are blessings bestowed by God for the benefit of mankind as a whole.

b) All human beings are entitled to earn their living according to the Law.

c) Every person is entitled to own property individually or in association with others. State ownership of certain economic resources in the public interest is legitimate.

d) The poor have the right to a prescribed share in the wealth of the rich, as fixed by Zakah, levied and collected in accordance with the Law.

e) All means of production shall be utilised in the interest of the community *(Ummah)* as a whole, and may not be neglected or misused.

f) In order to promote the development of a balanced economy and to protect society from exploitation, Islamic Law forbids monopolies, unreasonable restrictive trade practices, usury, the use of coercion in the making of contracts and the publication of misleading advertisements.

g) All economic activities are permitted provided they are not detrimental to the interests of the community *(Ummah)* and do not violate Islamic laws and values.

XVI Right to Protection of Property

No property may be expropriated except in the public interest and on payment of fair and adequate compensation.

XVII Status and Dignity of Workers

Islam honours work and the worker and enjoins Muslims not only to treat the worker justly but also generously. He is not only to be paid his earned wages promptly, but is also entitled to adequate rest and leisure.

XVIII Right to Social Security

Every person has the right to food, shelter, clothing, education and medical care consistent with the resources of the community. This obligation of the community extends in particular to all individuals who cannot take care of themselves due to some temporary or permanent disability.

XIX Right to Found a Family and Related Matters

a) Every person is entitled to marry, to found a family and to bring up children in conformity with his religion, traditions and culture. Every spouse is entitled to such rights and privileges and carries such obligations as are stipulated by the Law.

b) Each of the partners in a marriage is entitled to respect and consideration from the other.

c) Every husband is obligated to maintain his wife and children according to his means.

d) Every child has the right to be maintained and properly brought up by its parents, it being forbidden that children are made to work at an early age or that any burden is put on them which would arrest or harm their natural development.

e) If parents are for some reason unable to discharge their obligations towards a child it becomes the responsibility of the community to fulfil these obligations at public expense.

f) Every person is entitled to material support, as well as care and protection, from his family during his childhood, old age or incapacity. Parents are entitled to material support as well as care and protection from their children.

g) Motherhood is entitled to special respect, care and assistance on the part of the family and the public organs of the community *(Ummah)*.

h) Within the family, men and women are to share in their obligations and responsibilities according to their sex, their natural endowments, talents and inclinations, bearing in mind their common responsibilities toward their progeny and their relatives.

i) No person may be married against his or her will, or lose or suffer diminution of legal personality on account of marriage.

XX Rights of Married Women

Every married woman is entitled to:

a) live in the house in which her husband lives;

b) receive the means necessary for maintaining a standard of living which is not inferior to that of her spouse, and, in the event of divorce, receive during the statutory period of waiting *(iddah)* means of maintenance commensurate with her husband's resources, for herself as well as for the children she nurses or keeps, irrespective of her own financial status, earnings, or property that she may hold in her own rights;

c) seek and obtain dissolution of marriage *(Khul'a)* in accordance with the terms of the Law. This right is in addition to her right to seek divorce through the courts.

d) inherit from her husband, her parents, her children and other relatives according to the Law;

e) strict confidentiality from her spouse, or ex-spouse if divorced, with regard to any information that he may have obtained about her, the disclosure of which could prove detrimental to her interests. A similar responsibility rests upon her in respect of her spouse or ex-spouse.

XXI Right to Education

a) Every person is entitled to receive education in accordance with his natural capabilities.

b) Every person is entitled to a free choice of profession and career and to the opportunity for the full development of his natural endowments.

XXII Right of Privacy

Every person is entitled to the protection of his privacy.

XXIII Right to Freedom of Movement and Residence

a) In view of the fact that the World of Islam is veritably *Ummah Islamia,* every Muslim shall have the right to freely move in and out of any Muslim country.

b) No one shall be forced to leave the country of his residence, or be arbitrarily deported therefrom without recourse to due process of Law.

Explanatory Notes

1 In the above formulation of Human Rights, unless the context provides otherwise:

a) the term 'person' refers to both the male and female sexes.

b) the term 'Law' denotes the *Shari'ah*, i.e. the totality of ordinances derived from the Qur'an and the Sunnah and any other laws that are deduced from these two sources by methods considered valid in Islamic jurisprudence.

2 Each one of the Human Rights enunciated in this declaration

carries a corresponding duty.

3 In the exercise and enjoyment of the rights referred to above every person shall be subject only to such limitations as are enjoined by the Law for the purpose of securing the due recognition of, and respect for, the rights and the freedom of others and of meeting the just requirements of morality, public order and the general welfare of the Community *(Ummah)*.

The Arabic text of this *Declaration* is the original.

Glossary of Arabic Terms

SUNNAH - The example or way of life of the Prophet (peace be upon him), embracing what he said, did or agreed to.

KHALIFAH - The vicegerency of man on earth or succession to the Prophet, transliterated into English as the Caliphate.

HISBAH- Public vigilance, an institution of the Islamic State enjoined to observe and facilitate the fulfillment of right norms of public behaviour. The "Hisbah" consists in public vigilance as well as an opportunity to private individuals to seek redress through it.

MA'ROOF - Good act.

MUNKAR - Reprehensible deed.

ZAKAH - The 'purifying' tax on wealth, one of the five pillars of Islam obligatory on Muslims.

'IDDAH - The waiting period of a widowed or divorced woman during which she is not to re-marry.

KHUL'A - Divorce a woman obtains at her own request.

UMMAH ISLAMIA - World Muslim community.

SHARI'AH - Islamic law.

References

Note: The Roman numerals refer to the topics in the text. The Arabic numerals refer to the Chapter and the Verse of the Qur'an, i.e. 5:32 means Chapter 5, Verse 32.

I   1 Qur'an Al-Maidah *5:32*
          2 Hadith narrated by Muslim, Abu Daud, Tirmidhi, Nasai
          3 Hadith narrated by Bukhari

II   4 Hadith narrated by Bukhari, Muslim
          5 Sayings of Caliph Umar
          6 Qur'an As-Shura *42:41*
          7 Qur'an Al-Hajj *22:41*

III   8 From the Prophet's address
          9 Hadith narrated by Bukhari, Muslim, Abu Daud, Tirmidhi, Nasai
          10 From the address of Caliph Abu Bakr
          11 From the Prophet's farewell address
          12 Qur'an Al-Ahqaf *46:19*
          13 Hadith narrated by Ahmad
          14 Qur'an Al-Mulk *67:15*
          15 Qur'an Al-Zalzalah 99:7-8

IV   16 Qur'an An-Nisa *4:59*
          17 Qur'an Al-Maidah *5:49*
          18 Qur'an An-Nisa *4:148*
          19 Hadith narrated by Bukhari, Muslim, Tirmidhi
          20 Hadith narrated by Bukhari, Muslim
          21 Hadith narrated by Muslim, Abu Daud, Tirmdhi, Nasai
          22 Hadith narrated by Bukhari, Muslim, Abu Daud, Tirmidhi, Nasai
          23 Hadith narrated by Abu Daud, Tirmidhi
          24 Hadith narrated by Bukhari, Muslim, Abu Daud, Tirmidhi, Nasai
          25 Hadith narrated by Bukhari

V   26 Hadith narrated by Bukhari, Muslim
          27 Qur'an Al-Isra *17:15*
          28 Qur'an Al-Ahzab *33:5*

29 Qur'an Al-Hujurat *49:6*
30 Qur'an An-Najm *53:28*
31 Qur'an Al Baqarah *2:229*
32 Hadith narrated by Al Baihaki, Hakim
33 Qur'an Al-Isra *17:15*
34 Qur'an At-Tur *52:21*
35 Qur'an Yusuf *12:79*
VI   *36 Qur'an Al Ahzab 33:58*
VII   37 Hadith narrated by Bukhari, Muslim, Abu Daud, Tirmidhi, Nasai
38 Hadith narrated by Ibn Majah
VIII   39 From the Prophet's farewell address
40 Qur'an Al-Hujurat *49:12*
41 Qur'an Al-Hujurat *49:11*
IX   *42 Qur'an At-Tawba 9:6*
43 Qur'an Al-Imran *3:97*
44 Qur'an Al-Baqarah *2:125*
45 Qur'an Al-Hajj *22:25*
X   *46 Qur'an Al Baqarah 2:256*
47 Qur'an Al-Maidah 5:42
48 Qur'an Al-Maidah 5:43
49 Qur'an Al-Maidah 5:47
XI   *50 Qur'an As-Shura 42:38*
51 Hadith narated by Ahmad
52 From the address of Caliph Abu Bakr
XII   53 Qur'an Al-Ahzab *33:60-61*
54 Qur'an Saba *34:46*
55 Hadith narrated by Tirmidhi, Nasai
56 Qur'an An-Nisa *4:83*
57 Qur'an Al-Anam 6:108
XIII   58 Qur'an Al Kafirun *109:6*
XIV   59 Qur'an Yusuf *12:108*
60 Qur'an Al-Imran 3:104
61 Qur'an Al-Maidah 5:2
62 Hadith narrated by Abu Daud, Tirmidhi,Nasai, Ibn Majah
XV   63 Qur'an Al-Maidah *5:120*

64 Qur'an Al-Jathiyah 45:13
65 Qur'an Ash-Shuara 26:183
66 Qur'an Al-Isra 17:20
67 Qur'an Hud 11:6
68 Qur'an Al-Mulk 67:15
69 Qur'an An-Najm 53:48
70 Qur'an Al-Hashr 59:9
71 Qur'an Al-Maarij 70:24-25
72 Sayings of Caliph Abu Bakr
73 Hadith narrated by Bukhari, Muslim
74 Hadith narrated by Muslim
75 Hadith narrated by Muslim, Abu Daud, Tirmidhi, Nasai
76 Hadith narrated by Bukhari, Muslim, Abu Daud, Tirmidhi, Nasai
77 Qur'an Al-Mutaffifin 83:1-3
78 Hadith narrated by Muslim
79 Qur'an Al-Baqarah 2:275
80 Hadith narrated by Bukhari, Muslim, Abu Daud, Tirmidhi, Nasai

XVI 81 Qur'an Al Baqarah *2:188*
82 Hadith narrated by Bukhari
83 Hadith narrated by Muslim
84 Hadith narrated by Muslim, Tirmidhi

XVII 85 Qur'an At-Tawbah *9:105*
86 Hadith narrated by Abu Yala-Majma Al Zawaid
87 Hadith narrated by Ibn Majah
88 Qur'an Al-Ahqaf 46:19
89 Qur'an At-Tawbah 9:105
90 Hadith narrated by Tabarani-Majma Al Zawaid
91 Hadith narrated by Bukhari

XVIII 92 Qur'an Al-Ahzab *33:6*
XIX 93 Qur'an An-Nisa *4:1*
94 Qur'an Al-Baqarah 2:228
95 Hadith narrated by Bukhari, Muslim, Abu Daud, Tirmidhi, Nasai
96 Qur'an Ar-Rum 30:21

97 Qur'an At-Talaq 65:7
98 Qur'an Al-Isra 17:24
99 Hadith narrated by Bukhari, Muslim,Abu Daud, Tirmidhi
100 Hadith narrated by Abu Daud
101 Hadith narrated by Bukhari, Muslim
102 Hadith narrated by Abu Daud, Tirmidhi
103 Hadith narrated by Ahmad, Abu Daud
XX   104 Qur'an At-Talaq 65:6
105 Qur'an An-Nisa 4:34
106 Qur'an At-Talaq 65:6
107 Qur'an AtTalaq 65:6
108 Qur'an Al-Baqarah 2:229
109 Qur'an An-Nisa 4:12
110 Qur'an Al-Baqarah 2:237
XXI   111 Qur'an Al-Isra 17:23-24
112 Hadith narrated by Ibn Majah
113 Qur'an Al-Imran 3:187
114 From the Prophet's farewell address
115 Hadith narrated by Bukhari, Muslim
116 Hadith narrated by Bukhari, Muslim,Abu Daud, Tirmidhi
XXII   117 Hadith narrated by Muslim
118 Qur'an Al-Hujurat 49:12
119 Hadith narrated by Abu Daud, Tirmidhi
XXIII 120 Qur'an Al-Mulk 67:15
121 Qur'an Al-Anam 6:11
122 Qur'an An-Nisa 4:97
123 Qur'an Al-Baqarah 2:217
124 Qur'an Al-Hashr 59:9

b. The Cairo declaration on Islam and Human Rights[2]

Cairo Declaration on Human Rights in Islam,Aug. 5, 1990, U.N. GAOR, World Conf. on Hum. Rts., 4th Sess., Agenda Item 5,

U.N. Doc. A/CONF.157/PC/62/Add.18 (1993) [English translation]

The Nineteenth Islamic Conference of Foreign Ministers (Session of Peace, Interdependence and Development), held in Cairo, Arab Republic of Egypt, from 9-14 Muharram 1411H (31 July to 5 August 1990),

Keenly aware of the place of mankind in Islam as vicegerent of Allah on Earth;

Recognizing the importance of issuing a Document on Human Rights in Islam that will serve as a guide for Member states in all aspects of life;

Having examined the stages through which the preparation of this draft Document has so far, passed and the relevant report of the Secretary General;

Having examined the Report of the Meeting of the Committee of Legal Experts held in Tehran from 26 to 28 December, 1989;

Agrees to issue the Cairo Declaration on Human Rights in Islam that will serve as a general guidance for Member States in the Field of human rights.

Reaffirming the civilizing and historical role of the Islamic Ummah which Allah made as the best community and which gave humanity a universal and well-balanced civilization, in which harmony is established between hereunder and the hereafter, knowledge is combined with faith, and to fulfill the expectations from this community to guide all humanity which is confused because of different and conflicting beliefs and ideologies and to provide solutions for all chronic problems of this materialistic civilization.

In contribution to the efforts of mankind to assert human rights, to protect man from exploitation and persecution, and to affirm his freedom and right to a dignified life in accordance with the Islamic Shari'ah.

Convinced that mankind which has reached an advanced stage in materialistic science is still, and shall remain, in dire need of faith to support its civilization as well as a self motivating force to guard its rights;

Believing that fundamental rights and freedoms according to Islam are an integral part of the Islamic religion and that no one shall have the right as a matter of principle to abolish them either in whole or in part or to violate or ignore them in as much as they are binding divine commands, which are contained in the Revealed Books of Allah and which were sent through the last of His Prophets to complete the preceding divine messages and that safeguarding those fundamental rights and freedoms is an act of worship whereas the neglect or violation thereof is an abominable sin, and that the safeguarding of those fundamental rights and freedom is an individual responsibility of every person and a collective responsibility of the entire Ummah;

Do hereby and on the basis of the above-mentioned principles declare as follows:

ARTICLE 1:

(a) All human beings form one family whose members are united by their subordination to Allah and descent from Adam. All men are equal in terms of basic human dignity and basic obligations and responsibilities, without any discrimination on the basis of race, colour, language, belief, sex, religion, political affiliation, social status or other considerations. The true religion is the guarantee for enhancing such dignity along the path to human integrity.

(b) All human beings are Allah's subjects, and the most loved by Him are those who are most beneficial to His subjects, and no one has superiority over another except on the basis of piety and good deeds.

ARTICLE 2:

(a) Life is a God-given gift and the right to life is guaranteed to every human being. It is the duty of individuals, societies and states to safeguard this right against any violation, and it is prohibited to take away life except for a shari'ah prescribed reason.

(b) It is forbidden to resort to any means which could result in the genocidal annihilation of mankind.

(c) The preservation of human life throughout the term of time willed by Allah is a duty prescribed by Shari'ah.

(d) Safety from bodily harm is a guaranteed right. It is the duty of the state to safeguard it, and it is prohibited to breach it without a Shari'ah-prescribed reason.

ARTICLE 3:

In the event of the use of force and in case of armed conflict, it is not permissible to kill non-belligerents such as old men, women and children. The wounded and the sick shall have the right to medical treatment; and prisoners of war shall have the right to be fed, sheltered and clothed. It is prohibited to mutilate or dismember dead bodies. It is required to exchange prisoners of war and to arrange visits or reunions of families separated by circumstances of war.

(b) It is prohibited to cut down trees, to destroy crops or livestock, to destroy the enemy's civilian buildings and installations by shelling, blasting or any other means.

ARTICLE 4:

Every human being is entitled to human sanctity and the protection of one's good name and honour during one's life and after one's death. The state and the society shall protect one's body and burial place from desecration.

ARTICLE 5:

(a) The family is the foundation of society, and marriage is the basis of making a family. Men and women have the right to marriage, and no restrictions stemming from race, colour or nationality shall prevent them from exercising this right.

(b) The society and the State shall remove all obstacles to marriage and facilitate it, and shall protect the family and safeguard its welfare.

ARTICLE 6:

(a) Woman is equal to man in human dignity, and has her own rights to enjoy as well as duties to perform, and has her own civil entity and financial independence, and the right to retain her name and lineage.

(b) The husband is responsible for the maintenance and welfare of the family.

ARTICLE 7:

(a) As of the moment of birth, every child has rights due from the parents, the society and the state to be accorded proper nursing, education and material, hygienic and moral care. Both the fetus and the mother must be safeguarded and accorded special care.

(b) Parents and those in such like capacity have the right to choose the type of education they desire for their children, provided they take into consideration the interest and future of the children in accordance with ethical values and the principles of the Shari'ah.

(c) Both parents are entitled to certain rights from their children, and relatives are entitled to rights from their kin, in accordance with the tenets of the shari'ah.

ARTICLE 8:

Every human being has the right to enjoy a legitimate eligibility with all its prerogatives and obligations in case such eligibility is lost or impaired, the person shall have the right to be represented by his/her guardian.

ARTICLE 9:

(a) The seeking of knowledge is an obligation and provision of education is the duty of the society and the State. The State shall ensure the availability of ways and means to acquire education and shall guarantee its diversity in the interest of the society so as to enable man to be acquainted with the religion of Islam and uncover the secrets of the Universe for the benefit of mankind.

b) Every human being has a right to receive both religious and worldly education from the various institutions of teaching, education and guidance, including the family, the school, the university, the media, etc., and in such an integrated and balanced manner that would develop human personality, strengthen man's faith in Allah and promote man's respect to and defence of both rights and obligations.

ARTICLE 10:

Islam is the religion of true unspoiled nature. It is prohibited to exercise any form of pressure on man or to exploit his poverty or ignorance in order to force him to change his religion to another religion or to atheism.

ARTICLE 11:

(a) Human beings are born free, and no one has the right to enslave, humiliate, oppress or exploit them, and there can be no subjugation but to Allah the Almighty.

(b) Colonialism of all types being one of the most evil forms of enslavement is totally prohibited. Peoples suffering from colonialism have the full right to freedom and self-determination. It is the duty of all States peoples to support the struggle of colonized peoples for the liquidation of all forms of and occupation, and all States and peoples have the right to preserve their independent identity and econtrol over their wealth and natural resources.

ARTICLE 12:

Every man shall have the right, within the framework of the Shari'ah, to free movement and to select his place of residence whether within or outside his country and if persecuted, is entitled to seek asylum in another country. The country of refuge shall be obliged to provide protection to the asylum-seeker until his safety has been attained, unless asylum is motivated by committing an act regarded by the Shari'ah as a crime.

ARTICLE 13:

Work is a right guaranteed by the State and the Society for each person with capability to work. Everyone shall be free to choose the work that suits him best and which serves his interests as well as those of the society. The employee shall have the right to enjoy safety and security as well as all other social guarantees. He may not be assigned work beyond his capacity nor shall he be subjected to compulsion or exploited or harmed in any way. He shall be entitled - without any discrimination between males and females - to fair wages for his work without delay, as well as to the holidays allowances and promotions which he deserves. On his part, he shall be required to be dedicated and meticulous in his work. Should workers and employers disagree on any matter, the State shall intervene to settle the dispute and have the grievances redressed, the rights confirmed and justice enforced without bias.

ARTICLE 14:

Everyone shall have the right to earn a legitimate living without monopolization, deceit or causing harm to oneself or to others. Usury (riba) is explicitly prohibited.

ARTICLE 15:

(a) Everyone shall have the right to own property acquired in a legitimate way, and shall be entitled to the rights of ownership without prejudice to oneself, others or the society in general. Expropriation is not permissible except for requirements of public interest and upon payment of prompt and fair compensation.

(b) Confiscation and seizure of property is prohibited except for a necessity dictated by law.

ARTICLE 16:

Everyone shall have the right to enjoy the fruits of his scientific, literary, artistic or technical labour of which he is the author; and he shall have the right to the protection of his moral and material interests stemming therefrom, provided it is not contrary to the principles of the Shari'ah.

ARTICLE 17:

(a) Everyone shall have the right to live in a clean environment, away from vice and moral corruption, that would favour a healthy ethical development of his person and it is incumbent upon the State and society in general to afford that right.

(b) Everyone shall have the right to medical and social care, and to all public amenities provided by society and the State within the limits of their available resources.

(c) The States shall ensure the right of the individual to a decent living that may enable him to meet his requirements and those of his dependents, including food, clothing, housing, education, medical care and all other basic needs.

ARTICLE 18:

(a) Everyone shall have the right to live in security for himself, his religion, his dependents, his honour and his property.

(b) Everyone shall have the right to privacy in the conduct of his private affairs, in his home, among his family, with regard to his property and his relationships. It is not permitted to spy on him, to place him under surveillance or to besmirch his good name. The State shall protect him from arbitrary interference.

(c) A private residence is inviolable in all cases. It will not be entered without permission from its inhabitants or in any unlawful manner, nor shall it be demolished or confiscated and its dwellers evicted.

ARTICLE 19:

(a) All individuals are equal before the law, without distinction between the ruler and the ruled.

(b) The right to resort to justice is guaranteed to everyone.

(c) Liability is in essence personal.

(d) There shall be no crime or punishment except as provided for in the Shari'ah.

(e) A defendant is innocent until his guilt is proven in a fast trial in which he shall be given all the guarantees of defence.

ARTICLE 20:

It is not permitted without legitimate reason to arrest an individual, or restrict his freedom, to exile or to punish him. It is not permitted to subject him to physical or psychological torture or to any form of maltreatment, cruelty or indignity. Nor is it permitted to subject an individual to medical or scientific experiments without hisconsent or at the risk of his health or of his life. Nor is it permitted to promulgate emergency laws that would provide executive authority for such actions.

ARTICLE 21:

Taking hostages under any form or for any purpose is expressly forbidden.

ARTICLE 22:

(a) Everyone shall have the right to express his opinion freely in such manner as would not be contrary to the principles of the Shari'ah.

1. Everyone shall have the right to advocate what is right, and propagate what is good, and warn against what is wrong and evil according to the norms of Islamic Shari'ah.

(c) Information is a vital necessity to society. It may not be exploited or misused in such a way as may violate sanctities and the dignity of Prophets, undermine moral and ethical Values or disintegrate, corrupt or harm society or weaken its faith.

(d) It is not permitted to excite nationalistic or doctrinal hatred or to do anything that may be an incitement to any form or racial discrimination.

ARTICLE 23:

(a) Authority is a trust; and abuse or malicious exploitation thereof is explicitly prohibited, in order to guarantee fundamental human rights.

(b) Everyone shall have the right to participate, directly or indirectly in the administration of his country's public affairs. He shall also have the right to assume public office in accordance with the provisions of Shari'ah.

ARTICLE 24:

All the rights and freedoms stipulated in this Declaration are subject to the Islamic Shari'ah.

ARTICLE 25:

The Islamic Shari'ah is the only source of reference for the explanation or clarification of any of the articles of this Declaration.

c. The Arab Charter on Human Rights[3]

League of Arab States, Arab Charter on Human Rights, May 22, 2004, *reprinted in* 12 Int'l Hum. Rts. Rep. 893 (2005), *entered into force* March 15, 2008.

Arab Charter on Human Rights

Based on the faith of the Arab nation in the dignity of the human person whom God has exalted ever since the beginning of creation and in the fact that the Arab homeland is the cradle of religions and civilizations whose lofty human values affirm the human right to a decent life based on freedom, justice and equality,

In furtherance of the eternal principles of fraternity, equality and tolerance among human beings consecrated by the noble Islamic religion and the other divinely-revealed religions,

Being proud of the humanitarian values and principles that the Arab nation has established throughout its long history, which have played a major role in spreading knowledge between East and West, so making the region a point of reference for the whole world and a destination for seekers of knowledge and wisdom,

Believing in the unity of the Arab nation, which struggles for its freedom and defends the right of nations to self-determination, to the preservation of their wealth and to development; believing in the sovereignty of the law and its contribution to the protection of universal and interrelated human rights and convinced that the human person's enjoyment of freedom, justice and equality of opportunity is a fundamental measure of the value of any society,

Rejecting all forms of racism and Zionism, which constitute a violation of human rights and a threat to international peace and security, recognizing the close link that exists between human rights and international peace and security, reaffirming the principles of the Charter of the United Nations, the Universal Declaration of Human Rights and the provisions of the International Covenant on Civil and Political Rights and the International Covenant on Economic, Social and Cultural Rights, and having regard to the Cairo Declaration on Human Rights in Islam,

The States parties to the Charter have agreed as follows:

Article 1

The present Charter seeks, within the context of the national identity of the Arab States and their sense of belonging to a common civilization, to achieve the following aims:

1. To place human rights at the centre of the key national concerns of Arab States, making them lofty and fundamental ideals that shape the will of the individual in Arab States and enable him to improve his life in accordance with noble human values.

2. To teach the human person in the Arab States pride in his identity, loyalty to his country, attachment to his land, history and common interests and to instill in him a culture of human brotherhood, tolerance and openness towards others, in accordance with universal principles and values and with those proclaimed in international human rights instruments.

3. To prepare the new generations in Arab States for a free and responsible life in a civil society that is characterized by solidarity, founded on a balance between awareness of rights and respect for obligations, and governed by the values of equality, tolerance and moderation.

4. To entrench the principle that all human rights are universal, indivisible, interdependent and interrelated.

Article 2

1. All peoples have the right of self-determination and to control over their natural wealth and resources, and the right to freely choose their political system and to freely pursue their economic, social and cultural development.

2. All peoples have the right to national sovereignty and territorial integrity.

3. All forms of racism, Zionism and foreign occupation and domination constitute an impediment to human dignity and a major barrier to the exercise of the fundamental rights of peoples; all such practices must be condemned and efforts must be deployed for their elimination.

4. All peoples have the right to resist foreign occupation.

Article 3

1. Each State party to the present Charter undertakes to ensure to all individuals subject to its jurisdiction the right to enjoy the rights and freedoms set forth herein, without distinction on grounds of race, colour, sex, language, religious belief, opinion, thought, national or social origin, wealth, birth or physical or mental disability.

2. The States parties to the present Charter shall take the requisite measures to guarantee effective equality in the enjoyment of all the rights and freedoms enshrined in the present Charter in order to ensure protection against all forms of discrimination based on any of the grounds mentioned in the preceding paragraph.

3. Men and women are equal in respect of human dignity, rights and obligations within the framework of the positive discrimination established in favour of women by the Islamic Shariah, other divine laws and by applicable laws and legal instruments. Accordingly, each State party pledges to take all the requisite measures to guarantee equal opportunities and effective equality between men and women in the

enjoyment of all the rights set out in this Charter.

Article 4

1. In exceptional situations of emergency which threaten the life of the nation and the existence of which is officially proclaimed, the States parties to the present Charter may take measures derogating from their obligations under the present Charter, to the extent strictly required by the exigencies of the situation, provided that such measures are not inconsistent with their other obligations under international law and do not involve discrimination solely on the grounds of race, colour, sex, language, religion or social origin.

2. In exceptional situations of emergency, no derogation shall be made from the following articles: article 5, article 8, article 9, article 10, article 13, article 14, paragraph 6, article 15, article 18, article 19, article 20, article 22, article 27, article 28, article 29 and article 30. In addition, the judicial guarantees required for the protection of the aforementioned rights may not be suspended.

3. Any State party to the present Charter availing itself of the right of derogation shall immediately inform the other States parties, through the intermediary of the Secretary-General of the League of Arab States, of the provisions from which it has derogated and of the reasons by which it was actuated. A further communication shall be made, through the same intermediary, on the date on which it terminates such derogation.

Article 5

1. Every human being has the inherent right to life.

2. This right shall be protected by law. No one shall be arbitrarily deprived of his life.

Article 6

Sentence of death may be imposed only for the most serious crimes in accordance with the laws in force at the time of commission of the crime and pursuant to a final judgment rendered by a competent court. Anyone sentenced to death shall have the right to seek pardon or commutation of the sentence.

Article 7

1. Sentence of death shall not be imposed on persons under 18 years of age, unless otherwise stipulated in the laws in force at the time of the commission of the crime.

2. The death penalty shall not be inflicted on a pregnant woman prior to her delivery or on a nursing mother within two years from the date of her delivery; in all cases, the best interests of the infant shall be the primary consideration.

Article 8

1. No one shall be subjected to physical or psychological torture or to cruel, degrading, humiliating or inhuman treatment.

2. Each State party shall protect every individual subject to its jurisdiction from such practices and shall take effective measures to prevent them. The commission of, or participation in, such acts shall be regarded as crimes that are punishable by law and not subject to any statute of limitations. Each State party shall guarantee in its legal system redress for any victim of torture and the right to rehabilitation and compensation.

Article 9

No one shall be subjected to medical or scientific experimentation or to the use of his organs without his free consent and full awareness of the consequences and provided that ethical, humanitarian and professional rules are followed and medical procedures are observed to ensure his personal safety pursuant to the relevant domestic laws in force in each State party. Trafficking in human organs is prohibited in all circumstances.

Article 10

1. All forms of slavery and trafficking in human beings are prohibited and are punishable by law. No one shall be held in slavery and servitude under any circumstances.

2. Forced labor, trafficking in human beings for the purposes of prostitution or sexual exploitation, the exploitation of the prostitution of others or any other form of exploitation or the exploitation of children in armed conflict are prohibited.

Article 11

All persons are equal before the law and have the right to enjoy its protection without discrimination.

Article 12

All persons are equal before the courts and tribunals. The States parties shall guarantee the independence of the judiciary and protect magistrates against any interference, pressure or threats. They shall also guarantee every person subject to their jurisdiction the right to seek a legal remedy before courts of all levels.

Article 13

1. Everyone has the right to a fair trial that affords adequate guarantees before a competent, independent and impartial court that has been constituted by law to hear any criminal charge against him or to decide on his rights or his obligations. Each State party shall guarantee to those without the requisite financial resources legal aid to enable them to defend their rights.

2. Trials shall be public, except in exceptional cases that may be warranted by the interests of justice in a society that respects human freedoms and rights.

Article 14

1. Everyone has the right to liberty and security of person. No one shall be subjected to arbitrary arrest, search or detention without a legal warrant.

2. No one shall be deprived of-his liberty except on such grounds and in such circumstances as are determined by law and in accordance with such procedure as is established thereby.

3. Anyone who is arrested shall be informed, at the time of arrest, in a language that he understands, of the reasons for his arrest and shall be promptly informed of any charges against him. He shall be entitled to contact his family members.

4. Anyone who is deprived of his liberty by arrest or detention shall have the right to request a medical examination and must be informed of that right.

5. Anyone arrested or detained on a criminal charge shall be brought promptly before a judge or other officer authorized by law to exercise judicial power and shall be entitled to trial within a reasonable time or to release. His release may be subject to guarantees to appear for trial. Pre-trial detention shall in no case be the general rule.

6. Anyone who is deprived of his liberty by arrest or detention shall be entitled to petition a competent court in order that it may decide without delay on the lawfulness of his arrest or detention and order his release if the arrest or detention is unlawful.

7. Anyone who has been the victim of arbitrary or unlawful arrest or detention shall be entitled to compensation.

Article 15

No crime and no penalty can be established without a prior provision of the law. In all circumstances, the law most favorable to the defendant shall be applied.

Article 16

Everyone charged with a criminal offence shall be presumed innocent until proved guilty by a final judgment rendered according to law and, in the course of the investigation and trial, he shall enjoy the following minimum guarantees:

1. The right to be informed promptly, in detail and in a language which he understands, of the charges against him.

2. The right to have adequate time and facilities for the preparation of his defense and to be allowed to communicate with his family.

3. The right to be tried in his presence before an ordinary court and to defend himself in person or through a lawyer of his own choosing with whom he can communicate freely and confidentially.

4. The right to the free assistance of a lawyer who will defend him if he cannot defend himself or if the interests of justice so require, and the right to the free assistance of an interpreter if he cannot understand or does not speak the language used in court.

5. The right to examine or have his lawyer examine the prosecution witnesses and to on defense according to the conditions applied to the prosecution witnesses.

6. The right not to be compelled to testify against himself or to confess guilt.

7. The right, if convicted of the crime, to file an appeal in accordance with the law before a higher tribunal.

8. The right to respect for his security of person and his privacy in all circumstances.

Article 17

Each State party shall ensure in particular to any child at risk or any delinquent charged with an offence the right to a special legal system for minors in all stages of investigation, trial and enforcement of sentence, as well as to special treatment that takes account of his age, protects his dignity, facilitates his rehabilitation and reintegration and enables him to play a constructive role in society.

Article 18

No one who is shown by a court to be unable to pay a debt arising from a contractual obligation shall be imprisoned.

Article 19

1. No one may be tried twice for the same offence. Anyone against whom such proceedings are brought shall have the right to challenge their legality and to demand his release.

2. Anyone whose innocence is established by a final judgment shall be entitled to compensation for the damage suffered.

Article 20

1. All persons deprived of their liberty shall be treated with humanity and with respect for the inherent dignity of the human person.

2. Persons in pre-trial detention shall be separated from convicted persons and shall be treated in a manner consistent with their status as unconvicted persons.

3. The aim of the penitentiary system shall be to reform prisoners and effect their social rehabilitation.

Article 21

1. No one shall be subjected to arbitrary or unlawful interference with regard to his privacy, family, home or correspondence, nor to unlawful attacks on his honour or his reputation.

2. Everyone has the right to the protection of the law against such interference or attacks.

Article 22

Everyone shall have the right to recognition as a person before the law.

Article 23

Each State party to the present Charter undertakes to ensure that any person whose rights or freedoms as herein recognized are violated shall have an effective remedy, notwithstanding that the violation has been committed by persons acting in an official capacity.

Article 24

Every citizen has the right:

1. To freely pursue a political activity.

2. To take part in the conduct of public affairs, directly or through freely chosen representatives.

3. To stand for election or choose his representatives in free and impartial elections, in conditions of equality among all citizens that guarantee the free expression of his will.

4. To the opportunity to gain access, on an equal footing with others, to public office in his country in accordance with the principle of equality of opportunity.

5. To freely form and join associations with others.

6. To freedom of association and peaceful assembly.

7. No restrictions may be placed on the exercise of these rights other than those which are prescribed by law and which are necessary in a democratic society in the interests of national security or public safety, public health or morals or the protection of the rights and freedoms of others.

Article 25

Persons belonging to minorities shall not be denied the right to enjoy their own culture, to use their own language and to practice their own religion. The exercise of these rights shall be governed by law.

Article 26

1. Everyone lawfully within the territory of a State party shall, within that territory, have the right to freedom of movement and to freely choose his residence in any part of that territory in conformity with the laws in force.

2. No State party may expel a person who does not hold its nationality but is lawfully in its territory, other than in pursuance of a decision reached in accordance with law and after that person has been allowed to submit a petition to the competent authority, unless compelling reasons of national security preclude it. Collective expulsion is prohibited under all circumstances.

Article 27

1. No one may be arbitrarily or unlawfully prevented from leaving any country, including his own, nor prohibited from residing, or compelled to reside, in any part of that country.

2. No one may be exiled from his country or prohibited from returning thereto.

Article 28

Everyone has the right to seek political asylum in another country in order to escape persecution. This right may not be invoked by persons facing prosecution for an offence under ordinary law. Political refugees may not be extradited.

Article 29

1. Everyone has the right to nationality. No one shall be arbitrarily or unlawfully deprived of his nationality.

2. States parties shall take such measures as they deem appropriate, in accordance with their domestic laws on nationality, to allow a child to acquire the mother›s nationality, having due regard, in all cases, to the best interests of the child.

3. Non one shall be denied the right to acquire another nationality, having due regard for the domestic legal procedures in his country.

Article 30

1. Everyone has the right to freedom of thought, conscience and religion and no restrictions may be imposed on the exercise of such freedoms except as provided for by law.

2. The freedom to manifest one›s religion or beliefs or to perform religious observances, either alone or in community with others, shall be subject only to such limitations as are prescribed by law and are necessary in a tolerant society that respects human rights and freedoms for the protection of public safety, public order, public health or morals or the fundamental rights and freedoms of others.

3. Parents or guardians have the freedom to provide for the religious and moral education of their children.

Article 31

Everyone has a guaranteed right to own private property, and shall not under any circumstances be arbitrarily or unlawfully divested of all or any part of his property.

Article 32

1. The present Charter guarantees the right to information and to freedom of opinion and expression, as well as the right to seek, receive

and impart information and ideas through any medium, regardless of geographical boundaries.

2. Such rights and freedoms shall be exercised in conformity with the fundamental values of society and shall be subject only to such limitations as are required to ensure respect for the rights or reputation of others or the protection of national security, public order and public health or morals.

Article 33

1. The family is the natural and fundamental group unit of society; it is based on marriage between a man and a woman. Men and women of marrying age have the right to marry and to found a family according to the rules and conditions of marriage. No marriage can take place without the full and free consent of both parties. The laws in force regulate the rights and duties of the man and woman as to marriage, during marriage and at its dissolution.

2. The State and society shall ensure the protection of the family, the strengthening of family ties, the protection of its members and the prohibition of all forms of violence or abuse in the relations among its members, and particularly against women and children. They shall also ensure the necessary protection and care for mothers, children, older persons and persons with special needs and shall provide adolescents and young persons with the best opportunities for physical and mental development.

3. The States parties shall take all necessary legislative, administrative and judicial measures to guarantee the protection, survival, development and well-being of the child in an atmosphere of freedom and dignity and shall ensure, in all cases, that the child›s best interests are the basic criterion for all measures taken in his regard, whether the child is at risk of delinquency or is a juvenile offender.

4. The States parties shall take all the necessary measures to guarantee, particularly to young persons, the right to pursue a sporting activity.

APPENDIX 3

Article 34

1. The right to work is a natural right of every citizen. The State shall endeavor to provide, to the extent possible, a job for the largest number of those willing to work, while ensuring production, the freedom to choose one›s work and equality of opportunity without discrimination of any kind on grounds of race, colour, sex, religion, language, political opinion, membership in a union, national origin, social origin, disability or any other situation.

2. Every worker has the right to the enjoyment of just and favourable conditions of work which ensure appropriate remuneration to meet his essential needs and those of his family and regulate working hours, rest and holidays with pay, as well as the rules for the preservation of occupational health and safety and the protection of women, children and disabled persons in the place of work.

3. The States parties recognize the right of the child to be protected from economic exploitation and from being forced to perform any work that is likely to be hazardous or to interfere with the child›s education or to be harmful to the child›s health or physical, mental, spiritual, moral or social development. To this end, and having regard to the relevant provisions of other international instruments, States parties shall in particular:

(a) Define a minimum age for admission to employment;

(b) Establish appropriate regulation of working hours and conditions;

(c) Establish appropriate penalties or other sanctions to ensure the effective endorsement of these provisions.

4. There shall be no discrimination between men and women in their enjoyment of the right to effectively benefit from training, employment and job protection and the right to receive equal remuneration for equal work.

5. Each State party shall ensure to workers who migrate to its territory the requisite protection in accordance with the laws in force.

Article 35

1. Every individual has the right to freely form trade unions or to join trade unions and to freely pursue trade union activity for the protection of his interests.

2. No restrictions shall be placed on the exercise of these rights and freedoms except such as are prescribed by the laws in force and that are necessary for the maintenance of national security, public safety or order or for the protection of public health or morals or the rights and freedoms of others.

3. Every State party to the present Charter guarantees the right to strike within the limits laid down by the laws in force.

Article 36

The States parties shall ensure the right of every citizen to social security, including social insurance.

Article 37

The right to development is a fundamental human right and all States are required to establish the development policies and to take the measures needed to guarantee this right. They have a duty to give effect to the values of solidarity and cooperation among them and at the international level with a view to eradicating poverty and achieving economic, social, cultural and political development. By virtue of this right, every citizen has the right to participate in the realization of development and to enjoy the benefits and fruits thereof.

Article 38

Every person has the right to an adequate standard of living for himself and his family, which ensures their well-being and a decent life, including food, clothing, housing, services and the right to a healthy environment. The States parties shall take the necessary measures commensurate with their resources to guarantee these rights.

Article 39

1. The States parties recognize the right of every member of society to the enjoyment of the highest attainable standard of physical and mental health and the right of the citizen to free basic health-care services and to have access to medical facilities without discrimination of any kind.

2. The measures taken by States parties shall include the following:

(a) Development of basic health-care services and the guaranteeing of free and easy access to the centres that provide these services, regardless of geographical location or economic status.

(b) efforts to control disease by means of prevention and cure in order to reduce the morality rate.

(c) promotion of health awareness and health education.

(d) suppression of traditional practices which are harmful to the health of the individual.

(e) provision of the basic nutrition and safe drinking water for all.

(f) Combating environmental pollution and providing proper sanitation systems;

(g) Combating drugs, psychotropic substances, smoking and substances that are damaging to health.

Article 40

1. The States parties undertake to ensure to persons with mental or physical disabilities a decent life that guarantees their dignity, and to enhance their self-reliance and facilitate their active participation in society.

2. The States parties shall provide social services free of charge for all persons with disabilities, shall provide the material support needed by those persons, their families or the families caring for them, and shall also do whatever is needed to avoid placing those persons in institutions. They shall in all cases take account of the best interests of the disabled person.

3. The States parties shall take all necessary measures to curtail the incidence of disabilities by all possible means, including preventive health programmes, awareness raising and education.

4. The States parties shall provide full educational services suited to persons with disabilities, taking into account the importance of integrating these persons in the educational system and the importance of vocational training and apprenticeship and the creation of suitable job opportunities in the public or private sectors.

5. The States parties shall provide all health services appropriate for persons with disabilities, including the rehabilitation of these persons with a view to integrating them into society.

6. The States parties shall enable persons with disabilities to make use of all public and private services.

Article 41

1. The eradication of illiteracy is a binding obligation upon the State and everyone has the right to education.

2. The States parties shall guarantee their citizens free education at least throughout the primary and basic levels. All forms and levels of primary education shall be compulsory and accessible to all without discrimination of any kind.

3. The States parties shall take appropriate measures in all domains to ensure partnership between men and women with a view to achieving national development goals.

4. The States parties shall guarantee to provide education directed to the full development of the human person and to strengthening respect for human rights and fundamental freedoms.

5. The States parties shall endeavour to incorporate the principles of human rights and fundamental freedoms into formal and informal education curricula and educational and training programmes.

6. The States parties shall guarantee the establishment of the mechanisms necessary to provide ongoing education for every citizen and shall develop national plans for adult education.

Article 42

1. Every person has the right to take part in cultural life and to enjoy the benefits of scientific progress and its application.

2. The States parties undertake to respect the freedom of scientific research and creative activity and to ensure the protection of moral and material interests resulting from scientific, literary and artistic production.

3. The state parties shall work together and enhance cooperation among them at all levels, with the full participation of intellectuals and inventors and their organizations, in order to develop and implement recreational, cultural, artistic and scientific programmes.

Article 43

Nothing in this Charter may be construed or interpreted as impairing the rights and freedoms protected by the domestic laws of the States parties or those set force in the international and regional human rights instruments which the states parties have adopted or ratified, including the rights of women, the rights of the child and the rights of persons belonging to minorities.

Article 44

The states parties undertake to adopt, in conformity with their constitutional procedures and with the provisions of the present Charter, whatever legislative or non-legislative measures that may be necessary to give effect to the rights set forth herein.

Article 45

1. Pursuant to this Charter, an "Arab Human Rights Committee", hereinafter referred to as "the Committee" shall be established. This Committee shall consist of seven members who shall be elected by secret ballot by the states parties to this Charter.

2. The Committee shall consist of nationals of the states party to the present Charter, who must be highly experienced and competent in the Committee's field of work. The members of the Committee shall serve in their personal capacity and shall be fully independent and impartial.

3. The Committee shall include among its members not more than one national of a State party; such member may be re-elected only once. Due regard shall be given to the rotation principle.

4. The members of the Committee shall be elected for a four-year term, although the mandate of three of the members elected during the first election shall be for two years and shall be renewed by lot.

5. Six months prior to the date of the election, the Secretary-General of the League of Arab States shall invite the States parties to submit their nominations within the following three months. He shall transmit the list of candidates to the States parties two months prior to the date the election. The candidates who obtain the largest number of votes cast shall be elected to membership of the Committee. If, because two or more candidates have an equal number of votes, the number of candidates with the largest number of votes exceeds the number required, a second ballot will be held between the persons with equal numbers of votes. If the votes are again equal, the member or members shall be selected by lottery. The first election for membership of the Committee shall be held at least six months after the Charter enters into force.

6. The Secretary-General shall invite the States parties to a meeting at the headquarters the League of Arab States in order to elect the member of the Committee. The presence of the majority of the States parties shall constitute a quorum. If there is no quorum, the secretary-General shall call another meeting at which at least two thirds of the States parties must be present. If there is still no quorum, the Secretary-General shall call a third meeting, which will be held regardless of the number of States parties present.

7. The Secretary-General shall convene the first meeting of the Committee, during the course of which the Committee shall elect its Chairman from among its members, for a two-year n which may be renewed only once and for an identical period. The Committee shall establish its own rules of procedure and methods of work and shall determine how often it shall et. The Committee shall hold its meetings at the headquarters of the League of Arab States. ~ay also meet in any other State party to the present Charter at that party's invitation.

Article 46

1. The Secretary-General shall declare a seat vacant after being notified by the Chairman of a member's:

(a) Death;

(b) Resignation; or

(c) If, in the unanimous, opinion of the other members, a member of the Committee has ceased to perform his functions without offering an acceptable justification or for any reason other than a temporary absence.

2. If a member›s seat is declared vacant pursuant to the provisions of paragraph 1 and the term of office of the member to be replaced does not expire within six months from the date on which the vacancy was declared, the Secretary-General of the League of Arab States shall refer the matter to the States parties to the present Charter, which may, within two months, submit nominations, pursuant to article 45, in order to fill the vacant seat.

3. The Secretary-General of the League of Arab States shall draw up an alphabetical list of all the duly nominated candidates, which he shall transmit to the States parties to the present Charter. The elections to fill the vacant seat shall be held in accordance with the relevant provisions.

4. Any member of the Committee elected to fill a seat declared vacant in accordance with the provisions of paragraph 1 shall remain a member of the Committee until the expiry of the remainder of the term of the member whose seat was declared vacant pursuant to the provisions of that paragraph.

5. The Secretary-General of the League of Arab States shall make provision within the budget of the League of Arab States for all the necessary financial and human resources and facilities that the Committee needs to discharge its functions effectively. The Committee›s experts shall be afforded the same treatment with respect to remuneration and reimbursement of expenses as experts of the secretariat of the League of Arab States.

Article 47

The States parties undertake to ensure that members of the Committee shall enjoy the immunities necessary for their protection against any form of harassment or moral or material pressure or prosecution on account of the positions they take or statements they make while carrying out their functions as members of the Committee.

Article 48

1. The States parties undertake to submit reports to the Secretary-General of the League of Arab States on the measures they have taken to give effect to the rights and freedoms recognized in this Charter and on the progress made towards the enjoyment thereof. The Secretary-General shall transmit these reports to the Committee for its consideration.

2. Each State party shall submit an initial report to the Committee within one year from the date on which the Charter enters into force and a periodic report every three years thereafter. The Committee may request the States parties to supply it with additional information relating to the implementation of the Charter.

3. The Committee shall consider the reports submitted by the States parties under paragraph 2 of this article in the presence of the representative of the State party whose report is being considered.

4. The Committee shall discuss the report, comment thereon and make the necessary recommendations in accordance with the aims of the Charter.

5. The Committee shall submit an annual report containing its comments and recommendations to the Council of the League, through the intermediary of the Secretary-General.

6. The Committee›s reports, concluding observations and recommendations shall be public documents which the Committee shall disseminate widely.

Article 49

1. The Secretary-General of the League of Arab States shall submit the present Charter, once it has been approved by the Council of the League, to the States members for signature, ratification or accession.

2. The present Charter shall enter into effect two months from the date on which the seventh instrument of ratification is deposited with the secretariat of the League of Arab States.

3. After its entry into force, the present Charter shall become effective for each State two months after the State in question has deposited its instrument of ratification or accession with the secretariat.

4. The Secretary-General shall notify the States members of the deposit of each instrument of ratification or accession.

Article 50

Any State party may submit written proposals, though the Secretary-General, for the amendment of the present Charter. After these amendments have been circulated among the States members, the Secretary-General shall invite the States parties to consider the proposed amendments before submitting them to the Council of the League for adoption.

Article 51

The amendments shall take effect, with regard to the States parties that have approved them, once they have been approved by two thirds of the States parties.

Article 52

Any State party may propose additional optional protocols to the present Charter and they shall be adopted in accordance with the procedures used for the adoption of amendments to the Charter.

Article 53

1. Any State party, when signing this Charter, depositing the instruments of ratification or acceding hereto, may make a reservation to any article of the Charter, provided that such reservation does not conflict with the aims and fundamental purposes of the Charter.

2. Any State party that has made a reservation pursuant to paragraph 1 of this article may withdraw it at any time by addressing a notification to the Secretary-General of the League of Arab States.

Notes
[1] Text from http://www.alhewar.com/ISLAMDECL.html
[2] Text from http://www1.umn.edu/humanrts/instree/cairodeclaration.html
[3] Text from http://www1.umn.edu/humanrts/instree/loas2005.html

APPENDIX 4

A HINDU DECLARATION OF HUMAN RIGHTS

A Universal Declaration of Human Rights by the Hindus.[1]

Whereas the secular and the sacred are the two main avenues whereby human beings are led to affirm that there is more to life than life itself;

Whereas the Universal Declaration of Human Rights' as adopted by the General Assembly of the United Nations on 10 December 1948 draws mainly upon only one of them as a resource.

Whereas at the time of the adoption of the Universal Declaration of Human Rights religion had retreated from the public square but has since reappeared in a major way;

Whereas religions are meant to serve humanity and not humanity to serve religion;

Whereas one must not idealize the actual but strive to realize the ideal;

Whereas the various communities constituting the peoples of the world must exchange not only ideas but also ideals;

Whereas not to compensate victims of imperialism, racism, casteism and sexism is itself imperialist, racist, casteist and sexist;

Whereas any further exclusion of world's religions as positive resources for human rights is obnoxious to the evidence of daily life;

Whereas rights are independent of duties in their protection but integrally related to them in conception and execution:

Whereas in the case of human beings in general rights and duties are correlative ; subhuman creatures may have rights without corresponding duties and in exceptional cases persons, like mothers in relation to infants, duties without corresponding rights;

Whereas rights can serve both as ends in themselves (upeya) and as means (upaya) to ends and to each other;

Whereas a Hindu is like any other human being, only more so;

Whereas to be a Hindu is to possess the natural right to pursue the good (dharma); goods (artha); the good life (kama): and the highest good (moksa),like all other human beings, as children of the same earth and descended from the same Manu;

Whereas Hindus subscribe to universal norms such as non-violence (ahimsa); truth (satya): non-appropriation (asteya); purity (sauca), and self-restraint (indriyanigrahah) which find their expressions in rights and duties in relation to oneself, to others, and the state and that, in relation to the state, non-violence denotes the right protection against arbitrary conduct; truth denotes presumption of innocence until proven guilty, non-appropriation denotes right to property; purity denotes freedom from pollution, and self-restraint denotes the right that the organs of the state do not compromise the privacy and dignity of the individual.

Now therefore, on this, Sunday, Twenty Seventh Day of June, One Thousand Nine Hundred Ninety-Nine the Hindu community, as assembled at the Hindu Mission of Canada (Quebec), at 955 Bellechasse, Montreal, adopts this Declaration, as heaven and earth are our father and mother and all people brothers and sisters.

Article 1

All human beings have the right to be treated as human beings and have the duty to treat everyone as a human being.

Article 2

Everyone has the right to freedom from violence, in any of its forms, individual or collective; whether based on race, religion, gender, caste, or class, or nation, or arising from any other cause.

Article 3

(1) Everyone has the right to food.

(2) Everyone has the right to life, longevity and liveability and the right to food, clothing and shelter required to sustain them.

(3) Everyone has the duty to support and sustain the life, longevity, and liveability of all.

Article 4

(1) No one shall be subjected to slavery or servitude, forced labour, bonded labour, or child labour. Slavery and the slave trade shall be prohibited in all its forms.

(2) No one shall subject anyone to slavery or servitude in any of its forms .

Article 5

(1) No one shall be subjected to torture or to cruel, inhuman, or degrading treatment or punishment inflicted either physically or mentally, whether on secular or religious grounds, inside the home or outside it.

(2) No one shall subject anybody to such treatment.

Article 6

(1) Everyone has a right to recognition everywhere as a person before the law; and by everyone everywhere as a human being deserving humane treatment, even when law and order has broken down.

(2) Everyone has the duty to treat everyone else as a human being both in the eyes of law and one's own.

Article 7 All are equal before law and entitled to equal protection before law without any discrimination on grounds of race, religion, caste, class, nationality, sex, and sexual orientation. It is the right of everyone to be so treated and the duty of everyone to so treat others.

Article 8

(1) Everybody has the right to demand restitution for historical, social,

economic, cultural, and other wrongs in the present and compensation for such wrongs committed in the past, provided that the victims shall always have the right to forgive the victimizers.

(2) Everybody has the duty to prevent the perpetuation of historical, social, economic, cultural, and other wrongs.

Article 9

(1) No one shall be subjected to arbitrary arrest, detention or exile by the state or by anyone else. The attempt to proselytize against the will of the person shall amount to arbitrary detention, so also the detention, against their will, of teenage children by the parents, and among spouses.

(2) It is the duty of everyone to secure everyone's liberty.

Article 10

Everybody has the right to public trial when facing criminal charges and it is the duty of the state to ensure it. Everyone who cannot afford a lawyer must be provided one by the state.

Article 11

Everyone charged with a penal offence has the right to be considered innocent by everyone until proven guilty.

Article 12

(1) Everyone has the right to privacy. This right includes the right not to be subjected to arbitrary interference with one's privacy; or of one's family, home or correspondence.

(2) Everyone has the right to one's good name.

(3) It is the duty of everyone to protect the privacy and reputation of everyone else.

(4) Everyone has the right not to have one's religion misrepresented in the media or the academia.

(5) It is the duty of the follower of every religion to ensure that no religion is misrepresented in the media or the academia.

Article 13

(1) Everyone has the right to freedom of movement und residence anywhere in the world.

(2) Everyone has the duty to abide by the laws and regulations applicable in that part of the world.

Article 14

Everyone has the right to seek and secure asylum in any country from any form of persecution, religious or otherwise, and the right not to be deported. It is the duty of every country to provide such asylum.

Article 15

(1) Everyone has the right to a nationality;

(2) No one shall be arbitrarily deprived of one's nationality nor denied the right to change one's nationality.

(3) Everyone has the duty to promote the emergence of a federal but single global government-The Parliament of Humanity.

Article 16

(1) Everyone has the right to marriage.

(2) Parties to a marriage have the right to retain and practise their own religion or ideology within a marriage.

(3) Everyone has the right to raise a family.

(4) Everyone has the right to renounce the world and join a monastery, provided that one shall do so alter making adequate arrangement for one's dependents.

(5) Marriage and monasticism are two of the most successful

institutional innovations of humanity and are entitled to protection by the society and the state.

(6) Motherhood and childhood are entitled to special care and assistance. It is the duty of everyone to extend special consideration to mothers and children. Everyone shall promote the outlook that the entire world constitutes a single family.

Article 17

(1) Everyone has the right to own property, alone as well as in association with others. An association also has a similar right to own property.

(2) Everyone has a right not to be deprived of property arbitrarily. It is the duty of everyone not to deprive others of their property arbitrarily, or appropriate it in an unauthorized manner. Property shall be understood to mean material as well as intellectual, aesthetic and spiritual property.

Article 18

There shall be no compulsion in religion. It is a matter of choice.

Everyone has the right to retain one's religion and to change one's religion.

All human beings are entitled to participate in all the religions of the world as much as their own, for all are legatees of the religious heritage of humanity

Everyone has the duty to promote peace and tolerance among religions and ideologies.

Article 19

(1) Everyone has the right to freedom of opinion and expression, where the term expression includes the language one speaks: the food one eats; the clothes one wears; the religion one practises and professes provided that one conforms generally to the accustomed rules of

decorum recognized in the neighbourhood.

(2) It is the duty of everyone to ensure that everyone enjoys such freedom.

Article 20

(1) Everyone has the right to freedom of assembly and association, and the duty to do so peacefully.

(2) No one may be compelled to belong to an association, or to leave one without due process.

Article 21

(1) Everybody over the age of eighteen has the right to vote, to elect or be elected and thus to take part in the government or governance of the country, directly or indirectly.

(2) Everyone has the right of equal access to public service in and the duty to provide such access.

(3) It is the duty of everyone to participate in the political process.

Article 22

Everyone, as a member of society, has a right to social security and a duty to contribute to it.

Article 23

(1) Everyone has the right to work and seek gainful employment.

(2) It is the duty of the state and society to ensure that everyone is gainfully employed.

(3) Everyone has the right to equal pay for equal work and a duty to offer equal pay for equal work.

(4) Everyone has the right for just remuneration for one's work and the duty to offer just recompense for work done.

(5) Everyone has the right to form and to join trade unions for the protection of one's interests.

Article 24

(1) Everyone has the right to work and to rest, including the right to support while seeking work and the right to periodic holidays with pay.

(2) The right to rest extends to the earth itself.

Article 25

(1) Everyone has the right to health and to universal medical insurance. It is the duty of the state or society to provide it.

(2) Every child has the right to an unencumbered childhood and it is the duty of the parents, society and state to provide it.

Article 26

Everyone has the right to free education and the right to equality of opportunity for any form of education involving restricted enrolment.

Article 27

(1) Everyone has the right to freely participate in the cultural life of the community and the right to freely contribute to it.

(2) Everyone has the right to share in scientific advances and their benefits, the duty to disseminate them, and wherever possible, contribute to such advance.

(3) Everyone has the right to the protection of their cultural heritage' It is the duty of everyone to protect and enrich everyone's heritage, including one's own.

Article 28 Everyone has the right to socio-economic and political order at a global, national, regional, and local level which enables the realization of social, political, economic, racial and gender justice and the duty to give precedence to universal, national, regional and local interests in that order.

Article 29

(1) One is duty-bound, when asserting one's rights, to take the rights of other human beings; of past, present, and future generations; the rights of humanity; and the rights of nature and the earth into account.

(2) One is duty-bound, when asserting one's rights, to prefer non-violence over violence.

Article 30

As the entire earth constitutes one extended family, all human beings possess unrestricted right of freedom of movement across all countries, nations and states all over the world.

Article 31

All human beings possess the right to due compensation should aforesaid rights be violated, irrespective of whether the violation occurs in the past, present, or future.

Article 32

(1) Everyone has the right over his or her body and mind to use it in any manner one wishes.

(2) Everyone has the duty to use his or her body and mind to further the well-being of all.

(3) One's body and mind possess the right not to be abused by oneself, as the right of the part against the whole.

(4) It is one's duty to cultivate one's body and mind.

Article 33

(1) Everyone has the right to require the formation of a supervisory committee within one's community, defined religiously or otherwise, to monitor the implementation of the articles of this Declaration; and to serve on it and present one's case before such a committee.

(2) It is everyone's duty to ensure that such a committee satisfactorily supervises the implementation of these articles.

Notes

Composed by Professor G.C. Pande, at the International Symposium on Indian Studies, held at Kovalam in Kerala, 28 November – 2 December 1994.

[1] Text in Sharma, *Hinduism and Human Rights*, Appendix II.

APPENDIX 5

A BUDDHIST DECLARATION OF HUMAN RIGHTS

Towards A Buddhist Culture of Non-Violence And Human Rights

Declaration

The International Network of Engaged Buddhists On Vesakh 2542 / 1998

On 10 May 1998 Buddhists all over the world celebrate Visakha-puja (Vesakh). It is the most important day of observance for Buddhists, the day we commemorate the Lord Buddha's Birth, Awakening, and Parinibbana. On this day Buddhists remind themselves of their undertaking to follow Buddha's path towards Enlightenment. The International Network of Engaged Buddhists (INEB) would like to take the opportunity of this holy day to invite everyone to work towards a culture and global implementation of Non-violence and Human Rights.

Buddhism and Human Rights

Notions of rights derive from ethical principles. There is a clear convergence between Buddhist ethics and modern discussions on human rights, particularly in the common focus on responsibility and indivisibility/interdependence. The non-dual understanding of Buddhism gives rise to an ethics of inter-responsibility, or Bodhicitta – what His Holiness the Dalai Lama calls Universal Responsibility. In the Theravada we speak of Samma-sankappa or Right Thought, which leads to Bodhi, the Awakened Mind. This principle is expressed in everyday terms by the teaching of loving-kindness, non-violence, compassion, and particular responsibilities. For monks and nuns these are set down in the rule or Vinaya; for lay people in the Sigalovada Sutta and for rulers in the Dasarajadhamma.

271

All human beings, according to Buddhism, are equal, and each has the potential to realize the truth by his or her own will and endeavour, and can help others to realize it. Buddhist concepts recognize the inherent dignity and the equal and inalienable rights of all human beings. The teaching of the Buddha holds that all human beings are endowed with reason and conscience. It recommends a Universal spirit of brotherhood and sisterhood. Buddhist theory holds that the "three poisons" of hatred, greed and delusion are at the root of violence in the world, and that the solution is for us to see so deeply into these factors that we are no longer dominated by them.

In the early, organic, societies the Buddha was addressing, these specific responsibilities were assumed to be adequate guidelines for human behaviour, with no need to identify the corresponding rights. In modern, fragmented societies, however, where the fulfilment of responsibilities cannot be guaranteed by the immediate community, these guidelines or skilful means (upaya) have been supplemented by corresponding rights. These are specified and protected by States and International Organisations. In large part these bodies derive their legitimacy from their promotion and protection of human rights. A State which does not guarantee the enjoyment of human rights by its people loses its claim to legitimacy.

Buddhism is widely regarded as the most tolerant of all religious traditions. However, Buddhist countries like Sri Lanka, Burma, and Cambodia have seen some of the highest levels of religious and ethnic intolerance in the world, with Buddhists among the main perpetrators. In other places it is Buddhists who are persecuted by the State, which fears the influence of Buddhism on the people. In Burma, Tibet and Viêt Nam, for instance, thousands of Buddhists (especially monks and nuns) have been persecuted, with well-documented instances of torture and executions. In Tibet most of the country's monasteries have been demolished.

The depiction of rights as simply a Western invention fails to understand the relationship of rights to responsibilities and ethical norms. The central values of all societies are very much the same. All ethical systems encourage people to respect each other, and discourage killing, violence and so on. Rights are skilful means designed to assist the implementation of these ethics.

Human Rights discourse has moved on during the past 50 years and has expanded and enriched the somewhat individualistic principles set out in the 'Universal Declaration of Human Rights' which was adopted and proclaimed by the General Assembly of the United Nations on 10 December 1948. The dialectic of universalism and cultural relativism, for instance, is an immensely creative process as well as a cause for countless conflicts. The work since 1982 on the rights of indigenous peoples - group rights - is another important development. The cultural, social and political development of a nation is a dynamic process. The orientation of the process should not only be based in our own roots and traditions, but must also be shaped by innovative new ideas. Cultural diversity is a factor that enriches the modern approach to human rights, rather than hindering the universal respect for and observance of human rights.

Buddhist Commitment to Human Rights

As H.H. the Dalai Lama stressed: "I truly believe that individuals can make a difference in society. Since periods of great change such as the present one come so rarely in human history, it is up to each of us to make the best use of our time to help create a happier world".

In this spirit:

1. we call on all Buddhists to look into themselves, their institutions and teachings, in order to renew Buddhism as a way of peace and non-violence, not only in individual, but also in collective practice and theory. Buddhists must adopt an active approach

to reducing suffering. This can be done by working for the active implementation of peace and human rights, including economic, social and cultural rights. The activities related to the 50th anniversary of the Universal Declaration of Human Rights offer an excellent opportunity to renew and expand our efforts in this field.

2. we request all Buddhists to show solidarity with those who are persecuted by their governments and to stand up for their human rights.

3. we urge all Governments, especially in Burma, Viêt Nam and the Peoples Republic of China, to stop immediately the severe human rights violations against Buddhists and others and to ensure that human rights become a reality in their countries.

4. we invite all Buddhist communities and organizations to include human rights education in their programs and to distribute information and educational materials.

5. we encourage Buddhist leaders to give importance to the human rights issues in their communities and countries.

6. we support the appeal of H.H. the Dalai Lama and other Nobel Peace Prize laureates, that the UN should declare the years 2000-2010 the "Decade for a Culture of Non-Violence".

APPENDIX 6

A UNIVERSAL DECLARATION OF RIGHTS BY THE WORLD'S RELIGIONS.[1]

Universal Declaration of Human Rights by the World's Religions
September 7, 2011

Whereas human beings are led to affirm that there is more to life than life itself by inspiration human and divine;

Whereas the Universal Declaration of Human Rights, as adopted by the General Assembly of the United Nations on December 10, 1948 bases itself on the former;

Whereas any exclusion of the world's religions as positive resources for human rights is obnoxious to the evidence of daily life;

Whereas the various communities constituting the peoples of the world must exchange not only ideas but also ideals;

Whereas religions ideally urge human beings to live in a just society and not just in any society;

Whereas one must not idealize the actual but strive to realize the ideal;

Whereas not to compensate victims of imperialism, racism, casteism and sexism is itself imperialist, racist, casteist and sexist;

Whereas rights are independent of duties in their protection but integrally related to them in conception and execution;

Whereas human rights are intended to secure peace, freedom, equality and justice — and to mitigate departures therefrom — when these come in conflict or the rights themselves;

Now, therefore, on the fiftieth anniversary of the Universal Declaration of Human Rights and the fiftieth anniversary of the founding of the Faculty of Religious Studies, at McGill University, Montreal, Quebec, Canada; The signatories to this Universal Declaration of Human Rights by the World's Religions, as legatees of the religious heritage of humanity do hereby propose the following as the common standard of achievement for the followers of all religions or none, on the 10th day of December, 1998, as all people are brothers and sisters on the face of the earth

ARTICLE 1

All human beings have the right to be treated as human beings and have the duty to treat everyone as a human being.

ARTICLE 2

Everyone has the right to freedom from violence, in any of its forms, individual or collective; whether based on race, religion, gender, caste or class, or arising from any other cause.

ARTICLE 3

(1) Everyone has the right to food.

(2) Everyone has the right to life, longevity and liveability and the right to food, clothing and shelter to sustain them.

(3) Everyone has the duty to support and sustain the life, longevity and liveability of all.

(4) Everyone has the right to be cared for with dignity at the end of life, to die with dignity, and to have one's dead body treated with dignity.

It is the duty of everyone to ensure this.

ARTICLE 4

(1) No one shall be subjected to slavery or servitude, forced labour, bonded labour or child labour. Slavery and the slave trade shall be prohibited in all its forms.

(2) No one shall subject anyone to slavery or servitude in any of its forms.

ARTICLE 5

(1) No one shall be subjected to torture or to cruel, inhuman or degrading treatment or punishment, inflicted either physically or mentally, whether on secular or religious grounds, inside the home or outside it.

(2) No one shall subject anybody to such treatment.

ARTICLE 6

(1) Everyone has a right to recognition everywhere as a person before law; and by everyone everywhere as a human being deserving humane treatment, even when law and order has broken down.

(2) Everyone has the duty to treat everyone else as a human being both in the eyes of law and one's own.

ARTICLE 7

All are equal before law and entitled to equal protection before law without any discrimination on grounds of race, religion, caste, class, sex and sexual orientation. It is the right of everyone to be so treated and the duty of everyone to so treat others.

ARTICLE 8

Everybody has the duty to prevent the perpetuation of historical, social, economic, cultural and other wrongs.

ARTICLE 9

(1) No one shall be subjected to arbitrary arrest, detention or exile by the state or by anyone else. The attempt to proselytize against the will of the person shall amount to arbitrary detention, so also the detention, against their will, of teenage children by the parents, and among spouses.

(2) It is the duty of everyone to secure everyone's liberty.

ARTICLE 10

Everyone is entitled in full equality to a fair and public hearing by an independent and impartial tribunal, in determination of his rights and obligations and of any criminal charge against themselves. Everyone who cannot afford a lawyer must be provided on by the state.

ARTICLE 11

Everyone charged with a penal offence has the right to be considered innocent until proven guilty.

ARTICLE 12

(1) Everyone has the right to privacy. This right includes the right not to be subjected to arbitrary interference with one's privacy; of one's own, or of one's family, home or correspondence.

(2) Everyone has the right to one's good name.

(3) It is the duty of everyone to protect the privacy and reputation of everyone else.

ARTICLE 13

(1) Everyone has the right to freedom of movement and residence anywhere in the world.

(2) Everyone has the duty to abide by the laws and regulations applicable in that part of the world.

ARTICLE 14

Everyone has the right to seek and secure asylum in any country from any form of persecution, religious or otherwise, and the right not to be deported. It is the duty of every country to provide such asylum.

ARTICLE 15

(1) Everyone has the right to a nationality.

(2) No one shall be arbitrarily deprived of one's nationality nor denied the right to change one's nationality.

(3) Everyone has the duty to promote the emergence of a global constitutional order.

ARTICLE 16

(1) All men and women have the right to marriage, dissolution of marriage, and single life.

(2) Members of a family have the right to retain and practice their own religion or beliefs.

(3) Everyone has the right to raise a family.

(4) Everybody has the right to renounce the world and join a monastery and to return to lay life, provided that adequate arrangement has been made for one's dependants.

(5) Marriage and monasticism are two of the most fundamental institutional innovations of humanity and are entitled to protection by the society and the state.

(6) Motherhood and childhood are entitled to special care and assistance. It is the duty of everyone to extend special consideration to mothers and children.

(7) Everyone shall promote the outlook that the entire world constitutes an extended family.

ARTICLE 17

(1) Everybody has the right to own property, alone as well as in association with others. An association also has a similar right to own property.

(2) Everyone has a right not to be deprived of property arbitrarily. It is the duty of everyone not to deprive others of their property arbitrarily. Property shall be understood to mean material as well as intellectual, aesthetic and spiritual property.

(3) Everyone has the duty not to deprive anyone of their property or appropriate it in an unauthorized manner.

ARTICLE 18

(1) There shall be no compulsion in religion. It is a matter of choice.

(2) Everyone has the right to retain one's religion, to change one's religion and to transmit one's religion.

(3) Everyone has the duty to promote peace and tolerance among different religions, ideologies and worldviews.

(4) Everyone has the right not to have one's religion denigrated in the media or the academia.

(5) It is the duty of the follower of every religion to ensure that no religion is denigrated in the media or the academia.

ARTICLE 19

(1) Everyone has the right to freedom of opinion and expression, where the term expression includes the language one speaks; the food one eats; the clothes one wears; the religion one practices and professes, without unjustly imposing them on others.

(2) It is the duty of everyone to ensure that everyone enjoys such freedom.

(3) Children have the right to express themselves freely in all matters affecting the child, to which it is the duty of their caretakers to give due weight in accordance with the age and maturity of the child.

ARTICLE 20

(1) Everyone has the right to freedom of assembly and association for peaceful purposes, and the duty to do so peacefully.

(2) No one may be compelled to belong to an association, or to leave one without due process.

(3) Everyone has the right to resist injustice either singly or jointly and it is one's duty to do so.

ARTICLE 21

(1) Everybody adult citizen has the right to vote, to elect or be elected and thus to take part in the government or governance of the country, directly or indirectly.

(2) Everyone has the right of equal access to public service in one's country and the duty to provide such access.

(3) It is the duty of everyone to participate in the political process.

ARTICLE 22

Everyone, as a member of society, has a right to social security and a duty to contribute to it.

ARTICLE 23

(1) Everyone has the right to same pay for same work and a duty to offer same pay for same work.

(2) Everyone has the right for just remuneration for one's work and the duty to justly recompense for work done.

(3) Everyone has the right to form and to join trade unions for the protection of one's interests.

(4) Everyone has the right not to join a trade union.

ARTICLE 24

(1) Everyone has the right to work and to rest, including the right to support while seeking work and the right to periodic holidays with pay, including medical and maternity/paternity leave if necessary

(2) The right to rest extends to the earth.

ARTICLE 25

(1) Everyone has the right to health and to medical insurance. It is the duty of the state or society to provide it.

(2) Every child has the right to a childhood free from violence of abuse and it is the duty of the parents to provide it.

ARTICLE 26

Everyone has the right to free education and the right to equality of opportunity for any form of education involving restricted enrollment.

ARTICLE 27

(1) Everyone has the right to freely participate in the cultural life of the community and the right to freely contribute to it.

(2) Everyone has the right to share scientific advances and its benefits and the duty to disseminate them, and wherever possible to contribute to such advances.

(3) Everyone has the right to the protection of their cultural heritage. It is the duty of everyone to protect and enrich everyone's heritage, including one's own.

ARTICLE 28

Everyone has the right to socio-economic and political order at a global, national, regional and local level which enables the realization of social, political, economic, racial and gender justice and the duty to give precedence to universal, national, regional and local interests in that order.

ARTICLE 29

(1) One is duty-bound, when asserting one's rights, to take the rights of other human beings; of past, present and future generations, the rights of humanity, and the rights of nature and the earth into account.

(2) One is duty-bound, when asserting one's rights, to prefer non-violence over violence.

ARTICLE 30

(1) Everyone has the right to require the formation of a supervisory committee within one's community, defined religiously or otherwise,

to monitor the implementation of the ARTICLEs of this Declaration; and to serve on it and present one's case before such a committee.

(2) It is everyone's duty to ensure that such a committee satisfactorily supervises the implementation of these ARTICLEs.

Note
[1] Text from http://gcwr2011.org/Universal_Declaration_of_Human_Rights_by_the_World%27s_Religions_2011.htm

FURTHER READING

Chapter 1
Clayton, Richard and Tomlinson, Hugh, *The Law of Human Rights*, 2ed, Oxford: OUP, 2007.
Ishay, Micheline, *The History of Human Rights*, Berkeley: University of California Press, 2004.
Lauren, Paul, *The Evolution of International Human Rights: Visions Seen*, Philadelphia: University of Pennsylvania Press, 2003.
Smith, Rhona and van den Anker, Christien, *The Essentials of Human Rights*, London: Hodder Arnold, 2005.
Woodiwiss, Anthony, *Human Rights*, London: Routledge, 2005.

Chapter 2
Adeney, Frances and Sharma, Arvind, *Christianity and Human Rights: Influences and Issues,* New York: State University of New York Press, 2007.
Brackney, William H, *Human Rights and the World's Major Religions: The Christian Tradition*, Westport: Praeger Publications, 2005.
Cronin, Kieran, *Rights and Christian Ethics*, Cambridge: CUP, 1992.
Sugden, Chris, *The Right to be Human*, Cambridge: Grove Books, 1996.
Witte Jr., John and Alexander, Frank S, *Christianity and Human Rights*, Cambridge: CUP, 2010.
Wolterstorff, Nicholas, *Justice, Rights and Wrongs*, Princeton: Princeton UP, 2010.
World Alliance of Reformed Churches, *Theological Basis of Human Rights*, Geneva: World Alliance of Reformed Churches, 1976.

Chapter 3
Bick, Etta, *Judaic Sources of Human Rights*, Ramsat Aviv, Israel-Diaspora Institute, 1989.
Cohen, Haim, *Human Rights in the Bible and Talmud*, Jerusalem: Ministry of Security, 1988.
Goodman, Lenn E, *Judaism, Human Rights and Human Values*, New York: OUP, 1998.
Haas, Peter J, *Human Rights and the World's Major Religions: Judaism*, Westport, Praeger, 2005.
Novak, David, *Covenantal Rights: A Study in Jewish Political Theory*, Princeton: Princeton University Press, 2000.

Chapter 4
'Abd Al-Rahim, Muddathir, *Human Rights and the World's Major Religions: Islam*, Westport: Praeger, 2005.
Dalacoura, Katerina, *Islam, Liberalism and Human Rights: Implications for International Relations* , London: I B Tauris, 2003.
Dwyer, Kevin *Arab Voices: The Human Rights Debate in the Middle East*, Berkeley: University of California Press, 1991.
Mayer, Elizabeth A, *Islamic Human Rights* (3ed), Boulder, Westview Publishing 1999.
Oh, Irene, *The Rights of God, Islam, Human Rights and Comparative Religion*. Washington: Georgetown University Press, 2007.

Chapter 5
Carman, John B, 'Duties and Rights in Hindu Society, in Leroy S Rouner (ed,) *Human Rights and the World's Religions*, Notre Dame: University of Notre Dame Press, 1988.
Coward, Harold, *Human Rights and the World's Major Religions: The Hindu Tradition*, Westport: Praeger, 2005.
Mitra, Kana, 'Human Rights in Hinduism,' *Journal of Ecumenical Studies*, 77, 1982, pp.77-84.
Rai, Lal Deosa, *Human Rights in the Hindu-Buddhist Tradition*, New Delhi: Nirala Publications, 1995.
Sharma, Arvind, *Are Human Rights Western?*, New Delhi: OUP, 2006.
Welch, Claude and Leary, V A, *Asian Perspectives on Human Rights*, Boulder: Westview Press, 1990.

Chapter 6
Florida, Robert E, *Human Rights and the world's Major Religions: The Buddhist Tradition*, Westport: Praeger, 2005.
Jeffreys, Derek S, 'Does Buddhism Need Human rights?', in Christopher Queen et al (eds.). *Action Dharma: New studies in Engaged Buddhism*, London: Routledge, 2003.
Taitetsiu, Uno, 'Personal Rights and Contemporary Buddhism' in Rouner, Leroy, (ed.), *Human Rights and the World's Religions*, Notre Dame: Notre Dame University Press, 1988, pp.129-147.
Tay, Alice, (ed.), *East Asia: Human Rights, Nation Building, Trade*, Baden-Baden: Nomos Verlagsgesellscghft, 1999.

Thurman, Robert F, 'Human Rights and Responsibilities in the Buddhist Civilizations' in Bloom, Irene (ed), *Religious Diversity and Human Rights*, New York: Columbia University Press, 1996.

Chapter 7
Cole, W O, Understanding Sikhism, Edinburgh: Dunedin Academic Press, 2004.
Cole, W O, and Sambhi, P S, *The Sikhs: Their Religious Beliefs and Practices*, Brighton: Sussex Academic Press, 1995.
Kalsi, S S, *Simple Guide to Sikhism*, Folkestone: Global Books, 1999.
Mandair, Arvin-Pal Singh, *Sikhism: a Guide for the Perplexed*, London: Bloomsbury, 2013.
McLeod, Hew, *Sikhism*, Harmondsworth: Penguin, 1997.

Lightning Source UK Ltd.
Milton Keynes UK
UKOW08f0020230616

276894UK00017B/511/P